NAVIG
INDIA

Bharat Joshi is the CEO of JCurve Ventures Pvt. Ltd. Prior to founding JCurve, Bharat has worked and trained with leading multinational and Indian companies in Malaysia, Denmark and India. He regularly writes for various print and online publications, including *The Wall Street Journal, CNN IBN* and *Economic Times*, and is visiting faculty at Shri Ram College of Commerce, University of Delhi. He can be reached at both bharatj@actlindia.com and bharat@jcurve.in

NAVIGATING INDIA
$18 TRILLION OPPORTUNITY

BHARAT JOSHI

RUPA

Published by
Rupa Publications India Pvt. Ltd 2017
7/16, Ansari Road, Daryaganj
New Delhi 110002

Sales centres:
Allahabad Bengaluru Chennai
Hyderabad Jaipur Kathmandu
Kolkata Mumbai

Copyright © Bharat Joshi 2017

The views and opinions expressed in this book are the author's own and the facts are as reported by him which have been verified to the extent possible, and the publishers are not in any way liable for the same.

All rights reserved.
No part of this publication may be reproduced, transmitted, or stored in a retrieval system, in any form or by any means, electronic, mechanical, photocopying, recording or otherwise, without the prior permission of the publisher.

ISBN: 978-81-291-4754-7

Second impression 2017

10 9 8 7 6 5 4 3 2

The moral right of the author has been asserted.

Printed at Parksons Graphics Pvt. Ltd, Mumbai

This book is sold subject to the condition that it shall not, by way of trade or otherwise, be lent, resold, hired out, or otherwise circulated, without the publisher's prior consent, in any form of binding or cover other than that in which it is published.

For Dakshayani and Devyani, this is your world to make; and for Mrida: Tri-Shakti.
For all those who can envision what India and the world can be, and are working towards a better future for its beings.

CONTENTS

Preface	ix
1. The Promise	1
2. Bazaar: The Indian Market	30
3. The GiST of Our Democracy (or Creative Cumulative Incrementalism)	86
4. Demographic Dividend (or We the People)	115
5. Ease of Doing Business in India	141
6. India has Law, China has Order	157
7. The Elephant in the Room	182
8. The End... And New Beginnings	203
Appendix 1: How We Got Here	221
Appendix 2: Chronicle of a PPP	233
Appendix 3: Key Features of 'Make in India'	239
Acknowledgments	241
Index	243

PREFACE

India has just been rediscovered!

Well, not quite in the manner Vasco Da Gama did in 1498, but by Indian and foreign investors alike, who have up-ended their previous positions on India. And this appetite has grown beyond taking quick (read fickle) money positions in Indian markets through the foreign institutional investor (FII) route, to the more committed foreign direct investment (FDI) channel.

The Indian business lexicon is rapidly being challenged and redefined by the Modi juggernaut: FDI means 'First Develop India', Made in India has given way to '*Make* in India', and unfamiliar notions like self-certification are being embraced.

The seduction of India, the market, has been reinforced through the temptation of India, the cheap source of goods and services.

Rising input costs in China and the European Union (EU), Brexit, Trump administration, embargoes on Russia (via Ukraine), and other geopolitical developments have only added to the draw of a relatively predictable India. The world should be paying a lot of attention to India, both economically and politically, i.e. we should see India being courted by economic powerhouses such as Japan and the United States of America (USA) looking for a big Asian ally (soon to be the world's third-largest economy), to counter the threat—real or imagined—posed by China's growth and increasing assertiveness in the international arena.

These rediscoveries are not new. The country has been host to foreign corporations for centuries—and that's not counting the East India Company. Siemens has been around since the 1800s, Philips and Bata are honestly thought to be homegrown enterprises by at least a billion Indian consumers, and Bofors (Saab AB) almost brought down governments.

In the finest traditions of noisy entrepreneurial ecosystems, India is home to a multitude of businesses, both Indian and foreign, ranging from corner stores to multinational corporations (MNCs), and sole proprietorships to public-listed companies. India's rapid rise up global rankings of wealthiest individuals and corporations (Jaguar Land Rover and ArcelorMittal are famously Indian-owned), has fuelled their growing influence beyond India on to the world stage.

As with any vibrant free-market economy, there are scores of thousands of businesses that operate at each level and scale. And as much as we are tempted to box these into neat generalizations (small and medium enterprises or SMEs, liaison offices, foreign-owned, export-oriented units or EOUs, information-technology enabled services or ITES firms, etc.), Indian companies are not immune and are faced with a range of problems with remorseless consistency.

Even companies that have been around for decades find their world order disrupted every few years, caused by sudden, unfathomable, often unfriendly legislative changes or decisions. The speed of the *elephant* (that has scored over *tiger* as the world's favourite metaphor for India), i.e. the rapidly evolving tastes and spending habits of its various strata of demographics, catches us all off guard. This disruption compels these businesses, large and small, to question, revisit and revise their practices if they are to sustain their success.

This book aims to dive into these issues and examine through the experiences of others; personal anecdotes and interviews; case studies from the public domain; and this author's impressively cerebral insights—all of which will hopefully illuminate the path to the promised land, the tourism tag line of which is something of a warning—'Expect the unexpected'.

WHAT *DOES* IT TAKE TO SUCCEED IN INDIA?

I was speaking to an audience of start-up entrepreneurs, investors, and wannabe entrepreneurs at an incubator in Delhi, when a young American lady at the back of the room asked the panel a question, 'What *does* it take to succeed in India?' Well, I'm paraphrasing. She spoke briefly about the difficulties and surprises she faced on a daily basis, and really wanted to know what she was missing.

I gave her two or three broad pointers, and then reminded her of the American maxim, 'If you can make it in New York, you can make it anywhere *except India.*' This was greeted with peals of laughter from the audience, who were in on the inside joke. Nevertheless, the question stayed with me over the next few days and I examined it at various levels. What did 'making it in India' really mean, and what would it take or did it take to 'make it'.

To the Make in India campaign, 'making it in India' means manufacturing. To a young, restless population, 'making it in India' is achieving a better life for themselves than their parents could. To companies, multinational and Indian, it is about realizing returns from the 'India story'. And to the government, 'making it in India' is about providing opportunities to primary school kids and private citizens alike to realize their fullest potential.

But whether you're an aspiring actor, entrepreneur or philanthropist, you need to 'get' India before you can make it here. Understanding the wheels within wheels that move business in India, is essential to succeeding and saving you a huge amount of infuriation and distress.

India remains one of those countries where the government and social networks are a huge factor in determining your success and ease of operations. These operations range from obtaining licences for manufacturing or distribution, to getting your kids that school admission, or registration at the Foreigner Regional Registration Office (FRRO).

Big government affects only the very large corporations in the West, and if you're in the new economy (increasingly defined by having Silicon Valley roots or investors); but in India even the smallest businesses have to deal with a soul-crushing amount of bureaucracy. Reading this book, you will constantly see the direct and indirect role and influence of government in most aspects of business and life in India. However, the book is not a step-by-step guide on procedural compliance.

Coming back to the question the young American entrepreneur asked me—'What *does* it take to make it in India?'—this still remains an impossibly broad question, and like most questions about India, even the most contradictory answers would be true.

I'm not sure if one book can answer the question conclusively, but I will try. The book will hopefully explain or steer you clear of some stereotypes. If you decide to not buy this book (and aren't Indian), please take this advice to heart—stop subjecting your captive Indian audience to the ABC formula: laboured conversations on Astrology, Bollywood and Cricket. And please stop doing the head-bob, it is not endearing until you've lived here long enough to have acquired it with a stomach that is resilient to Delhi-belly.

When I first conceived the book through deliberations with Kapish Mehra and Ritu Vajpeyi-Mohan at Rupa Publications, the audience in mind was essentially non-Indian. However, in the early days of writing, I was fortunate to have the opportunity to teach a full semester at one of India's finest commerce colleges—Sri Ram College of Commerce (SRCC).

As we discussed Indian and Harvard case studies, as well as new laws around corporate governance and Corporate Social Responsibility (CSR), it gave me some uncanny déjà vu moments—the tone and quality of questions were often what foreign business persons or journalists would ask me. So, these young Indian graduands were smart and enthusiastic, but still somewhat unaware of the realpolitik of business in India.

I imagine this phenomenon can be attributed to two factors.

One, that every generation has one profession which is the most sought after. In my father's time, young Indian graduates badly wanted to join the Civil Services. In his father's time, the armed forces were the profession of choice; for kids graduating university now, its business. Business could mean entrepreneurship—so starting the next Flipkart and taking on Amazon; or founding the next Oyo rooms, and taking on Airbnb. The other opportunity of 'business' participation is working for a respected corporation and making to the top of the pile.

Further, most of India's young graduates do not come from mercantile backgrounds, nor from families that run businesses, or have a tradition of working for MNCs; they are often not from the mercantile castes (which could impart some tacit knowledge). Their parents are farmers, tradesmen, civil servants, doctors and so on.

Two, we tend to still teach mostly foreign written and foreign context theories and cases in our commercial education (high school up). Having said that, it is possible that well-informed readers might pick up the book and disagree with some of the points I make. Here, it is pertinent to repeat the old adage about India, where everything you say about the country and its opposite are both equally true.

This is because India genuinely is the most heterogeneous country in the world—we are a very complex country; if sitting with an investor or potential future partner, you have to be open to say that India is not a country for beginners, and that it is a very difficult country to operate in.

This book is neither meant to be a prescriptive 'self-help' book on India, simply because there is hardly ever the 'one' solution to any problem. Nor is it an exhaustive treatise of the multiple topics covered by the book. Indeed, several volumes could be written on any single subject that has been attempted to be unravelled here.

I am equally aware that some readers might have enjoyed more of an India flavour and expansion of topics not covered herein. The toughest job I have had, has been to 'contain the sprawl', as Ruchir Sharma warned me. So the simple rule we used was thus: anything unrelated to business, no matter how fascinating, must be omitted from the book.

Therefore, here's my humble attempt at narrating, documenting and observing some very intriguing stories and trends, and seeing where the 'discussion' takes us.

If you do read the book, you'll hopefully have a good read, and form an understanding and opinion on how to address the many challenges India is sure to throw your way. And more importantly, form your own views on how India might mature in the years to come. This is a critical skill, as everything in India is long-term. And having braved heartburn and infuriation, you need to consider if it is worthwhile for you (which, it usually is).

Spoiler alert—the book discusses an inordinate amount of horror stories across sectors. This isn't because I'm particularly despondent about the country of my birth and business (I'm unreasonably sanguine, actually). It is because I find extreme examples (especially tragedies) the most instructive of devices.

As a European Ambassador to India once told me, 'You're assured one or two surprises every day.'

1
THE PROMISE

The two largest economies in the world have essentially had a symbiotic relationship wherein one (USA) buys cheap merchandise from the other (China). Imagine an economy which could be comparable to these in terms of both, demand and supply of merchandise *and* services (significantly, China is yet to crack services). For many, India remains the holy grail of business. A cheap source of goods, *and* a large home market.

The path to this Garden of Eden is peppered with a minefield of legislative, socio-cultural and economic challenges which dampen the hopes of even the most adventurous. In an increasingly globalized and 'flat' world, India is one of the large economies where contradictions coexist as amiably as passengers in Mumbai's overcrowded trains, or Hyderabad's plush new airport.

In the brave new world, you ignore India at your own peril. Competitors will source goods, services, or even top management from Indian shores, and gain an advantage; or sell their products, services, or ideas to this insatiable market. Either ways, your hand is forced. It is only a matter of time before virtually every business actively engages India, either proactively, or reactively.

And if you cannot but engage with India, is it really worth the trouble? It better be, because it is hard, it takes time, and failure often precedes success. So, what might make it worthwhile to begin or stay committed to your Indian journey?

Circa 2016, India is the world's quickest-growing large economy (third largest in terms of purchasing power parity or PPP) at 7.3 per cent, has the world's second-largest working population (soon to overtake China), the world's largest stock exchange (in terms of number of companies listed), over 900 million mobile phone subscribers (almost 200 million of whom carry smartphones), a gross domestic product (GDP) of USD 7 trillion (third largest in PPP terms), and at least two airports that see upwards of fifty million passengers annually. In other words, it is the world's largest free-market economy, with hundreds of thousands of foreign companies doing business here.

India's not the biggest or best at everything, it is only the world's second-largest market for mobile phones and motorcycles (or two-wheelers, more accurately), and the Delhi National Capital Region (NCR) is the world's second-largest urban metropolitan area. The nation's annual defence budgets are in the region of US$ 40 billion; infrastructure and industrial corridors worth hundreds of billions of dollars are being built, and in late 2015 India was said to have among the highest 'national brands' (after the USA, China, Germany and Japan).

Its per capita vehicle penetration is 0.03, its steel consumption at 60 kg is lowest amongst all the BRIC nations (South Korea leads with over 1,100 kg), and air travel in 2014 as per World Bank stood at 82 million. So we're far from saturation of demand.

TABLE 1.1

Apparent steel use per capita 2008–2014 (finished steel products)

Country	2008	2009	2010	2011	2012	2013	2014
India	43.8	48.6	53.9	57.1	58.5	58.8	59.4
China	332.8	408.1	432.1	468.6	479.4	530.6	510.0
South Korea	1,223.6	942.8	1,081.2	1,157.2	1,103.4	1,050.7	1,118.8
Russia	246.9	172.8	255.9	289.3	298.9	306.4	302.8
Brazil	125.4	96.0	133.7	127.1	126.8	131.9	121.9
South Africa	121.9	87.6	97.2	102.6	100.5	107.8	97.5

Source: World Steel Association, *World Steel in Figures 2015*

It is common knowledge that we are an emerging market, a BRICS[1] nation, and an undeniable investment destination for virtually any biggish company. Some numbers might be debated or challenged because there are different sources and multiple ways to slice and dice data, but 'numbers are like hand grenades: close enough counts', as Harvard Business School professor and prolific investor Felda Hardymon would remind us.

In a non-numeric sense, India has had a rather good run as a democracy, the rule of law is trusted, and the press is genuinely free. As an emerging economy, the country has tremendous potential. Business after all is a function of a number of complex factors, but the basic underlying factor in a market-driven economy is population—with nearly 1.3 billion people, and a large portion of them (64 per cent) being between the ages of fifteen and sixty-five—the Indian demographic exceeds the

---

[1]An association of 5 major emerging economies—**B**razil, **R**ussia, **I**ndia, **C**hina and **S**outh Africa.

combined similar demographic of the G7! So from a potential point of view there is no question that India has the basic ingredients in place.

To paraphrase, India is doing well, and is expected to continue as such. To India's credit this is the exception and not the norm in South Asia. In fact, the only neighbouring country with comparable (though softening) numbers is China. Often written-off, the pejorative 'Hindu rate of growth', refers to the low annual growth rate of the planned economy before the liberalization of 1991, which stagnated at around 3.5 per cent from the 1960s to the 1980s, while per capita income growth averaged 1.3 per cent.

Professor Ashish Nanda, dean of the Indian Institute of Management (IIM)-Ahmedabad, and former, and still visiting faculty at Harvard Business School and Harvard Law School, reminds us of how frightening the Malthusian spectre of the era around the 1950s was. With a burgeoning population and no clear means to feed it, India suffered the ignominy of importing 'red wheat' from the USA, which would probably be fit for cattle fodder in any developed nation of the time.

However, the impressive achievement of reaching where it has today does not give India a free pass from the criticisms and expectations of doing still better. Starting in the late 2000s, my interactions with the foreign press and foreign business associates often pivoted around the evil troika that plagued India *at the time*—first, crimes against women (mostly the heinous rapes that brought citizens of Delhi to the gates of the President's residence in protest); second, large-scale corruption scandals that initially shook Indians out of their ambivalence to everyday graft, and created leaders like Anna Hazare and Arvind Kejriwal; and third, the softening economic numbers that dampened the India story at a less emotive, but more numerical level. Despite India's impressive economic achievements and democratic credentials, you can see why I would be prepared for a different line of questioning during the interaction.

So, circa late 2014, the frame of the conversation had shifted to the promise of India—what the economy could deliver to its people and the world, and how all foreign investors could do as well as the Japanese, for instance, with their envied participation in the US$ 100 billion Delhi-Mumbai Industrial Corridor (DMIC).[2]

The newly anointed Prime Minister, Narendra Modi, was prompt in speaking to the usual pain points of foreign investors—red tape would be mitigated, investor grievances would be addressed, and infrastructural constraints tackled head on.

The following is a view from the other side—that of the investor; World Conquerors interviewed me in September 2014 regarding my consulting and investment company that assists foreign companies doing business in India. The interview appeared in the Dutch *Financial Times,* where I spoke on prospects for foreign companies in India.[3]

---

[2]The DMICDC (Delhi Mumbai Industrial Corridor Development Corporation) was set up in 2012, with active involvement of the Indian and Japanese governments. This initiative gained such traction, that there was a clamour by other prospective partners to jointly set up other industrial corridors. Subsequently, industrial corridors are being planned: the Bengaluru–Mumbai Economic Corridor (BMEC), the Chennai–Bengaluru Industrial Corridor, the Visakhapatnam–Chennai Industrial Corridor (VCIC), and the Amritsar–Kolkata Industrial Corridor (AKIC).

[3]The interview was translated using Google Translate, and then improved. The order in which the questions appear has been changed when presented here. The original article in Dutch can be found at: http://fd.nl/ondernemen/entrepreneur/wereldveroveraars/124930-1408/ondernemen-in-india-doe-je-voor-de-lange-termijn

ENTREPRENEURSHIP IN INDIA FOR THE LONG TERM

'Dutch entrepreneurs are not sufficiently aware of the opportunities that India offers' said Bharat Joshi, when World Conquerors spoke to him about opportunities and pitfalls in India and the importance of a strong regional business partner.

Are Dutch companies aware of the opportunities in India?

Still not enough. Companies from Japan and China all invest eagerly, but the Dutch still do not know and must find the way to India. This is unfortunate because the developments in the country [India] are going very fast.

Our country director in the Netherlands, Adriaan Mast, knows all. He gave advice on the construction of an airport in Hyderabad, which opened in 2008. In three-and-a-half years it was pounded from the ground out of nowhere. Something you make in Europe is not as fast!

What is also to be considered is that India's focus traditionally is more on the United Kingdom and the United States, and less on continental Europe. To get assignments it is important that Dutch business presents itself well in India, for example, through trade missions.

Where are the opportunities for Dutch companies?

The Indian Government wants the economy [to prosper], triggering a number of major projects. For example, there is one large plan to clean the River Ganga, so that there is a better ecosystem. At the same time the river has to be more navigable, there must be energy generated by hydropower, and adjacent agricultural land must be irrigated. Finally, tourism in the area should also get a boost.

Another ambitious project is the Delhi–Mumbai Industrial Corridor, an industrial zone that runs through six states and the cities of Delhi and Mumbai, and spans [roughly] 1,500 kilometres. The first phase is all about building infrastructure, such as highways, railways and airports. Later, new industrial clusters will arise, 'green cities' and SEZs [special economic zones], where companies can work under a favourable tax regime.

These are just two projects, but you can see that there is a lot of different expertise required—infrastructure, through agriculture to tourism and green energy. The Dutch can certainly contribute.

What is important when doing business in India?

I advise companies to go only if they want to do business there for the long term. In India it is very important to build relationships with local business partners—a good relationship. It takes time to build relationships like that.

Further, you need to know well in advance: how much risk do I want to take? How much capital do I want to invest? And how much time do I want to invest? If you have clear answers to these questions, it will be easier to find a suitable partner.

What are the pitfalls?

It is not easy to start a company in India. Do not expect that you can arrange everything quickly. Especially arranging little things like local permits, can sometimes take a long time. Therefore, it is important to have a local partner who knows the way and can help you get there. Moreover, if the permits and the contracts are in, the market is changing fast and the long-term results are enormous.

Finally, it is important to delve into the culture and economy of the region where you are doing business. India is sometimes regarded by Westerners as a homogeneous country, but it consists of 29 states, where a total of 1.2 billion people live. The differences in terms of culture and economy are large. In that respect you'd better compare India with the European Union (EU).

One of the focus markets is JCurve Netherlands. Why did you focus specifically on the Netherlands?

First, there is a long history of trade between the Netherlands and India. But in addition, there are currently a number of sectors in which the Netherlands is a leader. One is the agricultural sector, spurred by Wageningen University as a major research institute. In addition, the Netherlands has a lot of knowledge in the fields of water, IT and infrastructure.

What is the role of the new Prime Minister, Narendra Modi, who comes to power in May?

Prime Minister Modi is breathing new life into old projects. In addition, certain sectors of the economy have been opened up to foreign investment. The maximum foreign investment has increased from 26 to 49 per cent in sectors such as defence, the railways, insurance, and manufacturing. It has also become easier to get foreign investment approval in these sectors.

Mr Modi has declared promising campaigns to address India's most pressing needs for the domestic constituency (these programmes are covered in greater detail later in the book). Further, he has set measurable and tangible targets, including 100 million jobs and achieving 25 per cent of GDP from the manufacturing sector by 2022; placing India among the top

50 nations in World Bank's 'ease of doing business' ranking; universal mobile connectivity; and, the prospect that India could be a US$ 20 trillion economy in the next couple of decades.

Even Mr Anand Sharma, India's former Commerce Minister (and current member of opposition), expressed confidence in Mr Modi's reiteration at the Town hall Q&A with Mark Zuckerberg at the Facebook headquarters (HQ) in California, that the size of India's economy could grow to US$ 20 trillion. 'Yes that is achievable for India.' (*The Hindu*)

Now, getting from US$ 2 trillion to US$ 20 trillion would be a spectacular feat, indeed. But is this mere rhetoric or an achievable target, worth working towards?

THE INDIAN ECONOMY: FROM 2 TRILLION TO 20 TRILLION

To realize Prime Minister Modi's ambition to achieve a GDP of US$ 20 trillion in the next twenty-five years, India would require a compound annual growth rate (CAGR) of 9.65 per cent. While this seems to be a trifle optimistic, there is evidence to demonstrate that this is doable. Economies such as Taiwan, South Korea, China and Japan have all achieved economic growth of over 7 per cent per annum (CAGR), sustained over decades.

In India's favour is the demographic dividend—an unmatched pool of human resource with productive age on its side. India has been growing at an average rate of 6 to 7 per cent over the last few years, majorly on the back of its service sector—a rude reminder of the lagging manufacturing and agriculture sectors, which have grown at 3 to 4 per cent. Make in India, Digital India, Startup India, and other declaratory programmes could tap the potential of these sectors and make a 9.65 per cent CAGR possible.

Prime Minister Modi's signature initiative, Make in India, seeks to make India a manufacturing powerhouse. The initiative contains a raft of proposals designed to get local and foreign companies to invest in the Indian manufacturing sector. With a vision of 'zero defects and zero [negative] effect', this initiative seeks to ensure that none of our exports are returned to us or have a negative impact on the environment.

The following programmes will support the Make in India vision.

- **Skill India:** where the youth can acquire relevant skills that will not only help them in getting jobs but also create jobs.
- **Digital India:** where India can use its prowess in IT to enhance the nation's competitiveness and create an enabling investment climate through emphasis on e-governance, e-healthcare, and e-education—covering both urban and rural areas.
- **Start-up India, Stand-up India:** to promote bank financing for start-ups and offer incentives to boost entrepreneurship and job creation.
- **Jan Dhan Yojana:** to promote financial inclusion. The PM has envisioned this scheme to connect the poorest citizens to the facility of bank accounts and up to ₹1 lakh insurance through a debit card.
- **Swachh Bharat Abhiyan:** based on a vision of a clean India, this campaign aims to provide all schools with toilets and separate toilets for girls. The PM has urged every Indian to ensure that every road, school, office, locality and neighbourhood is clean.

Mr Modi's critics allege that many of these new programmes are just old wine in new bottles, but even if true, the programmes only serve to underline the consistency of thought across different governments. Also, it is uncommonly pragmatic to adopt good ideas, wherever they may be found.

In India's favour is its track record—in nominal terms, India's GDP grew fourfold over the past fifteen years, from US$ 450 billon in 2000, to over US$ 2 trillion at present. If we were to repeat the feat, it certainly seems possible to get to US$ 20 trillion and beyond!

We need to handhold and drive growth in two or three big states—possibly Bihar, Uttar Pradesh (UP), and West Bengal—all of which are populous and large. As per the 2012 census Bihar's population stood at 99 million, UP's at 204 million, and West Bengal's at 90 million. There is need to create new pockets of growth, and UP will be the key.

If we extrapolate the Chinese trend to India—China had a GDP of just over US$ 2 trillion in 2006, it now touches more than US$ 11 trillion through a CAGR of approximately 20 per cent, so India's US$ 20 trillion target would seem within grasp. Nevertheless, the Government of India has to work very hard to achieve this; policy paralysis must be replaced with continuous policy reforms plus a stable 'majority' government—as opposed to a less stable coalition. Taken together, these factors can provide a favourable environment for businesses.

India also needs rapid infrastructure development on the PPP model. According to the latest available data from the World Bank, India's GDP was US$ 2.067 trillion in 2014. On PPP basis, according to the latest available data—from the 2011 International Comparison Program in which the World Bank is involved—India went from the tenth-largest economy in 2005 to the third-largest, moving ahead of Japan, in 2011 with US$ 5.75 trillion GDP.

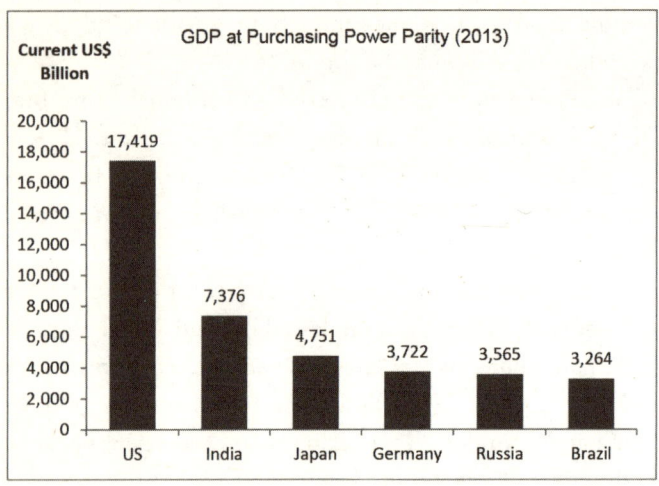

Figure 1.1: A comparative look at BRICS nations (excluding South Africa) vs the US, Japan and Germany—GDP at PPP

Source: IMF WEO April database

The study assesses economies based on PPP or an estimate of the comparable real living costs across countries by factoring in the differences in price levels and exchange rates.

However, the risk to India's US$ 20 trillion target is that economies are increasingly interconnected and a slowdown in a major economy leads to a drag in developing economies as well. With most of the developed economies (barring America) slowing down, double-digit growth would be tough to sustain at a continuous stretch. Moreover, even technologically-advanced countries like the US took approximately thirty-five years to cover the distance between US$ 2 trillion and US$ 17 trillion.

If we take the average growth rate of 7 per cent per annum, it is quite achievable and realistic that given all the others factors—growing demand, favourable demographics, and a promising track record—India will reach its target of US$ 20 trillion in 2049, i.e. thirty-three years from now. And if we take the average growth rate to be 5 per cent then it will take another thirteen years to reach the target. So going by the average growth rate and history, it appears that the target of US$ 20 trillion in thirty-five years is within reach for India.

TABLE 1.2
Number of years and CAGR required for India to achieve US$ 20 trillion target

Years Required	CAGR Required
25	9.6%
30	8.0%
34	7.0%
39	6.1%
47	5.0%

So, on paper, India should be able to achieve this target in about three decades, *ceteris paribus*. But as Ian Chappell famously commented about the all-star Indian team: 'Cricket is not played on paper'.[4]

Comfortingly, at least two other countries have achieved spectacular, sustained growth over time (certainly no paper tigers).

---

[4] 'Cricket isn't played on paper' an *India Today* interview in the late 1990s. Former Australia Captain Ian Chappell was in Mumbai for the CEAT Cricket Rating Awards. Known to be blunt, Chappell was pessimistic about India's chances in Australia. 'Q. Is India better prepared for Australia this time? A. On paper it looks like a better team, but cricket is not played on paper,' was Chappell's reply.

THE SINGAPORE MODEL

In 1959, Singapore—having remained under British control for over a century—was invaded by the Japanese during World War II and was also painfully expelled (after violent Malay–Chinese riots) from the Malaysian federation after spending two years as a part of the unified state. It could, therefore, hardly have been anticipated that it would become the next big thing in Southeast Asia.

When on 9 August 1965 Singapore became formally independent, the city-state was still experiencing unemployment, a housing shortage, and below par living standards—3 million people were unemployed and two-thirds of the population was living in slums. Further, the young nation lacked water supply, natural resources and proper infrastructure.

Singapore decided to adopt industrialization, with a focus on labour-intensive industries, but lacked the basic prerequisites for industrial development—a skilled labour force, and expertise of said industrialization. Its leaders went long on globalization and it paid off. They started connecting to the developed world and invited MNCs to manufacture in Singapore. Singaporeans realized early on, that to attract industries and multinational corporations (MNCs), their nation would have to offer a corruption-free environment with low taxation policies, which was still a challenge for Singapore.

To make all of this possible, Singapore adopted a rather autocratic style of governance. Prime Minister Lee Kuan Yew's People's Action Party (PAP), brought together all labour unions under one umbrella, that of the National Trade Union Congress (NTUC). Business-friendly laws appealed to the international investors. Two further advantages Singapore had were its geographical location, and its established port system.

Singapore's strategy of educating its workforce with the help of the MNCs also worked very well, and the nation adopted a three-pronged reform programme—enforcement, legislation, and the judiciary—to combat corruption. Singapore grew from a Third World island state to a model city-state, achieving Prime Minister Lee's vision of 'A First World Oasis in a Third World Region'.

This was a country behaving like a company.

Modi seems to have taken a leaf out of Mr Lee's book with his 'Swachh Bharat' (Clean India) programme. In 1959, Singapore undertook a similar programme to ensure a 'Clean and Green' Singapore. The nation instituted an infamous ban on chewing gum, imposed heavy fines for littering, and established an annual tree-planting day. Tough measures were taken to limit traffic congestion—heavy taxes were to be paid, and certificates of entitlement (COEs) were required to own and operate a vehicle.

Mr Modi's government, in addition to building affordable housing, has also adopted a programme of building millions of toilets across India, especially in schools (the lack of toilets being a major reason for girls dropping out of schools), and across rural India, where sanitation is poor or absent. However, building lavatories is one thing and maintaining them quite another, and toilets do need regular maintenance. Non-governmental organizations (NGOs) like Sulabh, have demonstrated that this is possible—they usually have a revenue-generating model in public toilets in high footfall areas. However, building and maintaining toilets nation-wide, remotest corners included, is easier said than done.

Sir Mark Tully narrates a telling incident of how far attitudes will need to change for these large-scale programmes to work. At Jaipur Railway Station, he observed some travellers eating from a bag of peanuts and as they did, they casually threw the shells on to the platform. Shortly thereafter a sweeper arrived and swept the shells off the platform on to the railway line. We can appreciate why, then, the short-term success of the Swachh Bharat programme is a tall order. It also entails cleaning the Ganges, India's most vital and revered river system, without which the vast plains of northern India would be barren desert.

I cannot help but draw parallels from these two very dissimilar states. India suffered a bloody and debilitating partition to achieve Independence, much like Singapore's own expulsion. The challenges India faces today are still those of Singapore's early days—corruption, lack of physical infrastructure, need to skill the workforce, and provision of basic housing for millions. India's better-managed public sector undertakings (PSUs) are now looking to expand overseas, which Singapore's Government-led corporations (GLCs) have been doing all along and betting on foreign investment to drive economic growth. Singapore has shown that it can be done. India will need to undertake serious legislative reform to emulate the 'Singapore model'.

India has the added advantage of its large English-speaking workforce, available (albeit depleting) water supply, and improving economic indicators, but India could draw inspiration from Singapore to tap its latent strengths. For one, India needs to educate its workforce as Singapore did post-independence. India also needs to tap its other strengths—a long coastline (of over 7000 km), and riverine network—by building more ports and port-based SEZ regions near these ports to make business more efficient and competitive, which will also reduce the cost of transportation and will attract more industries to these regions.

Singapore Indian Chamber of Commerce and Industry chairman R. Theyvendran has said, 'We want to go to India... We want to have a reliable partner,' but highlighted problems like corruption, and the lack of proper and centralized regulatory and information systems that keep investors away from India.

Mr Modi's plan of a 100 smart cities and the Make in India policy are the first initiatives to make India like Singapore, which is on the verge of becoming the first 'smart nation'.

While Singapore demonstrates how a nation with little or no resources can achieve an economic turnaround, its achievements are discounted by uncharitable observers as being possible only for a small city-state. China, however, attained an economic turnaround at scale.

THE CHINA MODEL

'Both will go on to become middle-income nations and would have pulled hundreds of millions of people out of poverty,' opines Gurcharan Das, referring to India and China. He has famously chronicled the economic rise of India through his bestselling books.

It is famously known that in AD 1700, India and China jointly accounted for almost half of the world's GDP. Having received the full benefits of colonization, their share had fallen to around 5 per cent a piece of global GDP by 1950. However, the recent growth of both Asian neighbours has been extraordinary, and it is commonly thought that if the trend is sustained, both economies could recapture their historic share of world GDP.

In 2004–2005, when India was growing at 7.5 per cent, Prime Minister Manmohan Singh's Government was praised by the International Monetary Fund (IMF), which stated,

'Notwithstanding high world oil prices and a weak monsoon, the economy showed remarkable resilience in 2004–2005, with growth (at 7.5 per cent) remaining robust and becoming broader-based.'

Around the same time (starting in the early 2000s), there were slightly different sentiments about China's even more impressive growth. Major trading partners, especially the USA and the EU, were becoming increasingly anxious about their 'Made in China' worries. Organized labour, politicians and experts were blaming China for the loss of millions of manufacturing jobs, a currency which was impervious to appreciation, and a ginormous trade imbalance giving China a trade surplus of hundreds of millions of dollars.

Like China, exports have aided India's economic growth, but with two notable differences—Indian exports have largely consisted of services (primarily IT)[5], and the absence of huge surpluses with trading partners also meant less dependence on foreign markets in bad times. This problem came to light in the global financial crisis of 2008, when China's exports fell for the first time since 1978.

Ironically, the 'Communist' State had a head start over India with regard to economic reform and economic growth, both of which India hopes to catch up with, putting interminable (and normally unflattering) comparisons to rest.

Deng Xiaopeng initiated economic reform in 1978, succeeding Mao and famously declaring that 'to get rich is

---

[5]Nevertheless, India has had its fair share of political resistance against loss of service and IT sector jobs to India, and 'Bangalored' became a hugely embarrassing verb for Indians—causing protectionist measures like a cap on working visas for Indians. To be fair, China ran a trade deficit with several Asian countries, from whence raw materials and natural resources are procured.

glorious', and by way of strategy offered, 'let many flowers bloom'. These simplistic statements represented a profound shift in the established Chinese policy of denouncing wealth (well, capitalism, but often evils of capitalism do create wealth), and a proliferation of enterprises, not state-owned enterprises (SOEs) alone owned ultimately by the monolithic government in Beijing.

China's population (962.6 million) and GDP (US$ 364.5 million), were both higher than India's (667.3 million, and US$ 139.7 million), but the per capita income of both economies was comparable (US$ 1090 China vs 1160 India in 1991). When India liberalized its economy in 1991, Chinese GDP was already twice as large as India's, and today, China's GDP is almost US$ 18 trillion (in PPP terms), whereas India's is over US$ 7 trillion.[6]

Economic reform in China can broadly be classified into two stages: pre- and post-China's accession to the World Trade Organization (WTO).

For three decades, China concentrated on strong, albeit insular, policies that drove staggering economic growth. Deng's famous innovation of SEZs allowed China to tinker with FDI and capitalism, while confining the potential downsides to said SEZs, both geographically and politically. China successfully reached out to its diaspora (initially from Hong Kong), as its earliest FDI investors—unlike India, which is still to truly leverage the full potential of a large and prolific diaspora.

China's success with agricultural reform was congruent to India's successful 'Green Revolution', which was substantive in creating food security for hundreds of millions. Deng

---

[6]Source: National Bureau of Statistics, China, *Statistical Yearbooks*; National Bureau of Statistics Plan Report; National Bureau of Statistics communiqués.

implemented 'Decollectivization', to help the disastrous farmers' collectives, by allowing them to sell surplus produce in the open market through the 'Household Responsibility' system. This market incentive worked, and China's agricultural output doubled over six years.

An intriguing by-product of the surplus earnings of farmers were the town and village enterprises (TVEs), essentially socialist organizations owned by local and provincial authorities to manufacture labour-intensive products. Eventually, 22 million TEVs grew 30 per cent annually, creating 140 million jobs.

Not everything worked per plan, though. The 'One Child' policy, enforced with great zeal through fines, sterilization, and worse, did halve the population growth to under 1 per cent, but has created a demographic worry of the 'inverted pyramid'. Juxtaposed with India's demographic dividend, this threatens to emerge as a potential spoiler to the China story.

Deng tried a version of agricultural reform, the 'Management Responsibility' system for SOEs (State Owned Enterprises), which controlled the market share and employment. Unlike agriculture, there wasn't a comparable open market for industrial goods, nor were employee layoffs an option, so it fell upon Deng's successor, Jiang Zemin to privatize SOEs. Intriguingly, India also undertook 'disinvestment' of its PSUs around the same time.

China used a dual currency system to great effect between 1978 and 1997, with great success. There was the domestic yuan (renminbi) and the foreign exchange certificate (fixed at 10 to the dollar), which investors bought on the open swap market. Deng initiated efforts to join the WTO in the 1990s but some of these policies—and more grievously, China's dismal human rights record—were a constant stumbling block. Though negotiations began under him, China failed to join the WTO under Deng.

China agreed to a swathe of reforms to gain WTO membership in 2001. These reforms were aimed at promoting free trade, facilitating foreign enterprises and making laws more transparent and predictable. Chinese growth really took off post WTO. Nominal GDP growth grew to 10–11 per cent, from the 8–9 per cent average of the previous two decades, commodity exports became more sophisticated than the earlier generation of labour-intensive products (toys, garments, etc.).

The common refrain is that Singapore could achieve growth because of its small size, and China due to an autocratic structure. On the flip side, India has strengths and weaknesses that neither of these countries have to the same degree. While appreciating that every country is unique and accepting that India has seen its share of missed chances, the US$ 20 trillion target does seem within reach.

China attained its spectacular growth by using the three drivers of growth—capital, labour, and total factor of productivity[7]—to great effect. Going forward, the means employed to achieve growth will produce diminishing returns (as economists would say). Massive governmental spending no longer sustains competitiveness, especially as demographics and rising labour rates chip away at price arbitrage. Technological and institutional reform could possibly pave the road to sustained growth, but as the recent economic slowdown demonstrates, it is difficult to shrug off economic sluggishness.

In contrast, India's demographic dividend and effective institutions will increase productivity (e.g. through capital allocation through banks that are not corrupt). The government

---

[7] The amount of productivity that can be achieved for the same factor of capital/labour.

will continue to create conditions to attract FDI (as against China's internal stimulus through spending), and by extrapolation, attract investment from Indian companies, which have been accumulating capital over the last couple of decades.

It is almost a given that India will grow, because capital formation has been increasing over time (i.e. not entirely dependent on foreign capital), we have inherited robust institutions (of financial governance and regulation), and a burgeoning home market. But India needs to solve some big issues—labour reform (so people hire more, and women participate more); judicial backlog; corruption; banking the unbanked; maintaining peaceful borders; ensuring ease of business for Indian and foreign businesses. Not an exhaustive list, but perhaps an overly simplified one.

One intriguing development is that as India tries to emulate the manufacturing-led Chinese growth model, China has now declared it wants to move away from investment and manufacturing-led growth, to a model based on services and consumption—very much the India model since the 1990s.

It is often said of governments that bold decisions are made only in a crisis, or when a bold person is at the helm. India's radical liberalization of the economy was the outcome of a dire economic crisis[8] in 1991 (and stipulated by the IMF). Mr Analjit Singh, who had a ringside view (as founder of Max Telecom), of India's legendary leapfrogging of copper wires and into mobile telephony, opines that leapfogging is possible in whatever is more technically or mechanically driven, and requires minimal human interface, bias, interpretation, or regulation. But he also credits

---

[8]For a brief vignette of Indian economic history (the Raj onwards)—turn to 'How we got here' (Appendix 1).

the leapfrogging to Sukhram, the Telecom Minister of the day as the only one person responsible for the telecom revolution.

Mr Singh, Chairman Emeritus of the US$ 2 billion Max Group, also warns of how far success stories can slide. 'Telecom was the golden goose of this country, and now, since A. Raja's[9] time, it's become an untouchable, and a few other sectors are also becoming so,' he cautions. Experienced and accomplished businessmen like Mr Singh often cite the Singapore government as an enabler of business. And looking at the example of its first Prime Minister Lee Kuan Yew and how Singapore was able to turn around the business climate of the small nation before World Bank's 'ease of doing business' rankings became a catchphrase, they allow themselves to be optimistic.

Mr Singh believes we could be in one of these inflection points. 'Our PM is very bold, and as the leader is giving right messages, there's criticism around: "Should the PM talk about clean toilets, or using unused infrastructure after 1.00 p.m. for vocational training?"—Yes! He should,' he asserts.

The prevailing omens—economic indicators, political stability, bold leadership and favourable demographics—would indicate that India should be growing at a much faster rate than China. So in some ways, the real question India faces is: How do we ensure we don't mess it up? But in asking this question, I don't want to give you the false impression that everything is perfect.

---

[9] A. Raja was a state Telecom Minister and a star player in a 2G Spectrum licence allocation scam where according to *The Hindu*, 'CBI had alleged there was a loss of ₹30,984 crore to the exchequer in allocation of 122 licences for 2G spectrum, which was scrapped by the Supreme Court on February 2, 2012.' http://www.thehindu.com/news/national/2g-case-a-raja-was-main-conspirator-favoured-firms-says-cbi/article7625584.ece

TABLE 1.3
Comparative look at agricultural profile of BRICS nations, the US, and the world

Date	2005	2005	2005	2005	2005	2005	2005
Total land area (km^2)	149,000,000	9,826,675	3,287,240	9,640,821	17,075,400	8,514,877	1,221,037
Other lands (%)	88.38	81.78	48.37	83.87	92.72	92.18	87.11
Other lands (km^2)	131,686,200	7,492,621	1,438,133	7,822,060	15,185,442	7,795,211	1,062,665
Permanent crops (%)	1.04	0.21	2.8	1.27	0.11	0.89	0.79
Permanent crops (km^2)	1,549,600	19,240	83,249	118,445	18,016	75,263	9,637
Arable land (%)	10.57	18.01	48.83	14.86	7.17	6.93	12.1
Arable land (km^2)	15,749,300	1,650,062	1,451,810	1,385,905	1,174,284	586,036	147,609
Cultivated land (%)	11.61	18.22	51.63	16.13	7.28	7.82	12.89
Cultivated land (km^2)	17,298,900	1,669,302	1,535,063	1,504,350	1,192,300	661,299	157,246
Country	World	United States	India	China	Russia	Brazil	South Africa
Rank	—	1	2	3	4	5	20

Source: CIA World Factbook

Senior economists opine that many of the current government's programmes are a continuation of earlier programmes or the United Progressive Alliance's (UPA's) experiments and pilots. They may also question some of the reported results, as junior officers have in the past been known to manipulate programmes (or accounts) to meet targets.

The last decade has seen some sharp ups and downs as well. In 2008, India clocked over 10 per cent growth, but by 2013 growth had halved to 5-ish per cent. A key challenge will be achieving consistency. Here's an example to think over. A frequently cited constraint in economic forecasting and achieving consistency is the monsoon. A substantive portion of India's GDP still comes from agriculture, which is largely dependent on seasonal rainfall, so annual variations swing economic performance significantly. Intriguingly, India has the highest percentage of arable land (48.83 per cent) of any of the BRICS nations. If technology and mechanization could reduce dependence on rainfall, this could simultaneously provide economic prosperity for hundreds of millions in India's agrarian belt, while contributing to the world's food security.

Sir Mark Tully, self-confessed fan of the Indian Railways, once narrated a delightful anecdote of how India operates at sync with the weakest link in the chain. As a young BBC correspondent, Sir Mark was travelling by train when the TC (Ticket Collector) approached him to check his ticket. As he retrieved his ticket from his pocket, young Mark noticed an 'express surcharge' of a few rupees. 'Look, I don't mind paying this, but this clearly is not an express train,' he told the TC. The TC patiently explained 'Sir, this actually is an express train that happens to be travelling slow, and stopping at all stations.'

In some ways, that is the promise of what India could be:

an unrestrained express train, travelling at express speeds.

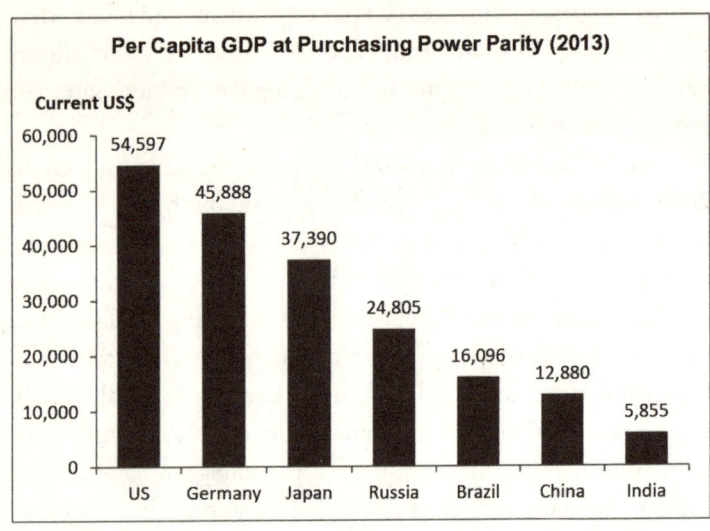

Figure 1.2: A comparative look at BRICS nations (excluding South Africa) vs the US, Japan and Germany—per capita GDP at PPP

Source: IMF WEO April database

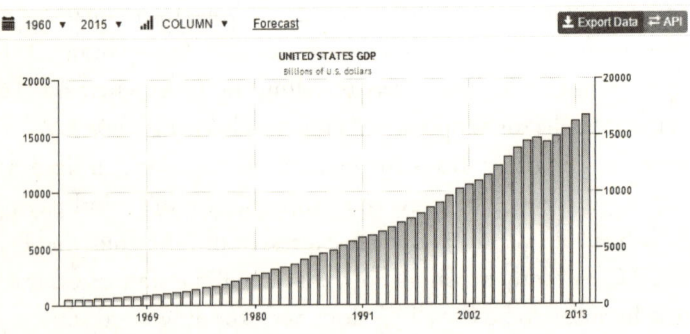

Figure 1.3: United States GDP charted from 1961 to 2014

FISCAL AND CAD: TWIN DEFICITS UNDER CONTROL

The Government of India has been successful in undercutting the fiscal deficit to 4 per cent of GDP in the financial year (FY) 2015, as against targeted 4.1 per cent of GDP.

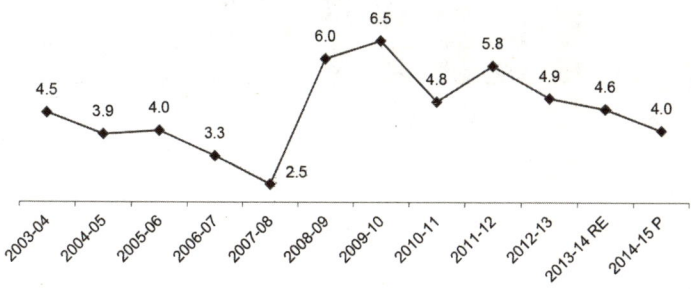

Figure 1.4: India's fiscal deficit from 2003-04 to 2014-15

Source: RBI, Planning Commission

Further, it is envisioned to lower the fiscal deficit progressively to 3 per cent by 2017-18, through measures aimed at increasing revenues and lowering expenses. India's current account deficit narrowed sharply to 1.3 per cent of GDP in financial year (FY) 2015 as against 1.7 per cent of GDP in FY2014, as merchandise trade deficit shrank while the export of services improved.

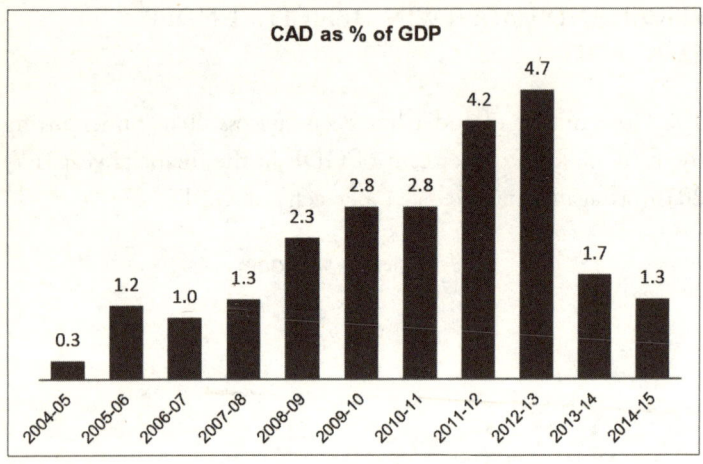

Figure 1.5: India's current account deficit (CAD) from 2003-04 to 2014-15

Source: RBI, Planning Commission

World Bank divides countries into four income groupings: low, lower-middle, upper-middle, and high. Income is measured using gross national income (GNI) per capita in US dollars. India is currently a lower-middle income economy but is expected to be the fastest growing country in 2015 and 2016.

TABLE 1.4
Global growth rates: World Economic Outlook

	2013	2014	2015 Projection	2016 Projection
World	3.4	3.4	3.1	3.6
Advanced Economics	1.4	1.8	2.0	2.2
USA	2.2	2.4	2.6	2.8

Euro Area	–0.4	0.9	1.5	1.6
Japan	1.6	–0.1	0.6	1.0
Emerging and Developing Economics	5.0	4.6	4.0	4.5
China	7.7	7.3	6.8	6.3
India[1]	6.9	7.3	7.3	7.5
Brazil	2.7	0.1	–0.3	–1.0

1. Output data and forecasts for India are on fiscal year basis and at market prices (base year–2011/12)

Source: IMF, *World Economic Outlook*, October 2015

2
BAZAAR: THE INDIAN MARKET

> It is pardonable to be defeated,
> but never surprised.
> —*Frederik the Great*
> *(King of Prussia, 1740-86)*

YOU'RE PROBABLY reading this book because of the compelling Indian market, which is to say, the stirringly large numbers—a billion people—many of them unserved or underserved in precisely the product or service you can so effectively provide. Whether you're a corporation, consultant NGO, or multilateral—the singular Indian market is hard to ignore.

This, however, is a fallacy.

Or more precisely, it is reckless to consider India one single market, where seemingly everyone speaks English. All of its 29 states differ in demographics, topography, customs and even laws. Even socio-economic indicators exhibit great heterogeneity within the same metro.

For instance, as a foreign retailer, you might be granted the Foreign Investment Promotion Board's (FIPB's) 100 per cent FDI license, but individual states still have the power to disallow you from plying your trade in their territories.

Staying with the retail example, products you sell in one state (say liquor in Delhi), could be contraband in another (e.g.

Gujarat and Kerala are 'dry'[10] states, despite being on the coast).

Or the products could be constant, but use and positioning may differ. As the head of a leading retail chain reminds me, 'Coconut oil is simultaneously sold as a cooking medium in Kerala, and hair-care product in West Bengal.' And as a retailer, you wouldn't possibly want to send your customers to the cosmetics section to get their kitchen supplies.

Taxes differ significantly from state to state,[11] as do minimum wage, real estate prices, availability of talent, purchasing power and 'ease of doing business' (I've tried to explain this broad term in a separate chapter). To break it down—knowing what India isn't, is most useful when trying to define what it is.

Having said this, MNC's have been operating in India for centuries, profitably and happily. Here are a few examples of MNCs and their year of entry into India.

Goodyear	1822
StanChart	1858
HSBC	1860
BNP Paribas	1860
Siemens	1867
HUL (Unilever)	1888
Citibank	1902
GE	1902
Ericsson	1903

---

[10]Dry states forbid sale and (public) consumption of liquor. Certain establishments are, however, allowed to serve 'permit holders' and non-residents.
[11]We have Central Sales Tax (CST), Local Sales Tax (LST), Excise, Octroi, and a myriad web of taxes that have spawned a thriving economy of tax experts and consultants.

Castrol	1910
Reckitt Benckiser	1911
Nestle	1912
Glaxo SmithKline	1919
Ingersoll Rand	1922
SKF	1923
Philips Electronics	1930
Bata	1931
Alfa Laval	1937
Colgate Palmolive	1937

- IBM is India's second-largest employer and largest foreign employer, with over 100,000 employees
- Indian units of Nestle, Proctor & Gamble, Colgate post higher margins than their parent companies
- Microsoft is India's top MNC in terms of turnover

THE PIO TRAP

Young (or naïve) Indians are more likely than expats to make the same rookie mistakes expats do, but with the added handicap of overestimating their own insight and astuteness—believing all of India to function like where they grew up, especially big city kids. Los Angeles-based businessman, Rajiv, believes that his fellow persons of Indian origin (PIOs) are more gullible than non-Indians. PIOs, 'don't know what they don't know,' laments Rajiv, 'and this is a trap most PIOs and NRIs [Non-Resident Indians] fall into.'

But this equally describes Rajiv's paisan from Kolkata or

Kochi as well.[12] Confucius said that 'real knowledge is to know the extent of one's ignorance'. Having written this book, reviewers will no doubt remind me of the extent of my ignorance, but for my compatriots without said benefit, this is a real risk.

Rajiv feels overseas Indians can get emotional about investing in the motherland, and believe in the absolute power of Chief Ministers (CMs)—another fallacy. While CMs are unquestionably at the summit of administrative powers at state-level, the petty bureaucracy seems to have a formidable rule of its own. Also, there are subjects (such as environmental clearances), that are governed by the Central, not State government.

In Rajiv's case, he was invited by an Indian CM to invest in his state, and assured of a 'single-window clearance'.[13] While the single-window clearance didn't exist, he fell into the PIO trap. While waiting long weeks for the requisite permits to materialize, Rajiv got quite involved personally, and insisted that the official-in-charge expedite his clearances for his planned building. The officer was sympathetic, but explained the process would take its own time, which he couldn't help, but advised Rajiv to begin construction regardless—the licence was merely a question of 'when', and not 'if'.

Following this rather official counsel, Rajiv commenced and even completed construction of his factory and building before the permit was issued. In the meantime, the official who gave the above assurances was transferred, and his successor was livid.

---

[12]For those not familiar with the term, 'Paisan' is an informal usage, in the US, among people of Italian and Spanish origin, and roughly translates into 'brother', 'fellow Italian/Spanish American'; something like the subcontinental usage of 'bhai'.

[13]As an indicator of the clout and financial muscle of the enormous Indian diaspora, there's also a separate ministry for Overseas Indian Affairs.

He asked Rajiv to produce any documentary evidence of these assurances, which of course didn't exist, and was convinced his predecessor had made money on the arrangement. The implication was that Rajiv should similarly 'take care of' the successor or face the consequences. In time, Rajiv was able to establish his bonafides, but not without delays and heartburn. 'Make sure you get papers in hand,' advises a wiser (and somewhat older) Rajiv.

In my experience, self-effacing PIOs have been more successful (like Amar of Clove Dental, whom we meet later in the book), than have returning Indians, and PIOs (the self-effacing ones), have often been more successful than even Indian entrepreneurs.

Twenty-something Naman Shah graduated from Stanford, worked with an NGO in rural Rajasthan (India's vast desert expanse), left for his MBA at Harvard, only to return to Delhi to co-found a startup with fellow PIOs, while starring in a Harvard Business School case-study. After residing in Delhi for a couple of years, he's moved back to the US where his latest venture is headquartered, with technical support and product development in Delhi (he now shuttles).

At time of going to press, at least three ambassadors to India are PIOs—including the US Ambassador Richard Verma; Canadian High Commissioner Nadir Patel and Australian High Commissioner Harinder Sidhu.

In the development sector too, PIOs are returning in significant numbers to work in impact investment funds, and social entrepreneurship start-ups—upending the conventional NGO-only space for societal, socio-economic, or ecological development.

It may be hard to believe, given India's position—low in the depths of World Bank's ease of doing business ranking[14]—but it is an enormously easier place to work and live in, than it was a decade ago. And a decade ago, it was an easier place to do business in, than in the preceding decade. So, the trajectory has been in the right direction, though the rate of reforms may vary within narrower periods of the decade. There's possibly no greater evidence of this, than the immense number of successful first-generation entrepreneurs, both Indian and foreign.

A number of Indian cities now see something of a proliferation of first-generation expatriate entrepreneurs, altogether a new species in India and a far cry from the 1980s, when expats would accept India as a hardship posting, with the customary hardship allowance. Diversity, brought in by the best and brightest from across the globe, is also rewarded by the changing skill-set required to 'make it' in India.

Until the early 1990s, the largest Indian conglomerates—Tata[15], Reliance, Birla, etc.—would concentrate on managing the regulatory environment, essentially securing licences for being allowed the privilege of conducting business. Now it is about discovering or creating new markets, innovative solutions and

---

[14] Among the main objectives of the Make in India programme, is to boost India's raking to the top fifty in World Bank's 'Ease of doing business' listings. We're currently ranked 130. Ironically, if we were to follow best practices of states across the country, we'd already be in the top fifty!

[15] Excerpt from Harvard Business School article titled 'India Arrives on the Global Stage': 'When I started in business in the 1960s, many of our companies didn't have a profit plan; instead, we had a production plan,' says Ratan Tata (HBS AMP 71, '75), chairman of the Tata Group, a $22 billion conglomerate with 93 companies operating in areas as diverse as IT and communications, steel, financial services, hotels, and consumer goods ranging from tea to china to automobiles. 'There was also very little focus on strategy. None was necessary, unless it had to do with how to make it through the various government gateposts in order to obtain a license.'

fund raising for expansion.

Dhruv Shringi's personal journey simultaneously chronicles the worst of the license raj and the best of the start-up culture that is fast gaining momentum.

A YATRA FROM BRICKS TO CLICKS

Doodh ka jala, chachh bhi phoonk phoonk ke peeta hai, (a Hindi saying which means 'once bitten twice shy', or literally, 'those scalded by milk, drink buttermilk cautiously too!')—the moral of this story is not to put you off old economy business (or dairy) in India, but to understand that there are second chances.

Dhruv Shringi of Yatra and its famous portal yatra.com ('yatra' is Hindi for 'journey') swore off industrial ventures years ago, when he witnessed governmental apathy and corruption first-hand. So put off was he by his failed enterprise, that his second venture was planned around a sector with little or no governmental interface.

Dhruv was still in college, when as a first-generation entrepreneur (his father was an army man) he invested most of his father's life savings in a venture with an acquaintance of his father's to set up a chemical factory near Delhi. After three excruciating years, the Shringis exited the business, Dhruv completed his education, and got a job in London. He returned a few years hence, and decided to risk it all once again with a foray in e-commerce.

But here's the story in slo-mo.

In 1991, the year after the Mandal Commission,[16] Dhruv

---

[16]There's a separate section on caste, but briefly: the recommendations of quotas (affirmative action) for Scheduled Castes and Tribes in government jobs and

entered college, and 'since not much was happening in college', decided to take the entrepreneurial plunge at eighteen.

The aforementioned chemical factory was set up in Bhiwadi. His father, whose savings financed Dhruv's share of the equity, was as naïve as him in matters of commerce (having retired from the army). The business partner had an existing business of the same nature, so gave the Shringis comfort on the execution front.

After a long process of obtaining approvals and licenses, the venture commenced production. However, governmental interface proved to be a daunting challenge on an ongoing basis with various local bodies including the Rajasthan State Industrial Development Corporation (RSIDC; Bhiwadi is in Rajasthan), Departments of Excise, and Sales Tax, the Rajasthan State Pollution Control Board (RSPCB), and of course, labour-related challenges. Dhruv realized that unless you knew how to manage the system at the grassroots level, you couldn't scale-up the business.

'Demands (read, bribes) were made for the most random things,' recalls Dhruv—for things that should be taken for granted. For example, power supply. The route to getting power supply was 'convoluted' and he observed that established industries also had established machinery to pay out 'the maximum bribes most efficiently.'

It was a challenge to get an Excise Officer to visit his factory when goods needed to be shipped, says Dhruv. He would hold on to the inventory for days waiting for the Inspector, because the Inspector felt he hadn't 'been adequately rewarded' the first time

---

higher education were implemented. These suggestions were made by the Mandal Commission, and carried out by the government of Prime Minister V.P. Singh. This was a period of great political and social volatility.

round. In addition, Dhruv's partner felt the Shringis were being 'disruptive' by being upright, and adding cost to the business by not paying bribes as per the prevailing norm.

Anyhow, after three long years at the school of hard knocks, the Shringis decided to exit a loss-making business. Dhruv's father lost a fair amount of money (substantially his commuted pension and savings), in the venture which ended in an acrimonious parting of ways.

Dhruv, who had become quite a cynic by this time, was left to learn that legally enforcing a contract was hard and required an inordinate amount of time and effort, especially for a small, unlisted company. A useful jab in the ribs came from a well-wisher in the police, who bluntly advised the Shringis, 'Economic offenses are not a priority for the police.' The prospect of waiting twenty or thirty years before getting redress is discouraging to even the most litigious businessmen, which the Shringis were not.

The story doesn't end here. Due to the timing and negotiating the exit from the chemical business, Dhruv missed out on the CAT exams (Common Admission Test, required for applying to MBA courses). His mom was flabbergasted at the prospect of his skipping a year waiting for the next CAT (this really is a big thing for middle-class Indian families; a 'gap year' is almost always not an option). Luckily, he got a job at Arthur Anderson, and completed his Chartered Accountancy exams simultaneously.

He worked with Anderson in India and UK and by 2000 felt he had enough consulting experience, so quit his job and went to INSEAD for an MBA. Day one of campus recruitment was 9/11—the very day of the attack. All employers were grounded for two days, and no recruitment happened.

Dhruv really just wanted highfalutin management consulting, but got a job at Ford, which was fortunate, given the business climate. After two years with Ford, he realized that you can't make too much of a difference with an employee ID that was beyond 178,000. With an employee strength that big came a large bureaucratic structure, with ten-plus years before he would be in a position to make a difference to the fortunes of his employer.

So, he joined a smaller company called 'e-bookers' in the online travel space as Head of Strategy in 2003, and promptly got promoted to Chief Operating Officer (and headed operations and technology), but after a couple of years, the company got acquired by a large international conglomerate and Dhruv was laid-off.

Dhruv had already been thinking of starting India operations at e-bookers, but Cendant (the buyer) had other plans. So at the customary farewell drinks, five e-bookers team members, including Dhruv, decided to found Yatra and its portal yatra.com, and shook on it. However, only two of the five—Manish and Dhruv—made it to India.

Other than ambition, Dhruv confesses there were other reasons for his repatriation—nostalgic memories of vacations with family and friends, and the Bollywood hit film, *Swades,* the story of a NASA scientist of Indian origin who gives it all up to bring science to a small Indian village. So yatra.com tied in perfectly with his desire to do something in India.

However, he was forced to rush to India even before funding for yatra.com could be closed. His heavily pregnant wife would not be permitted to fly if they waited any longer.

This was clearly an eventful year.

His first surprise on returning to India in 2006 was the cost of living, which had climbed sharply since his last stay in India in 1997, when he lived with his parents. His negotiations with investors were also based upon this dated sense of the cost of living, and so his take-home was not comfortable for the first couple of years.

In 2005–06, the period when yatra.com was taking off, it was very hard to sell an Internet start-up in India to investors, employees or clients. Investors had to be convinced that Indians would use a credit card, debit card or direct transfer; they were also doubtful about the extent of credit/debit card penetration in the Indian market.

Another big challenge was convincing people to join the yatra.com team. In the West, people are more accustomed to joining start-ups, and mid to senior executives routinely leave a stable environment for a start-up. Building a customer base was tough as well. Dhruv narrates instances of early cynicism—the Vice President (VP) of an airline ('not even the President'), made him wait for hours before meeting him. Only a few years later, the same VP was in the job market and approached yatra.com for a job.

There was a silver lining though, discernable now with the 20/20 vision of hindsight. In 2005–06, as the internet sector was perceived to be very small, it had minimal regulation and governmental intervention, and yatra.com flourished because it was under the radar.

Cash being a major contributor to online sales in India, Yatra began dealing with cash for holiday packages, keeping in mind that the average customer's credit card limit might not be high enough. To action this the company built a network of 14,000 rather novel travel agents—for instance, the chemist with a high footfall who puts up a computer terminal and acts as a cash collection point for cash-on-delivery (COD) sales.

Compared to his previous foray into business in India, Dhruv says he's hardly seen demands of any kind at Yatra, though he faced other challenges of an evolving industry—grappling with questions such as how to treat sales tax, or interstate sales. With Yatra in the second stage now, the challenge is sustaining the rate of growth, i.e. 'Are you growing fast enough?' notes Dhruv.

Yatra emerged at a time when the Indian economy was doing well, and consequently, a healthy respect for India prevailed till about 2011. Investors looked at 'macros' and the management team, and invested. Matters held good until around 2013, which became an especially bad time to raise funds.

Investors were deterred by public scams, growing cynicism about the speed of governmental or political action, wild currency fluctuations—from the mid-50s to 68 rupees vs the US dollar—and 'nobody wanted to come to India'.

Again, nobody looked beyond macros.

Thankfully for Dhruv, things changed as they usually do, and Yatra has seen renewed momentum and improved sentiment 2013 onwards, on the back of favourable tailwinds; little did anyone expect smartphones or the stunning internet scale-up.

Yatra is today a well-known brand, which pays Bollywood star Salman Khan millions of rupees (millions of dollars, probably) for endorsement. Salman adds recall, more than anything, as Bollywood is big only in India's Hindi-speaking belt (whereas cricket is everywhere). But like anywhere in the world, creating a sense of brand ownership among employees is a challenge—for instance, if a customer has a bad experience on the phone, or for instance if Yatra staff don't call for two days, after promising to call in six hours.

But for Dhruv, managing the 2,000 people in yatra.com

is less challenging than tackling the 150 employees in the old chemical factory. And unlike the traditional sector (still controlled by old-school families of India), the new economy is teeming with first-generation entrepreneurs, with no baggage, and also no knowledge of how to manage the system—which intriguingly, has become an asset. New economy sectors are very democratized, and with talk of net neutrality, there's 'little need to manage the external system', says Dhruv, which now better allows IT entrepreneurs focus on innovation, rather than spending time managing the ecosystem.

Contrast this with Dhruv's first venture, wherein a third, if not half, of his time went into managing the environment. There was just no time to think of optimizing production, or to innovate. The sheer frequency of perfunctory rituals was crushing. There wasn't a day when the factory was deprived of a visit by some inspector, and if that didn't happen Dhruv and partner were at the RSIDC complex, meeting government people.

Just consider the opportunity cost of the collective time of all entrepreneurs that went into managing inspectors, rather than in creating world-class products.

Not that he's complaining, but visits by inspectors to Yatra are few and far between, and for minor oversights like not displaying a licence properly, for instance.

By the very nature of their business, e-commerce entrepreneurs who pioneered travel portals, taxi cab aggregators, online shopping portals, or even movie ticket sellers, have had a ringside view of the changing Indian scenario.

The sentiment-driven holiday business is a useful barometer for economic trends too—you spend on a holiday if you feel your future is bright. But the holiday culture is a very new thing for Indians, it has only really picked up in the last couple of years. All travel previously, was object oriented—business, annual holiday, pilgrimage, and so forth. Impulse travel, for an earlier generation, was a ridiculous notion. 'Experiences' are a new thing—writing trips, snow leopard trails (in the Himalayas), dhaba (authentic, rustic Indian highway eateries) trails led by celebrity chefs, writers or environmentalists as fellow travellers—all of this is new.

What has not changed, is the famous Indian emphasis on 'value', which doesn't mean 'cheap'. Even a five-star vacation to the Maldives needs to be a 'good deal' (but still far from inexpensive).

There's a bit of a geographic skew to spending habits too. Metro (big city) clients have similar buying habits. They are usually well-travelled, and now crave experiential travel, while the middle class is more aspirational and wants to 'tick the box'. The middle-class traveller will often pack ten to twelve hours of sightseeing a day, for all-important bragging rights.

Most non-metro clients have similar buying habits too, for them visiting an Indian metro is an aspirational holiday—for instance, tours from South India to Delhi to visit historic monuments, or to Mumbai on a Bollywood trail to see the homes of film stars. This was a learning for Yatra, that there might actually be a client-base that would rather see Delhi or Mumbai before hill stations, or a foreign jaunt.

There are multiple ways marketers slice and dice the 'Indian market' to make sense of it—as do employers. Other than the metro/non-metro classification, common ones are state-wise, East/West, zonal (usually with Central or Northeast added for further filtration), and of course, North/South.

Shrivats Singhania, whose family runs the large and

ubiquitous JK Group (encompassing paper, tyres, cement, energy, insurance, etc.) believes differences in behaviour and attributes are attributable to geography, and sees the North/South (as opposed to metro/non-metro) manifest in his businesses.

In general, Southern consumers are more brand conscious and loyal but very discerning and unforgiving. 'Brand conscious' down South means these discerning customers go with established and trusted brands. Dutch electronics giant Philips, for example, is a dominant player in the South, because of the trust and confidence built over time, while new age giants like Samsung need to catch up when faced with brand loyalty built over decades. *The Hindu* is the leading English language newspaper, having built its reputation over generations, even though its national presence is relatively small. Some regional brands like CavinKare and Arun Icecreams have established themselves despite multinational brands dominating the segment. However, loyal Southern customers are also more demanding in terms of quality and service standards.

Many marketers view tests conducted in South Indian states as the litmus test for new launches, as consumers are conservative and not 'Early Adapters'. Rarely distracted by glitzy packaging and product features, they focus on quality, price and after sales service.

Mr G.R. Anand, CEO of the widely respected GRT Group of Chennai, run a successful chain of jewellery stores in South Indian states, Dubai and Malaysia—and none in North India. Mr Anand is clear in the strategy of entering markets with a significant South Indian market.

The South, typically, displays a more disciplined approach to managing business and a propensity to more ethical conduct. It leads the country in major human development indices such as literacy, health and sanitation. Organized retail started and prospered in the South as compared to rest of the country. Business automation is greater in the South than elsewhere. This has led to comparatively better business practices; in fact automation and IT penetration is highest in the South leading to more organized business practices.

Coming back to Yatra, its Delhi offices see people troop into work at 10.00 or 10.30 a.m. (for a 10.00 a.m. start), but are happy to stay on and work late. In offices in the South and Mumbai, people are usually more punctual, and these differences might cause challenges in getting to work in diverse teams.

But hiring remains a challenge for the IT and e-commerce industry, regardless of location. A dearth of engineering talent on product development means there are only a few quality employees in the pool, who are in high demand and constantly poached.

This sounds counter-intuitive, given India's well-established IT credentials and large pool of engineering graduates, but let's put this into perspective. Historically, India has been a software development services hub. The more creative aspects like innovation were happening somewhere else, say in the US, and Indian firms were asked to execute and write code, which was part of a larger piece, so the solution was not conceived in India.

In the new world order of the burgeoning home-grown e-commerce market, companies require a different skill-set—analysing a problem or need, thinking of solutions for the end consumer and coming up with a product for that consumer.

E-commerce companies today look for 'transferable skills', for techies to be able to train on an existing product and perform. So, companies are looking beyond their immediate business—

flash sales, travel, cloud computing—to see if there are skills that can be transferred.

Practical new economy businesses are looking beyond IIT, IIM, and the other schools that comprise the Indian Ivy league. They have found that they can only attract mid to bottom league students from premium institutes, who only look at these companies as a stepping stone for Facebook or other aspirational employers; whereas for smaller, but also solid schools, the Indian company is an aspirational brand, and commands loyalty from its pick of the crop.

With over 100 million smartphones and over 200 million internet connections, the consuming class is around 65–70 million households, 250–300 million consumers, which is almost as large as the US population. The online revolution is here to stay.

There is another reason why the recent surge in online businesses is not a bubble in the squalid physical infrastructure. Customer experience in the virtual world is as good as the best in the world, while the physicality is infuriating—unmanageable traffic snarls (especially around Diwali and other shopping events), parking problems, few pleasant venues of shopping, etc.

This is both, a cynical reminder of present constraints and future potential. The future potential of e-commerce, which ironically is helped by the poor physical infrastructure; and the potential to build quality infrastructure for India.

Despite the massive opportunity, Dhruv has sworn off physical businesses for good. He certainly won't go back to manufacturing, but also eschews temptations to enter the hotel business for instance, due to the 'laws around a blue-collar workforce'. Online travel operators have found other ways to offset a slump in the big domestic travel business, by booking hotels, and offering holiday packages, for example.

Needless to say, they are impacted by anything that hits travel. A recent shock to travel agents, and travellers alike, was the sudden insolvency of the flamboyant Kingfisher airlines, causing yatra.com to refund forward sales to customers.

Despite business risks that no sector is impervious to, Yatra has managed to clock 10 per cent growth at present. Well, it's almost embarrassing compared to the 50-60 per cent year-on-year growth they saw for few years, but perhaps it is the sign of the stabilizing of a sector. The IT sector has since attracted the benign attention of the government, which is doing what it can to 'regulate' this previously ignored sector.

Dhruv has since developed more of an appetite for working with the government, and as an elder statesman of the industry, is now working with industry bodies and government committees to help shape the legislation for the sector.

That's some journey.

YOUR INDIA PLAYBOOK

Permission to Conquer

The puja ceremony is an essential part of any mountaineering expedition in the Himalayas that wishes to use the indispensable support of Sherpas[17].

The Sherpas (usually Buddhist or Bonpo) believe the summits are the abode of mountain gods, who must be appeased before

---

[17] Sherpas are an ethnic group from the most mountainous region of the high Himalayas (shared by four neighbouring nations), the most famous of whom was Tenzing Norgay, who accompanied Sir Edmund Hillary on his climb to the summit of the Everest.

setting foot on the mountain. A platform of rocks with a small furnace for burning juniper branches and incense is placed in a prominent location at base camp. During the puja ceremony, a lama (monk) chants mantras, blesses equipment—ice axes, boots, crampons, etc.—and makes offerings to ask the mountain gods for safe passage during the climb. Finally, a flagpole is erected on the puja platform and prayer flags draped from it point to all corners of the base camp, and rice is thrown into the air three times (an auspicious number) to the cry of 'lakalu' or 'victory to the gods'.

The Sherpas believe that it is only after the puja, that they are allowed to climb the mountain, instead of 'conquering' the mountain—a term even Western mountaineers are becoming reluctant to use.

Evolving through the complex Indian ecosystem can induce some very special attributes indeed, for ventures that can survive the baptism by fire. Almost without exception, Darwinian Indian conditions make companies smarter and leaner (or at least meaner), equipping them to take on different markets. But more tangible benefits accrete as well. The learnings in product and service offerings can often be successfully exported to global markets.

McDonald's succeeded when it adapted to Indian preferences—a menu free of beef and pork, a family dining experience, and home-deliveries (which since have been started in several countries)—all at an affordable price point. Further, McDonald's was able to demonstrate to governments that they were generating stable and well-paying jobs for the local population, that they undertook CSR projects from the beginning (before CSR was recently mandated by law), and that they have developed a supply chain for ingredients, such as the right kind of potato for the fries, for which they engaged with Indian farmers.

Issues beyond customer preferences and competition play a critical role as well. Visible examples include those of retail giant WalMart, which experienced very public and very embarrassing setbacks (stemming from compliance issues); and Coca-Cola and PepsiCo, both accused of their beverages containing pesticides.

Cracking the Indian market is not confined to the need to Indianize products or services, or understanding why Indian consumers look for different things than Western consumers. Nor is it merely adjusting to lower margins and price-sensitivity in business negotiations ('price is never off the table'). A hyper-competitive environment breeds tough negotiators. And often humbles brands before they are allowed to reap returns.

When Kellogg's first entered India, it didn't truly understand the market. Nor did Kellogg's heed the advice of its own market research, which said that Indians liked their cornflakes with warm milk. In early 1996, defending the company's products, Managing Director Avronsart declared, 'True, some people will not like the way it tastes in hot milk. And not all consumers will want to have it with cold milk. But over a period of time, we expect consumer habits to change. Kellogg's is a past master at the art, having fought and won against croissant-and-coffee in France, biscuits in Italy and noodles in Korea.'

Kellogg's cornflakes, designed for cold milk, shrivelled to a soggy mass in warm milk. The company probably couldn't appreciate that Indians didn't really have refrigeration till the 1960s, and the best method of storage and preservation was boiling milk, and hence mostly warm milk stayed available through day in Indian kitchens, even in the summer.

Also, Indians like to add sugar to their milk. On rare

occasions when Kellogg's flakes were consumed with cold milk, they were (by themselves) not sweet enough because the sugar added by Indian consumers did not dissolve as easily in cold milk.

It is estimated that Kellog's made losses of around ₹500 crore before it turned a corner. The turnaround probably started with Kellog's asserting that the company was not trying to change traditional habits (unlike croissants, biscuits and noodles, in the past); the idea was to purely position its products on the health attribute, and make consumers see the benefit of this healthier alternative.

Home-grown companies, too, have found that replicating a foreign business model, as is, seldom works.

As Founder-CEO of Credit Rating and Intelligence Systems India Limited (CRISIL), India's first credit rating agency, Mr Pradip Shah had his task cut out for him. When first set up, it was thought that CRISIL was ahead of its time in India. CRISIL adapted its market to Indian conditions. Standard & Poor's (S&P) and Moody's always considered investors their solitary market, and named and shamed companies with sliding ratings. CRISIL rated companies, and would help them achieve better scores if they so wished. It did not make ratings public, unless the companies did so themselves (in which case, CRISIL would monitor).

> The trouble with being pioneers
> is that you get arrows in the front and in the back.
> —*Felda Hardymon, Harvard Business School
> and Bessemer Venture Partners*

Sesame Street came into the country with no brand legacy, and found a big (and enduring) gap in the Education Entertainment (aka Edutainment) market. Organizations like BBC and

UNICEF had some initiatives around adult edutainment mostly, so Sesame was left to address the mass, young audience space. In this virgin market, Sesame Street worked around the pivots of accessibility and affordability, to create a new genre. Favourably, the company found that broadcasters in India were more open to Sesame Street content than it had anticipated.

Since those early days, Sesame Street has grown to offer programming in multiple Indian languages very successfully in India (through multiple audio feeds, I am told), and is presently exploring the option of its own 24/7 channel. With increasing television reach, awareness and digitization, companies like Sesame Street are well poised to seize the opportunity a burgeoning market will provide.

Another first for Sesame, pioneered in India, is its 'Robin Hood Model', under which it runs 30 pre-schools in India for children of higher-income parents. The idea is to use surplus from the schools to fund other programmes, such as the production of *Gali Gali Sim Sim*, educational programmes, and fulfilling its overall mission.

When proven, this model could be exported overseas, as schools have never been run anywhere else by Sesame Street.

The best way to conquer the Indian market, perhaps, is to not try and conquer. Much like Mount Everest.

A LONG-TERM RELATIONSHIP

The phenomenally successful Japanese projects and ventures in India are widely considered the gold standard of bilateral economic ties. An especially impressive feat, given that most of the substantial Indo-Japanese projects were launched only in the last fifteen years or so.

It is commonly thought that Indo-Japanese friendship adopted a higher trajectory, when Prime Minister Atal Bihari Vajpayee (BJP, or NDA coalition), reached out to his Japanese counterpart. His successor, Dr Manmohan Singh, saw that this alliance resulted in some rather spectacular projects. As Principal Secretary to Prime Minister Singh, and later as his Principal Advisor, Mr T.K.A. Nair had a ringside view of the blossoming relationship.

According to Mr Nair:

Undoubtedly, Indo-Japanese engagement has been on the upswing from the Vajpayee–Manmohan days and continues to be so. The impact of the economic reforms in India initiated in the 1990s, the international trade and economic development affecting Japan and its perception about India and its economic prospects, continues to create conditions conducive to greater Indo-Japanese cooperation, the seeds of which were sown during the Vajpayee era and blossomed in the days of Manmohan.

Significant involvement of Japanese industry, more than its Indian counterpart in this area of Indo-Japanese engagement has its own implications for the Indian economy, which would be felt in the years to come. At the Japanese industry-level the preparatory homework done before making investment decision, is indeed remarkable and worth emulating by us.

To prospective investors in India, I would quote the oft-repeated observation of former Premier Manmohan Singh that investment in a country is a matter of faith and add that it would be prudent not to flirt with India, and be prepared for a long-term relationship!

Good advice, clearly, as the Indo-Japanese bilateral relationship transcends governments in power, and is currently as robust as ever.

As is demonstrated in virtually every India success story, you require a huge amount of patience, as:

1. Almost everyone will tell you—red tape takes time.
2. Indians are relationship-oriented, not transactional (and building personal ties takes time).
3. The courts are slow.

One of India's more prominent expatriates, who has been around for a while, advises that companies need to be prepared for a ten to fifteen-year runway, because of a unique curve wherein most overnight successes are ten years in the making.

Foreign companies looking to flirt with the Indian market would do well to commit to a longer relationship. And also be very clear about whom they ally with and why.

Ironically, very few joint ventures (JVs) succeed long-term, because the reasons for the alliance are not long-term. Typically, the MNC wants to enter India, an unknown, albeit attractive market; while the local partner wants foreign expertise to enable him to compete globally. It's the classic 'race to learn', as more experience or cynical observers sometimes describe JVs.

JVs work extremely well if a foreign partner has found the 'right' local partner and, more importantly, if both are on the same page in terms of time horizon. Indian companies are often family-owned or controlled, giving them a unique ability to plan or commit to rather long-term alliances and business plans.

However, if the value for either (or both) partner is expected to be short-term, alternatives to JVs can be about as good.

Possible solutions include acquiring a small company (Indian or foreign, depending on the acquirer); clear roles (supplier/vendor, forward/backward linkages, but control over governance, etc); and understanding the underlying motivations and priorities of partners—family-owned companies (Indian- or foreign-owned), tend to focus on control, whereas professionally managed or public-listed companies focus on profit (often quarterly).

Foreign professionals and investors, who have committed to the long-term relationship, unanimously appreciate the change for the better over the last couple of decades. To these frequent travellers, the once daunting process of flying into and out of India is now a breeze. Airport infrastructure is at par with the best in the world, and more importantly, Customs and Immigration staff is also more benign. The Delhi Metro Rail Corporation (DMRC; building metro systems in several Indian cities), is often quoted as an example of 'first world' efficiency and infrastructure in India. Socially, it fills one of the large public transport gaps for many commuters between the taxi and bus (or bicycles).

Also, the business climate has changed for the better. In a persistent attempt to attract FDI, the government has actually created conditions that are considered quite fair (India's 'Ease of doing business' rankings notwithstanding). For instance, economists describe how, in the hugely successful auto sector, the policies encourage 'tariff jumping' (where car makers initially began producing in India to bypass high import duty on cars), but once they were invested there was no local content requirement, no export obligation, and no limits on repatriation of funds. It's a different matter altogether, that the earliest foreign investors in the auto sector established their local supplier ecosystems (often JVs with foreign companies), and are now exporting large volumes of vehicles—making even RO-RO (roll-on, roll-off ships, which are especially designed to carry vehicles) operations viable.

Significantly, the recent trend is that even Indian politics is becoming more long-term. Governments at the Centre and States are lasting the full term, with voters giving strong mandates. And even if there is a coalition government, the alliance is formed prior to, not after elections (pre-poll alliances).

COLA WARS: COKE'S MANY BATTLES

Coca-Cola's chequered history in India started with a bottling plant in 1950; and in just five years, the drink grew so popular, that a Hindi movie, *Miss Coca Cola*, was released in 1955, with the biggest stars of the day. The company went on to become the market leader in India and stayed there solidly until 1977.

In 1977 there was a push for MNCs to dilute their stake to less than 50 per cent. Some agreed, while others like IBM and Coke (which didn't want to share the 'secret formula') left. PepsiCo entered the country in the late 1980s. Coke, not wanting to be left out, had an opportunity to re-enter in 1991 and found a willing partner in Parle Beverage. Through Parle, Coke acquired the biggest brands of the day (Thums Up, Limca, Maaza), their entire bottling network, and launched Coke (and the range of Coke's own global brands) nationally.

The last twenty-five years have been as interesting for Coke, who Venkatesh Kini, President of Coca-Cola for South Asia, believes is the whipping boy of all. Brands like Coke (and other visible brands such as McDonalds, Pepsi, etc.) are 'lightning rods' for anti-globalization, anti-business, anti-MNC, religious, anti-capitalism.

This is, of course, a global, not an Indian, phenomenon, wherein consumer brands are seen as visible representatives of the new world order (i.e. globalized, capitalist consumerist).

It is probably a good thing then, that the Coca-Cola stable also houses the reigning champion, Thums Up (a homegrown brand), which still outsells both Coke and Pepsi. However, the largest aerated beverage brand in the country is Sprite (an international brand, launched as late as 1999), as dark colas were vilified (clear one seen as safer, healthier, etc.). Sprite doesn't use Bollywood stars, except Shah Rukh Khan, whom it used for only a year.

Cola, as it turns out, is a capital-intensive product, which is highly localized since it cannot be imported and assembled. But the bigger concern is intellectual property rights (IPR), as local imitators will step up and try and imitate the look and taste of Coke.

As we've discussed earlier, for any business to shut down in India is a long, painful process. The labour laws add to this, as there is a real concern about job losses, and also nothing makes governments as unpopular as layoffs. And there's self-imposed pressure as well, explains Kini, 'In some parts of the country, it's extremely hard to enter, so there's huge pressure to keep the company going. You can check out anytime you want, you can never leave,' he muses, borrowing a line from the Eagles' song 'Hotel California'.

Bottling plants are sizeable investments, upward of ₹150 crore each (plus cost of land), and are currently present in 20 states. In an encouraging sign of federal competitiveness, Coke now sees states encouraging industry, competing with one another for investment and for companies to set up shop.

The Japanese, for instance, have a problem of plenty, as

virtually every other month they receive a delegation from an Indian state, often led by the CM. The Japanese PM, Shinzo Abe, had committed an investment of some US$ 35 billion, so states are actively competing for a share of the Japanese pie.

To return to Coke, the company has remained viable in the face of business challenges as well. Counter-intuitively, India is amongst the highest-cost places to do business for Coke. Land is expensive, labour is cheap but inflexible, ability to hire-fire-retrain is limited, productivity is low, the cost of power is among the highest in the world (mostly captive in the case of Coke), and Coke provides services like water, effluent treatment, etc. itself, as opposed to these being provided by the government as in other parts of the world.

Coke's revenue realization on per unit basis, is amongst the lowest in world, but volumes are high and optimizing (for cost) on areas like packaging (a 200 ml glass bottle at ₹10/15 US cents is still profitable, despite being among the lowest in world). This is not unlike telecom in India, which has been hugely successful despite amping the lowest average revenue per user (ARPU) worldwide. Indian telecom companies like Bharti (Airtel) have gone global, on the back of a large home-grown business.

The lessons from Coke could be extrapolated to virtually every sector and company, regardless of size. Other than its public tribulations, Coke has demonstrated how to thrive with a standardized product in a heterogeneous country.

Friction in an economy creates opportunities for players to benefit from friction. For example, a large market for captive power (which Coke is a large consumer of)—this business of providing captive power for energy needs of an industry is a virtual monopoly, as energy is not a globally traded commodity (for instance, you can't choose to purchase from a neighbouring country if terms are more favourable, or supply is more reliable), and India's appetite for energy will only grow with rising income levels and GDP. Overcoming constraints in logistics, a labyrinthine police system, sales tax, or bureaucracy makes it gainful for those who can navigate the system, while the environment creates natural barriers to entry for competitors.

Even with low margins—as often happens in industries where you compete globally, or depend on millions of consumers—Coke has remained in stable flight.

Persisting with the aviation metaphor, Kini analyzes India vis-à-vis China, 'There's less competition in India as the runway is bumpy, but if and when you take off, the skies are clear. In China, on the other hand, the runway is smooth, but you soon realize that skies are crowded.'

FRISKING AND OTHER COMMONALITIES

> The mean is mean, but the variance is meaner.
> —*Anonymous*

There's an interesting theory, with which I'm inclined to agree. Essentially how the development index of a country (social, economic, other), is inversely proportionate to the special status and privileges accorded to its VIPs. I'm also inclined to add: inversely proportionate to the number of VIPs and a stratified VIP culture (e.g. VVIP or Very, Very Important Person).

The Indian landscape is not always quite the dramatic divide of the haves and have-nots. But there are two ubiquitous classes of Indians that deserve special mention—the very privileged (by political power, formal authority, or tremendous wealth), and the rest of us.

The privileged (and their near and dears), expect special treatment everywhere, and their wish is widely formalized—exemptions for holders of public office from paying toll on highways, or from being frisked at airports or other public places.

Sadly, the trappings of this class of VVIP's are mistaken for the reason they are 'special' in some way. Noveau riche Indians, today, are inventing insignias for themselves, hiring PSOs (bodyguards), and cultivating a VIP air—often, as status symbols, rather than for utility, almost believing that having access to some privileges can create true power, rather than the other way around.

Personal security is a great example of this. Budding politicians or rising entrepreneurs may seldom have a real threat perception, but will hire a security detail (or at the least, a bodyguard in grey Safari suit mimicking the government-issued suit worn by VIP politicos' bodyguards), to create an air of VIP'ness'.

Indians are frisked more than probably any other people anywhere, essentially because of a sense of insecurity caused by multiple terrorist attacks on Indian soil. The defining attack though was the one in 2011 in Mumbai. The city's landmarks were assailed—hotels Taj Mahal and Trident, the popular Café Leopold, a Jewish hostel, Nariman House, and even a train station: Chhatrapati Shivaji Terminus.

The instant and enduring consequence of the attack on our daily lives is the ubiquitous security check carried out by private security—when entering hotels, shopping malls, office complexes, residential buildings and just about any gated perimeter. If you drive, your car is 'frisked' (boot and hood peeked into, and occasionally some sort of serious looking electronic device used), and if you walk, you are frisked often after passing through a door frame metal detector.

But if you're a VIP or in the company of a VIP, you will be spared the above mentioned and other commonalities. The VIP culture is very well structured and followed in India, and so is the fickleness of such vaulted status (usually co-terminus with position of office, financial success, or friendship with powers that be).

Sir Mark Tully explains how this VIP culture is endemic:

> Bureaucracy is still based on the British Raj system—the structure and attitude is exactly the same. The purpose is to maintain law and order, and (public servants) behave as if they have no duty to serve you, but you should be grateful if they do anything for you... The guy who sells the railway ticket is a petty bureaucrat. And the Block Development Officer is the highest bureaucrat an average villager will ever see.

In fact officious hubris invariably is inversely proportionate to the seniority of the officer.

Economists and social workers alike have been warning of the widening gap (variance), between the rich and poor, and how average (or mean) incomes do not accurately reflect those on the margins of this bell curve (the concern being the BPL or below poverty line households, and not billionaires).

VERY IMPORTANT PEACOCKS (OR POSEURS)

'We are a semi-feudal society trying to become a proper republic,' is Swaminathan Aiyar's unforgiving observation on how we face a 'double problem of class plus caste'. Swami's explanation somewhat explains the rather amusing displays of class (class as in socio-economic status, not accusing these wannabe VIPs of being classy).

The sense of entitlement endemic amongst our elite leads to a very clear code of 'thou shalt not':

1. Stand in a queue.
2. Subject yourself to security checks.
3. Obey traffic rules.
4. Park more than 50 metres away from the entrance of a building.
5. Sit beyond the first two rows of any event or performance you are invited to.
6. Carry your own gym bag from your car to your weight-training session.
7. Show up in time for meetings (or anything).
8. Cancel appointments last minute with due reason or remorse.
9. Settle for VIP or security status at any event or occasion that has potential for upgrading through strata (VVIPs, VVVIPs, etc./ X, Y and Z-plus security).
10. Go a day without loudly and publicly asking, 'Do you know who I am?'

I might be guilty of exaggeration (the rich and powerful are known to have parked 55 metres away), but you get the message. Also, this list is hardly exhaustive, but certainly exhausting, hence limited to ten commandments.

The business risk is that foreign investors think India is different (which it is), so does not have similar approach to that which would work in Japan or Germany. For instance, in Germany you don't shake hands till you conduct due diligence.

In India you meet people at a party and join hands after the potential Indian partner drops some heavy names. This, somehow, is considered a suitable substitute to a confidential credit report, or even Googling the company.

Where there's fear, greed is never far behind, so there's also some hope of getting something for free in India (unlikely—but if you do get something for free, tell me about it).

But back to the non-privileged, Indian precociousness is best observed watching the average Jai sidestep intelligently conceived and expertly drafted laws that govern their ventures, and even private lives. This is very distinct from the sense of entitlement some compatriots (certainly not 'average Jai' by any measure) suffer from.

Disclaimer: Three of my dear friends are called Jai. I promise, I'm referring to none of them.

THE GAME (AND TRAP OF JUGAAD)

According to Yatra's Dhruv Shringi:

> North India is a hustle—everyone is trying to hustle. Maybe it is a part of our DNA as we have been invaded so many times. We see a need for jugaad even when a completely straightforward way is available. For instance, when updating or developing a new app, a product engineer may put a hack in an app to save four hours of coding (and demonstrate his ingenuity), where another few hours of writing code would give you the proper long form way to doing it. In the South though, processes are more streamlined and focused around the task at hand.

While I am wont to disagree with his sweeping generalization,

I thank Dhruv for a rather effective segue into jugaad. For the book, I feel obliged to discuss a couple of subjects that have been done to death, and frankly jugaad is one of them.

Jugaad, or improvization, has become something of a pejorative in recent times. It started off with touristy wonder at how impoverished Indian villagers (or city slickers) would tinker with meagre resources to create innovative solutions—honestly, the very personification of 'necessity is the mother of invention'. Sadly, the lazy and unscrupulous started using jugaad as a justification for cutting corners, compromising on quality, and not meeting standards. As if to say to foreign observers that whatever they did was good enough for India, because we are the land of jugaad.

This has done a great disservice to sincere, conscientious and genuinely innovative Indian companies and professionals.

The flipside of this depressing jugaad mindset is Frugal Innovation. A case in point is the Tata Nano. When Tata Motors committed itself to delivering a sub-one lakh[18] rupee car, it was thought a tall order, especially if the company hoped to meet safety and emission standards. Impressively, the Tatas achieved this with some very innovative cost engineering. Transnational original equipment manufacturers (OEM) like Bosch and Continental repatriated some of these learnings to their home country (the uber quality conscious Germany), and were able to serve existing customers (BMW, Porsche and the ilk) at a lower cost point. The German government now advocates frugal engineering as one of the pivots of Indo-German business relations.

---

[18] 1 lakh is 1,00,000; 1 crore is 1,00,00,000 (i.e. ten million, and yes, that's where we place the commas). 1 US$ is around 65 INR.

So that's my tuppence on jugaad, and now back to our national sport: gaming the system.

> Ninety per cent of the time, business is painting on a big canvas with all the paints, 10 per cent of it is like trying to push the mountain which is not moving.
> —*Prof. Ashish Nanda*

To be fair, this trait of gaming the system is something of a survival skill in a nation where laws drafted almost two-hundred years ago are still in force. Seasoned civil servants and businessmen confess how it is impossible to comply with all the legislation (which is often contradictory), in some sectors. Add to this the easy rationalization that this levels the playing field, viz. the privileged lot, and the fun that people have doing this.

Here's an example. A friend recounts a recent ordeal. Starting a business requires approximately twenty-seven approvals, at last count, in Karnataka (his business is in Bengaluru, formerly Bangalore). Now, some of these approvals involve factory or site inspections by the concerned department. 'I don't understand what they will see, but they have to come,' he sighs. 'And this is, of course, not free. It is understood that some type of payment is required to "move the file".'

Companies like his that don't pay have to wade through numerous inspections, interminable questions and endless delays. It took him four months to start a company in 2015. This was after being promised a single-window clearance.

Once his business started, a constant and ceaseless stream of pollution control people, the excise inspector, sales tax official, labour officer, inspector of factories, the local MLA and so forth, kept popping in. 'Which just makes working and doing business as inefficient as can be imagined,' and he sighs more dramatically. Understandably, this friend wishes to be identified as, 'A businessman in Bengaluru who, while making the comments and observations, did not want to be named for fear of reprisals.'

This illustrative example would evidence rather neatly, why Indians have long depended on networks, communities, and informal structures to traverse the terrain. But to be fair, we also enjoy the *game*. Beating the system is something of a national sport. Its worst forms manifest in endemic tax evasion, and worse.

One theory is that the need for instant gratification is inbuilt into Indian DNA because we have been in relative shortage and poverty for so long, that our ability to plan long-term and exercise 'deferred gratification' is impeded. This is as true as the converse is and the converse manifests in Indians being among the world's largest savers, or buyers of gold and university education.

Further, the need to create alternative support structures to supplement a formal governance structure, has led to an immense reliance on networks and relationships. These are not considered unprofessional or undesirable, instead they fit rather well with Indian culture that places a high amount of importance on community bonds. Indian businessmen will see even a one-off transaction as a relationship, whereas for some other cultures, an extant relationship might be seen as a mere series of transactions.

This leads in India, to an inordinate amount of time in building the 'relationship' and, having established kinship, entering into some rather emotionally-charged negotiations.

This structure of the very rich and powerful, is described as a 'semi feudal' system by Swaminathan Aiyar. In other cultures, this divide (demographic and digital), could have created serious challenges, what with transformational events like the Arab Spring and the Jasmine Revolution being broadcast real-time. So it begs the question, how have unprivileged (if not underprivileged), impatient, and well-informed Indians resisted a violent overthrow of the status quo?

The answer may lie in India's model of Market Welfarism. 'In many ways, the USA is more socialist than India,' explains the outspoken Swaminathan Aiyar, 'while we use "socialist" to mean "welfare".'[19] Most of young India, and by extrapolation most of India has witnessed the power of private-sector jobs, investment and enterprise to improve lifestyles, enable class (even caste mobility), and create wealth.

CSR @ 2 PER CENT

Corporate social responsibility (CSR) since 2014 (the new Companies Act of 2013) is mandated by law. All companies above a certain size (in profit, net worth or turnover) must

---

[19]Swaminathan Aiyar explains that freebies are fine as long as the state's fiscal position can afford it. The Indian style welfare benefit (electoral promises of laptops by Akhilesh Yadav in Uttar Pradesh; of pressure cookers and rice cookers, or 'Amma Kitchen', by Jayalalithaa in Tamil Nadu), is different from the Western style welfare in capitalism and, 'this is the only reason capitalism has survived, which is unlike the Marxist model of capitalism)'. Even the astute Kejriwal, who is seen as 'socialist' in his ways (which might actually be welfare-ist), and promises free water and electricity (among other things) to the poor, has said at different points of time that private business is a wealth creator, and that honest businessmen must be encouraged. Perhaps appealing to voters who want to see the private sector flourish, and the rising tide to lift all boats.

apportion two per cent of profit towards CSR activities.

The CSR legislation may well have been rolled out with the best of intentions, but large corporations (mostly large firms will fall under the compliance) fear that it will become just another box to check, if the government doesn't have the right mechanism in place.

A significant number of Indian and multinational corporations were already spending far in excess of two per cent on CSR, but now complain that they have to contend with yet another inspector.

On the other hand, unsavoury practices are already being alleged—that companies are giving CSR rupees to the Chief Minister's Relief Fund under duress (which complies with the letter, not the spirit of law); or crooked businesses are setting up their own foundations, which is permissible, but some are using their foundations to circulate funds back to themselves; and unscrupulous NGOs are promising a share of funds (so businessmen don't need to set up their own foundation). This 'round-tripping' would typically work as follows: crooked company (A) and unscrupulous NGO (B) agree upon an amount (say, the entire 2 per cent CSR obligation) to 'comply' with the regulation. A transfers the CSR funds to B, who are an eligible NGO running CSR compliant projects, and B retains a small 'fee' and refunds the money to A (well, to the officer who authorized this transaction, typically).

Even pre-CSR law, companies were driven either by an enlightened self or by gaps in governance and public goods to direct copious amounts of earnings towards similar goals. The head of a large conglomerate setting up a plant in a tribal area claimed to have built great public infrastructure, to which a cynical friend retorted that the development was not entirely selfless CSR, but had to be built to attract employees. However, he did concede that there was nothing wrong with this either—it being a win-win for local communities and the corporation.

The private sector has long been forced to fill the gap, and will continue to do so in the foreseeable future. Infosys, for instance, set up Infosys University for its burgeoning in-house requirement of skilled manpower.

Ideologically, though, there are a few issues with this kind of compulsory CSR. 'In theory, CSR (law) is bad,' warn hard-nosed economists, for three reasons.

1. Welfare is the job of the government, if it cannot do its job why ask the private sector to do so?
2. How can you ensure no leakage in the 2 per cent?
3. As the shareholder of a listed company, why should a portfolio company (say, ITC or Tata) do CSR, and not the individual—so, *individual social responsibility*, anyone?

Other economists believe that the CSR law is a way of cutting out 'friction'. The 2 per cent goes directly from the tax-paying corporation to active projects. Corporations are also discovering that in many ways, the 2 per cent spend can benefit the companies, depending on how they put the CSR to work. Skill/vocational training is an obvious example, which can simultaneously create employment opportunities for communities, while widening the talent pool for the company to hire from.

Lawyers are already examining how a well-conceived and executed CSR programme can help overcome problems related to land acquisition. Rural development can create the right conditions and goodwill to negotiate potentially hairy land acquisition transactions with local communities.

In these early days of CSR, companies have demonstrated enlightened self-interest in their philanthropy, often seeking to fill gaps in governance and public goods.

CORPORATE GOVERNANCE

The Companies Act, 2013 has been progressive on a couple of accounts, in particular, mandating at least one woman director on every corporate board.

But first the bad stuff. Women directors are usually family members of major shareholders or promoters, and sadly this is also the trend in sizeable, and even listed companies. On the other hand, truly independent women directors (or any independent directors, really) are reluctant to join boards due to the disproportionate amount of legal exposure the position entails. Finance or legal professionals might insist on a position on the audit committee, for instance, to have some oversight into potentially hairy matters.

To put this into context, the recent onerous laws that place liability on executive and independent directors alike, were framed in the aftermath of large Indian corporate scams. The most notable of these cases of corporate avarice, has been that of the ironically named Satyam (Sanskrit for 'truth').

TRUTH BACKWARDS

Mr Ramalinga Raju, the Chairman and founder of Satyam, ran a well-respected and profitable corporation, but shocked the world with his sudden confession of falsifying company accounts for years.

Prior to Raju's confession in early 2009, Hyderabad-based Satyam was doing well by all counts. The IT giant (consulting, enterprise business solutions, engineering solutions, and infrastructure management) was among the four largest Indian IT services company in revenue terms, had close to 53,000 employees spread across 65 countries, was listed on both Indian and US stock exchanges, and boasted 690 global customers, 185 of them Fortune 500 companies. Raju was named *Fortune* magazine's Entrepreneur of the Year in 2003, and in 2007 won the Ernst and Young Entrepreneur Award.

The story unravelled when on 16 December 2008, the Board of Satyam met to decide on a proposal for Satyam to acquire a stake in two companies owned by Raju's sons—Maytas (Satyam backwards) Properties and Maytas Infrastructure. The Board of Satyam approved the purchase of a 51 per cent stake in Maytas Infrastructure, and a 100 per cent stake in Maytas Properties at an investment of US$ 0.3 billion and US$ 1.3 billion, respectively.

Then Raju told the Board that he had learnt that IBM was planning to mount a takeover bid on Satyam, and advised the Board that a 'poison-pill' strategy was the best defence. A diversification in unrelated assets by assuming a large liability would discourage potential investors from mounting an aggressive bid on the company.

Raju's announcement of this diversification, non-core to Satyam's IT business, which was decided without shareholder consent, made investors furious. Overnight, Satyam's stock price nosedived in both the Indian (30 per cent) and US exchange markets (55 per cent). The decision was reversed the following day, but the damage couldn't be undone. Investors and clients remained wary of Satyam, fearful of a more extensive fraud.

On 7 January 2009, Raju shocked the corporate world with his confessional letter addressed to Satyam's Board of Directors. He disclosed that the company's accounts had been falsified for several years—that he had overstated the receivables, understated the liabilities, and inflated cash balances for the second quarter ending September 2008. Raju said of his immersion in the violation, 'It was like riding a tiger, not knowing how to get off without being eaten.'

> (Letter from Raju)
>
> To the Board of Directors
> Satyam Computer Services Ltd.
> From B. Ramalinga Raju
> Chairman, Satyam Computer Services Ltd.
> January 7, 2009
>
> Dear Board Members,
>
> It is with deep regret, and tremendous burden that I am carrying on my conscience, that I would like to bring the following facts to your notice:
>
> 1. The Balance Sheet carries as of September 30, 2008:
>   a. Inflated (non-existent) cash and bank balances of 50.40 billion rupees ($1.04 billion) (as against 53.61 billion reflected in the books).
>   b. An accrued interest of 3.76 billion rupees which is non-existent.
>   c. An understated liability of 12.30 billion rupees on account of funds arranged by me.
>   d. An overstated debtors position of 4.90 billion rupees (as against 26.51 billion reflected in the books).
> 2. For the September quarter (Q2) we reported a revenue

of 27.00 billion rupees and an operating margin of 6.49 billion rupees (24 per cent of revenues) as against the actual revenues of 21.12 billion rupees and an actual operating margin of 610 million rupees (3 per cent of revenues). This has resulted in artificial cash and bank balances going up by 5.88 billion rupees in Q2 alone.

The gap in the Balance Sheet has arisen purely on account of inflated profits over a period of last several years (limited only to Satyam standalone, books of subsidiaries reflecting true performance). What started as a marginal gap between actual operating profit and the one reflected in the books of accounts continued to grow over the years. It has attained unmanageable proportions as the size of company operations grew significantly (annualized revenue run rate of 112.76 billion rupees in the September quarter, 2008, and official reserves of 83.92 billion rupees). The differential in the real profits and the one reflected in the books was further accentuated by the fact that the company had to carry additional resources and assets to justify higher level of operations—thereby, significantly, increasing the costs.

Every attempt made to eliminate the gap failed. As the promoters held a small percentage of equity, the concern was that poor performance would result in a takeover, thereby exposing the gap.

The aborted Maytas acquisition deal was the last attempt to fill the fictitious assets with real ones. Maytas' investors were convinced that this is a good divestment opportunity and a strategic fit. Once Satyam's problem was solved, it was hoped that Maytas' payments can be delayed. But that was not to be.

What followed in the last several days is common knowledge. I would like the Board to know:

1. That neither myself, nor the Managing Director (including our spouses) sold any shares in the last eight years—excepting for a small proportion declared and sold for philanthropic purposes.
2. That in the last two years a net amount of 12.30 billion rupees was arranged to Satyam (not reflected in the books of Satyam) to keep the operations going by resorting to pledging all the promoter shares and raising funds from known sources by giving all kinds of assurances (statement enclosed, only to the members of the Board). Significant dividend payments, acquisitions, capital expenditure to provide for growth did not help matters. Every attempt was made to keep the wheel moving and to ensure prompt payment of salaries to the associates. The last straw was the selling of most of the pledged share by the lenders on account of margin triggers.
3. That neither me, nor the Managing Director took even one rupee/dollar from the company and have not benefitted in financial terms on account of the inflated results.
4. None of the Board members, past or present, had any knowledge of the situation in which the company is placed. Even business leaders and senior executives in the company, such as, Ram Mynampati, Subu D., T.R. Anand, Keshab Panda, Virender Agarwal, A.S. Murthy, Hari T., S.V. Krishnan, Vijay Prasad, Manish Mehta, Murali V., Sriram Papani, Kiran Kavale, Joe

> Lagiola, Ravindra Penumetsa, Jayaraman, and Prabhakar Gupta are unaware of the real situation as against the books of accounts. None of my or Managing Director's immediate or extended family members has any idea about these issues.

Having put these facts before you, I leave it to the wisdom of the Board to take the matters forward. However, I am also taking the liberty to recommend the following steps:

1. A Task Force has been formed in the last few days to address the situation arising out of the failed Maytas acquisition attempt. This consists of some of the most accomplished leaders of Satyam: Subu D., T.R. Anand, Keshab Panda and Virender Agarwal, representing business functions and A.S. Murthy, Hari T. and Murali V. representing support functions. I suggest that Ram Mynampati be made the Chairman of this Task Force to immediately address some of the operational matters on hand. Ram can also act as an interim CEO reporting to the Board.
2. Merrill Lynch can be entrusted with the task of quickly exploring some merger opportunities.
3. You may have a 'restatement of accounts' prepared by the auditors in light of the facts that I have placed before you.

I have promoted and have been associated with Satyam for well over twenty years now. I have seen it grow from few people to 53,000 people, with 185 Fortune 500 companies as customers and operations in sixty-six countries. Satyam has established an excellent leadership and competency base at all levels. I sincerely apologize to all Satyamites and stakeholders, who have made Satyam a special organization, for the current situation. I am confident they will stand by the company in this hour of crisis.

In light of the above, I fervently appeal to the Board to hold together to take some important steps. Mr T.R. Prasad is well placed to mobilize support from the government at this crucial time. With the hope that members of the Task Force and the financial advisor, Merrill Lynch (now Bank of America), will stand by the company at this crucial hour, I am marking copies of this statement to them as well.

Under the circumstances, I am tendering my resignation as the chairman of Satyam and shall continue in this position only till such time the current Board is expanded. My continuance is just to ensure enhancement of the Board over the next several days or as early as possible.

I am now prepared to subject myself to the laws of the land and face consequences thereof. (B. Ramalinga Raju) Copies marked to:
1. Chairman SEBI
2. Stock Exchanges ($1= ₹48.6)

The government quickly sensed the potentially disastrous consequences that this incident involving a highly respected, internationally traded company could have on international confidence in the hitherto respected Indian technology sector, and India's competitiveness in a sector vital to the economy.

India's Ministry of Corporate Affairs swung swiftly into action. The Ministry announced that there would be no financial bailout for Satyam, but the government would provide a 'managerial bailout' in order to avert the company imploding, by finding a strategic investor. The collapse of Satyam, the single largest employer in the state of Andhra Pradesh, would have catastrophic economic and political ramifications in the state. The Ministry then asked the Company Law Board (CLB) to suspend Satyam's Board. The CLB is an independent quasi-judicial body with powers to oversee the behaviour of companies.

The story has a happy ending. Satyam was acquired by the much smaller Tech Mahindra (though part of the immense Mahindra Group), and was able to overcome scepticism and challenges to emerge as one of the top five Indian IT companies, with a market capitalization of almost US$ 7 billion as of January 2016. In a signal that investors reward good governance (Mahindra Group has a reputation for high integrity), Satyam's shares started climbing soon after Tech Mahindra was announced as the winner bidder.

Also, the three-member government-appointed Satyam Board steered the company through the storm and was successful in its goal of finding a credible, strategic buyer for the beleaguered company.

The Satyam story probably explains why the seemingly harsh laws were drafted—like any laws, a product of the prevailing mood and times. These are still early days for the law. There is hope that good governance can be achieved without scaring away good independent talent for boards.

Some corporate governance experts are already calling for scrapping of this legislation, which has seemingly limited utility. However, a familiar challenge plagues all new policymaking, taxes and legislation. The challenge is to draft new, reformative and progressive laws. Also, to check potential misuse of the new law without diluting its ambitions.

The Satyam story also demonstrates excellent crisis management on the part of the government in protecting jobs and shareholder wealth. It also shows the fact that the Indian investor is mature enough to punish misdemeanour, and reward corporate integrity.

First generation entrepreneur, Mr Tulsi Tanti, who built India's largest wind power company through many ups and downs says, 'One of my biggest learnings from these multiple experiences was to always have my principles and values be the guiding factors in business. A building can only weather difficult storms if it has a strong foundation. With the right principles in place, you also ensure sustainability of the business.'

RISK TAKERS *AND* RISK AVOIDERS

While most Indians are enormously entrepreneurial, the well-established folk are rather risk averse (another of our contradictions).

Family businesses (the F word you'll frequently encounter in Indian business) are operating in a rational mode, to put it mildly, and not quite taking advantage of global realities and opportunities. These conservative businesses are resistant to moving a part of their production overseas, for instance. If we were to examine the EU value chain, no single product is produced entirely in one country, and the production network creates advantage—a competitive advantage.

The once thriving Indian textile sector is in disarray, having lost ground to other Asian competitors. This sector was rationally export dependent, but due to the changing economic landscape—especially after the Generalized System of Preferences (GSP, a quota for exports given to developing economies) was phased out as a response to the growing Indian economy—this sector began to struggle.

The efforts of Indian industry are focused around trying to revive the GSP, but not on pushing for Trade Agreements (for instance the Free Trade Agreement [FTA] with EU), where zero per cent market access gives them a huge market. The GSP, even if revived, will be temporary, and will at best give them a limited benefit (some percentage or volume), as opposed to say, a preferred 8 to 12 per cent duty where non-GSP exports pay 18 to 30 per cent.

However, a few progressive textile firms like Raymonds, Arvind Mills and Kanoria have decided to relocate their garment business to Ethiopia, in response to the Africa Growth and Opportunity Act. Export from Africa, especially African 'least developed countries' (LDCs), to EU is duty exempt, so with one deft move, they have killed the duty disadvantage without GSP or FTA.

THE RETURNING INDIAN

Professor Ashish Nanda returned to India after twenty-five years of teaching at Harvard Business School and Harvard Law School to head his alma mater, IIM, Ahmedabad (IIM-A). Needless to say, he took a significant economic haircut to come back, for a non-monetary reward, 'a feeling of fulfilment for doing something for an institute' he cares about.

His appointment as Dean of IIM-A was the outcome of all stakeholders—alumni, Board, students and faculty—recognizing a 'felt need for drastic change'. People were welcoming. The top three agenda items were: (i) talk and listen (ii) listen and talk (iii) be willing to learn without any prescription or preconceived notions.

IIM-A is an institute of national importance, so both state

and national governments have a big say in its decisions, though it is an autonomous body. Prof. Nanda says he was warned of attempts of bureaucratic control, but got the feeling that people (the government as well as Board members), and the Ministry of Human Resource Development (MHRD), wanted him to succeed. He says he has, 'not had conflict, and made demands yet, but they haven't been obstructive,' which he says, 'was a surprise'.

The 'infrastructure is terrible,' he adds. The 'workforce is loyal, but not terribly skilled. There is a sense of identity among the workforce, but there is a need to upgrade skills, while bringing in laterals. The opportunity exists to do things right—conservation instead of the shortcut of a quick repair,' he adds.

However, Prof. Nanda notes that, 'Faculty salaries are much lower than private sector salaries. Salaries are offered as per government norms, so they are as low as 12 per cent of what you could earn abroad.' There is thus an exodus of the best doctoral students who want to go abroad. He adds that 'The good guys who will come back will be absolutely patriotic, or will return due to family constraints.' So the new Dean of IIM-A got companies to endow Chairs, 'eleven Chairs were very rapidly raised, and the money earned goes towards compensation of faculty. They were also allowed outside consulting by faculty members, and the share of executive education fees.'

There is a constant change for the better, but often indiscernible to those who are too close to the scene.

EUROVISION

Bernard Steinruecke, head of Indo-German Chamber of Commerce sums up the most telling changes since he moved to India in 1993. 'The biggest change is scale,' says Steinruecke. Since he first arrived in India, the GDP has more than quadrupled, while market capitalization of listed exchanges (and listed companies) has 'attained unimaginable levels'. He offers the city of Pune, Mumbai's smaller, greener neighbour, as a case in point. Circa early 1990s, Pune had a million inhabitants, and most Germans would travel there only to get to the famous Osho Ashram. Today six million inhabitants comprise this emerging city, and if you meet a German, chances are that he works for Volkswagen (or another MNC).

Mumbai may long have been considered the financial capital of India, but the city's infrastructure was infamously deficient. Virtually all business, government and cultural activity clogged around Nariman Point, which was the world's most expensive neighbourhood to buy or rent. What made matters worse was that this 'city centre' of the megapolis was located at its southernmost point, on the coast.

If you visit Mumbai today, chances are your meetings or social engagements will be in lower Parel, BKC (Bandra-Kurla Complex, fast overtaking Nariman Point as the priciest business district in Mumbai), Powai, New Mumbai, Andheri, Worli or the many new neighbourhoods gaining acceptance. Mumbaikars surveying the scene from the Bandra–Worli sealink—which cuts travel time by up to half by connecting said areas by going around the coastline and avoiding congested roads—can see the impressive skyline, where all high-rise buildings were built in the last ten years.

Gurgaon (now Gurugram) is the 'Pudong' of Delhi, claims Steinruecke, referring to the famous über-modern district of Shanghai. Very much like Pudong of the late 1980s, Gurgaon, as recently as fifteen years ago, was mostly vast farmland. Gurgaon today feels like a mix of Dubai and Pudong—metro lines and skyscrapers being constantly constructed, with construction cranes being the only permanent landmark of the city.

Bengaluru in a similar timeframe has emerged as a vast urban sprawl, 'you drive and drive and the city doesn't end,' observes a long-term expat. Other changes noted include the fact that earlier there were fewer flights, and connections were cumbersome. Today private airlines like Indigo are always on time and comfortable (though all economy), while airports are efficient. Travelling in India is getting easy. Earlier there was no mobile telephony, today life is unimaginable without a mobile.

Another dramatic change is that the Indian is now a global person. Large European companies have, or have had, Indians at the helm—BASF, Deutsche Bank, and other DAX listed companies.

The speed of German plants coming up in India has been quite remarkable. Projects of Indian corporations have impressed international veterans equally. Adriaan Mast, who headed the Airport City Real Estate concept at Schiphol Amsterdam Airport later advised the Indian GMR Group (developers of the international airports of New Delhi and Hyderabad, and also of Istanbul in Turkey and of Male in Maldives), and discussed airport city development—retail, offices, hotels, parking and logistics. In Mast's estimation, comparable airport development projects that take over a decade in Europe, were up and running within a period of 4–5 years in India.

Mast attributes this impressive speed in an infamously difficult bureaucratic and physical environment, to the drive of Indian entrepreneurs (which meant open communication lines and fast decision-making), a leadership style which ensured buy-in of various business lines in decisions (Mast had to acclimatize to the large number of people at these lengthy meetings), and the strategy of hiring top advisors (Mast was one of many different consultants working on the project).

The new airports (including Mumbai, Bengaluru and Delhi) are considered among the best in the world. The consortium approach—with experienced foreign partners in the airport management, as well as financial partners—has clearly worked well.

Germans are no strangers to India. Einstein (the physicist) and Tagore (the poet) shared a famous friendship, Max Müller (the Indologist) instructed ICS (Indian Civil Services) recruits on India before they made their maiden journey to the subcontinent (think undivided India), and companies like Siemens have been in India since the late 1800s. And knowing full well the cultural differences between India and the Fatherland, German friends inform me that for them, it is 'comparatively easy to do business in India'.

And to explain this comparative ease of doing business (CEODB, to coin a term), I'm offered three arguments:

1. the right approach, people and strategy can give great results
2. people are highly motivated and *motivate-able*
3. somehow it all works out in the end

MNCs now consider India a strategic market and allocate it resources, funds and people. 'You must aim to be successful, you cannot be half-hearted. A lukewarm approach of "let's see if it works" is bound to fail,' Steinruecke notes.

The volume of German FDI in India is considered very low, though Steinruecke explains why this is a unique tribute to the success Germans have witnessed in India. Indian operations of

German companies, of all sizes, are typically highly profitable, and don't need funds from abroad. Add to this the trait of relatively low dividend payouts, which is usually 5 or 10 per cent of profit, means that these companies reinvest the bulk of their earnings in India. German corporations such as Bosch and Siemens are also known to repatriate profits, albeit within the prudent levels that German companies prefer.

A mascot of Indo-German success is Bajaj Allianz Insurance, which has grown within a decade from a staff of two employees to 25,000 employees and 100,000 exclusive agents. Its success is attributed to a mix of factors, including picking the right local partner (i.e. Bajaj); treating India as a strategic investment, which meant hiring brilliant people like Kamesh Goyal, who is now just one level below the Board of Allianz; product expertise, and the bold choice of Pune as main location (initially chosen because Mr Bajaj lived there, and also because it was not as expensive as Mumbai). Bosch has had a similar golden run in India.

There are, however, as many acrimonious divorces as ongoing honeymoons with local Indian partners. Luxury car maker BMW has disputes on import duties, wind power company Enercon famously has problems with its JV partner. To avoid a 'match made in heaven, but ended in hell', make sure you pick the right partner and right strategy (JV, licence agreement, special purpose vehicle or SPV, etc.) for your venture.

Adriaan Mast has further insight on the partner search, 'Make up your mind well in advance—how much risk you want to take, how much capital you want to invest, how much time you want to invest. If you have clear answers to these questions, it will be easier to find a suitable partner.'

In India, both airports Mast consulted on had foreign consortium partners from Malaysia (Delhi and Hyderabad), and Germany (Delhi), respectively. In addition to this, there were a large number of suppliers, employees and advisors from many other countries across the world.

Heads of multiple foreign-owned corporations insist that it makes lot of sense to get Indian CEOs and talent, as they are 'very loyal and brilliant', while the expats were good to ensure that the company's corporate philosophy was conveyed to the Indian subsidiary, and often a foreign face helps in marketing. But there's a consensus that loading a company with expensive expats is not a good idea. Depending on the scale and sector, a blend (in some proportion) is ideal.

When challenged with examples of German companies being deceived by Indian employees or partners, Steinreucke insists that none of the recent cases, including Reebok (where Adidas discovered after the takeover that the Indian management was cooking the books), are India-specific. He offers examples of Flowtex (where Indian companies were getting receipts that were fake), or the Schneider case viz. Deutsche Bank (where real estate was being built, but only on paper).

When approached for a bribe, what has worked for German companies is to say something along the lines of, 'Sorry, we are listed, and bound by rules and regulations. If you want to do business with us take it (our approach) or leave it.' Remember, corruption can also be private sector corruption. Siemens is one of the most unwavering on this issue, especially after its very public scandals, which blew all the way back to Germany.

Steinreucke has been on the boards of some of the largest German investors in India, and finds that embassies can sometimes be used to escalate hairy matters with the top at a local level, starting with the MLA or MP, and later the CMs, and at the Secretary level. These office bearers are consistently receptive and proactive in dealing with genuine grievances. The straight approach is the best he says, 'Tell them that the company will leave if the concerned department won't cooperate. The company is paying taxes, investing here, supporting the local school (as good corporate citizens would do in enlightened self-interest) for trained, employable talent.'

As Coke, Yatra, Kellogg's and Japanese investors demonstrate, the Indian market is about managing diversity and scale, and political shifting sands and red tape. It is probably a good idea to understand the 'what' and 'why', before the 'how to'.

3

THE GIST OF OUR DEMOCRACY[20]
(OR CREATIVE CUMULATIVE INCREMENTALISM)

> That old wheel, is gonna roll around once more.
> When it does, it will even up the score.
> —*Johnny Cash and Hank Williams Jr.*

We have arrived at a peculiar stage, in that India Inc. is pro economic reform, and pro FDI, while the resistance comes from political opposition.

Significantly, this is a 180 degree turn from the days of the 'Bombay Club' of the 1990s,[21] when a significant section of Indian industrial royalty created a pressure group and lobbied, unsuccessfully, against liberalization of the economy. Instead of being wiped out by competition, these companies, reared on protectionism, actually have done famously well, and achieved unimaginable (at the time) growth.

The Goods and Services Tax (GST),[22] is interchangeably

---

[20]India's Chief Economic Adviser, Arvind Subramanian, famously argued in Economic survey 2014–15 that India could achieve double digit growth without drastic reform through persistent incrementalism that could cumulate to big bang reform.

[21]See Appendix 1: How We Got Here

[22]The introduction: GST would be a trans-functional step in the reform of indirect taxation in India. Consolidating multiple Central and State taxes into a single tax would mitigate cascading or double taxation and facilitate a

quoted as a solution to problems, or a cause of many, or a missed chance, depending on whom you ask. Like most things in India, all of the above are partly true, and this has been the status quo for a while.

In August 2016, the long awaited GST Bill was passed by the Rajya Sabha (Upper House of Parliament), after a thirteen year journey (of which six were in Parliament).

Considerable effort was yet required to put GST into action. The amendments from Rajya Sabha had to be incorporated by the Lok Sabha (the Lower House), a minimum 50 per cent of state legislatures were to approve the Bill, the President needed to sign the Bill into law and the GST Council was to be formed. This was diligently followed through: The Constitution Amendment Bill for GST was cleared in both the Houses of the Parliament, ratified by the requisite number of states and received the President's consent.

Politically, it was a thorn in the side of the Modi administration, which pushed hard for legislation since he assumed office in May 2014 but was filibustered in the Rajya Sabha where the ruling party doesn't have a majority.

The Union Cabinet acceded to one of three key demands of the Opposition, and dropped the 1 per cent manufacturing tax, while providing a guarantee to compensate states for any revenue loss arising in the first five years of this indirect tax regime.

Foreign investors were keenly watching developments, having made clear that they considered the passage of GST as

---

common national market. The simplicity of the tax would also lead to easier administration and enforcement. In India's federal structure, GST would need to be implemented concurrently by the Central and State governments. Implementation of GST in the near future would necessitate all supply chains to be re-aligned.

the single most important reform the Government of India must enact. Some foreign observers called it the biggest tax reform since 1947, the year of India's Independence.

GST is seen as the silver bullet to replace the myriad state-by-state tax rules with a single indirect tax, and for the first time create a single national market for the movement of goods. GST has the potential to lead the economic integration of India, generate millions of new jobs, improve enterprise productivity and empower consumers and producers. Key benefits include easier compliance, uniformity of tax structures, improved competitiveness and removal of cascading. The National Council of Applied Economic Research has predicted GST implementation to boost India's GDP growth by between 0.9–1.7 per cent.

However, this is not a dream GST, as creating consensus has meant several compromises. The fine print of the GST is not for the faint hearted—which by the way is three GSTs- State (SGST), Central (CGST) and Integrated (IGST). And there will still be multiple agencies involved: Central for CGST and IGST, and State governments for SGST. But this still is a considerable improvement over the previous indirect tax regime, now to be subsumed under GST, including:

At the Central level, the following taxes are being subsumed:

1. Central Excise Duty
2. Additional Excise Duty
3. Service Tax
4. Additional Customs Duty, commonly known as Countervailing Duty
5. Special Additional Duty of Customs

At the State level, the following taxes are being subsumed:

1. Subsuming of State Value Added Tax/Sales Tax
2. Entertainment Tax (other than the tax levied by the local bodies)
3. Central Sales Tax (levied by the Centre and collected by the States)
4. Octroi and Entry tax
5. Purchase Tax
6. Luxury tax
7. Taxes on lottery, betting and gambling

There still isn't a single GST rate (as Swaminathan Aiyar had warned us in his book), but a range, depending on where a product lies on the essentials to 'demerit' scale.

Broadly

1. Exemption or zero per cent for essential items including food grains
2. 5 per cent lower rate for goods for mass consumption
3. 12 per cent merit rate for necessity goods
4. 18 per cent standard rate for all common goods
5. 28 per cent demerit rate for luxury goods like tobacco, aerated beverages, luxury cars (currently at 30–31 per cent)

A formidable IT framework, the GSTN is being established to implement the new legislation. The GSTN (or GST Network) provides for an Electronic Credit Ledger System (ECLS) programmed to capture data, assessee-wise.

The GSTN promises a common GST portal providing frontend services of registration, returns and payments; as well as the backend modules for states that could include processing of returns, registrations, audits, assessments, appeals etc. Manual intervention and manual filing of returns could be done away with, and self-assessment enabled.

The final shape of GST will become clear in due course, as the GST council refines and evolves the tax, but the implementation of GST in an increasingly digital economy (spurred on by the demonetization drive) holds exciting possibilities.

As importantly, 2016 was another big year for reform, which saw the government further overhauling India's FDI regime. The policy framework governing FDI in a variety of sectors, including strategic sectors like defence and aviation were further simplified, opened up under the automatic route, and FDI limits have been increased for those sectors that require approval.

Passage of the Insolvency & Bankruptcy Code Bill in the Parliament is another key reform (remember India's previously poor record at palliative care for companies?). This Bill is seen as a major step towards improving ease of doing business, and assuring greater legal certainty and speed in closure of businesses.

Other landmark reforms included announcement of the much awaited Intellectual Property Rights Policy and passage of Real Estate Bill.

Significantly, India jumped 21 places globally in terms of gender equality, having closed its gender gap by 2 per cent in a year. It now ranks 87 out of 144 countries according to the WEF's Global Gender Gap Report 2016. This is especially significant, given WEF's observation that the prospects of global workplace gender parity slipped further, in a 'dramatic slowdown in progress', globally.

It is often thought that the EU, in many ways, is more of an economic union than is India, though India is of course a stronger (federal) political union. While trucks zoom past international borders throughout most of the Eurozone, every Indian state has check posts at borders, with trucks and commercial vehicles backed up for miles before they can pass. It takes a truck about 6 days to traverse the distance of about 1500 km from Delhi to Mumbai, while transit time for vessels from Nhava Sheva (India's largest container port, off the coast of Mumbai) to Dubai is four days. It is estimated that implementation of GST alone (with no improvement in physical infrastructure), will condense this Delhi to Mumbai travel time to a 3 or 4-day journey. This, of course, would be accompanied by a cost saving of as much as 20 per cent. A telling example of how the legislative infrastructure undermines even the best physical infrastructure.

All states in India had different tax rates, and a system of taxation that often causes products to be taxed more than just once. This was in addition to the Central (federal) taxes. This created a huge amount of inefficiency in supply chains and complexity in doing business in more than one state in the country.

As a solution, GST was conceived as a single tax rate that would take care of all Central, State and inter-state taxes. The delivery, however, hasn't been as efficient as the conception. Studies estimate better tax administration, enhanced Ease of Business, a uniform market and a 2 per cent increase in GDP would be outcomes of GST implementation.

Reportedly, McKinsey attributes the success of MNCs in emerging markets to five factors:

1. localized management/empowered local team
2. making significant investment—with a long-term approach
3. investing in India-specific products at different price points

4. setting up a distribution channel and brand
5. building a supply chain to get the cost structure right

There's plenty of scope for doing the first, but appetite for companies of any size to carry through points two to four, depends on measures like the GST, as well as mitigating tax inefficiency, red tape, and wasteful physical infrastructure to mitigate double taxation. Onerous compliance essentially distracts management from really focusing on building business.

In studying and refining the supply-chain architecture of multiple companies, I have been repeatedly reminded of how legislative framework incentivizes (or disincentivizes) the behaviour of businesses.

For instance, a factory in Mumbai selling to cities in Punjab, Haryana and Delhi, might want to operate a hub-and-spoke warehouse out of Delhi. However, this would mean incurring taxes in Delhi, Mumbai, and at the point of sale—say, Jaipur in Rajasthan. To circumvent this, companies run 'virtual warehouses' in the state of sale to document a 'stock transfer' instead of an interstate sale. This is a legal grey area, but still in use by companies, to differing degrees.

Similarly, making your India-specific product might require you to source, supply and store at multiple locations around the country. This leaves you or your vendors to come up with a supply chain that's least inefficient. Pretty much all supply chains will incur some inefficiency, so your job is to figure out which permutation works best for you. The problem isn't purely physical either, i.e. affecting warehouses and trucks alone. Procedural red tape ties a neat bow around interstate transactions.

When selling interstate in India and in order to avoid higher rates of taxation, the Central government allows inter-state sales against 'C Forms'. This drops the taxation on goods from 12.5 per cent to a concessional 2 per cent. Sounds great? The devil as usual is in the details.

The seller of the goods, after declaring the sales under form C, must now ensure collection of the said form from the customer. The customer on the other hand, must get the C forms from local tax authorities in their state. If the company has a tax issue (a discrepancy, a summons, or has not filed returns) the department does not issue the forms. Further, the forms also get held up because the department doesn't issue due to its own inefficiency. I have heard of situations where delays were caused by reasons such as having run out of paper to print the forms, no signing officer, election duty, to name but a few.

So getting the form is challenging. Now for the real problem—even if the department does not issue the forms, the manufacturer is responsible for getting them and submitting them to the local tax department. If he does not, the transaction is charged the differential tax of 10 per cent, even though the fault may not lie with the manufacturer. The implementation of GST is expected to eliminate Sisyphean processes of the ilk.

The implementation of GST can lift the GDP by 1 to 2 per cent, which could generate an estimated 1.5 million new jobs, which in turn create another 4 indirect jobs for each direct job created.

IN INDIA MIRACLES TAKE A LITTLE LONGER

On managing expectations—if GST sounds too good to be true, maybe it really is. Implementation of GST is challenging to say the least, with states reluctant to act on what they see as relinquishing powers. A senior politician explained what was going on in the negotiations, 'Each clause has 70 to 90 per cent agreement, but [the degree of] disagreement is different in each state.'

And implementation of GST might not automatically mean the end of interstate check posts. You could abolish check posts if there was a uniform tax rate, but if some products are not covered by GST, you again need to check all trucks, or else this could lead to inter-state smuggling, as happens in US and Canada.

States are demanding a Constitutional amendment to promise GST will not exceed 18 per cent. If and when it will get done is anybody's guess. But all parties (especially political parties), agree it is required.[23] Parliamentary theatrics might lead us to believe that the Opposition and the ruling party and its allies have some irreconcilable differences on issues, including the GST, which also is true regardless of who is in power or in the Opposition. In principle, all parties are agreed on the merits and need for the uniform GST, but getting state governments to agree is akin to signing FTAs (Free Trade Agreements) with individual states.

Like most countries, reforms, traditionally were reactive, that is to say, they were usually preceded by a crisis.[24] Over the

---

[23] The passing of GST is meant to serve as an example of how the parliamentary process works, how the legal framework intersects with business, and the interplay of the federal (state + central) structure.

[24] 1st reform: IMF forced us to liberalize; 2nd reform: WTO forced agricultural reform; 3rd reform: easing quantitative restrictions, when balance of payments are favourable. India has never defaulted on international deadlines (even if paid at eleventh hour, at midnight). So commitments have also always been honoured, as in the case of the WTO judgements, i.e., even if rulings were not in India's favour. Crisis preceding reform goes back a long way. A watershed moment was the Great Depression of 1929. Until then, countries only went into debt to finance wars. Keynes's public letter to US President Roosevelt changed

last few years reforms are becoming proactive; governments no longer wait for a crisis to undertake reform. We could reform faster, but reforming without the external compulsions of a crisis is already a heartening development.

FOXIFICATION

This can get rather confusing. In a rather bizarre TV news show (even American journalist John Oliver lamented the 'foxification' of Indian news on *The Daily Show*), a popular anchor heckled a hapless MP for being inconsistent in voting in Indian Parliament. The accused MP tried to explain how voting on issues is more consistent than voting based on your seating in the Parliament (literally: seating is decided on whether you are in the Opposition or in the ruling coalition). For the last three decades, India has been ruled by one of two parties, individually or via coalition—the Congress (I), India's grand old party, whom we refer to as the Congress; and the Bhartiya Janata Party, whom we refer to as the BJP.

Over the last couple of decades, all parties (generally when in power), have agreed that the GST is essential to making a single market of India. The economic benefits, and the consequent political mileage that accrues from a uniform GST across the length and breadth of the country, are also fairly clear. Ergo, any opposition party is loath to allow this obviously beneficial law to be passed by a party other than itself.

Opposition takes, well, opposing rather seriously. Obstructionism has rather become the accepted norm in

---

all that. For the first time, a government—in this case the US—undertook debt to boost public spending.

Parliament. This is not to say there are no instances of bipartisanship. Resolutions to increase MP salaries and benefits are known to be passed unanimously and without debate. This isn't unique to the Indian Parliament, but an interesting stage in the lifecycle of our democracy, nonetheless. Most Western democracies went through this evolution, and the most telling might be the American example.

In the Gilded Age (the late nineteenth century), the US was rife with corruption, parliamentary boorishness and corporate cronyism (which we call Crony Capitalism in India)—think robber barons. Politics was very much the preserve of a few influential families, and entry of a first-generation politician was thought nigh impossible.

This was followed by the Progressive Age in the early twentieth century, when progressive reform of laws and, most importantly, the rise of the middle class led to cleaner, more rational, and egalitarian politics which eventually enabled a Barack Obama to occupy the White House, beating the formidable Hillary Clinton in the primaries, and twenty-year senator, McCain in the general elections.

It is just a matter of time until the majority of India is made up of the middle class.[25] And when this happens, it will transform the nature of politics and political process in the country at all levels.

Though still very much a work in progress, and we're still a long way, but are visible in the urbane, mostly middle-class areas. The NCR (neither city, nor quite state) of Delhi has voted

---

[25]The number of middle-class households is expected to double in ten years. This includes both the lower and upper middle-class, as the income range is ₹2–10 lakhs.

Arvind Kejriwal to power, on the back of some very impressive austerity and questionable economics.

TABLE 3.1
No. of Households (in millions)

Year	The Poor	Middle Class	The Rich
Annual household income (₹)	< 200,000	200,000 – 1,000,000	> 1,000,000
1995	160.1	4.6	0.3
2005	192.4	13.3	1.2
2015	180.1	60.6	3.3
2025	143.0	128.0	9.5

Source: National Council for Applied Economic Research/McKinsey Global Institute

KEJRIWAL'S BROOM

Arvind Kejriwal shot to fame, first as an Right to Information (RTI) activist, and later as a key player in India Against Corruption (IAC) and in the agitation/demand for the Lokpal (Ombudsman) law. He fell out with some other leaders of the movement, one thing led to another, and he formed the Aam Aadmi (common man) Party or AAP. And as if to signify an imminent clean-up, the AAP chose the humble broom as its electoral symbol.[26]

Eschewing the 40-person security detail, four-acre government bungalow, and cavalcades of screaming sirens and

---

[26] Symbology is big in India, especially in politics. A chief reason is illiteracy. To ensure the unlettered voter is not confused or deceived, each party has a symbol (e.g. Congress has the hand, BJP goes with the lotus and the Indian National Lok Dal or INLD, uses a pair of spectacles). In campaigns, voters are constantly reminded to choose the 'right' symbol.

red beacon lights, the new CM struck a chord with young India, sick of the VIP culture that Delhi had come to personify. In his first stint as CM, Mr Kejriwal travelled by the Delhi Metro to his own swearing-in ceremony. This was unprecedented; VIPs, including CMs, had hitherto eschewed all forms of public transport, not just the subway.

Mr Kejriwal quit less than forty-five days into his tenure, and caused great heartburn. Fast forward one year, and AAP managed to sweep (pardon the pun) the Delhi elections in its second attempt. This time with much greater majority, and despite the popular PM Modi campaigning for the BJP and against AAP. His administrative and economic record remains uninspiring, but Mr Kejriwal hasn't taken his eye off the ball. Speaking in radio advertisements, the Chief Minister of Delhi exhorts citizens to conduct 'sting operations' of their brush with graft, so corrupt officials can be jailed.[27]

Now, Delhi is not India, and India is not Delhi. But with the passage of time, much of India will look increasingly like Delhi, and therein lies the rub. Taking a cue from Mr Kejriwal, chief ministers of other states are increasingly adopting their own versions of austerity, lest the AAP be voted in to power for the distinctive frugalities that voters increasingly support.

Adam Smith noted that 'The real tragedy of the poor is the poverty of their aspirations.' Rural India is young, and increasingly impatient. And as incomes and education levels improve, so will memories and the quality of public discourse.

Bijayant 'Jay' Panda is one of our more scholarly

---

[27] Sting operations are a hugely popular way of exposing all manner of wrongdoings. Mr Kejriwal suggests the use of camera phones, but serious journalists have also used hidden cameras, going incognito to conduct scandalous exposés.

parliamentarians, and represents a rural constituency of Odisha, one of India's least developed states. Needless to say, he has an insider's view of India as well as Bharat (the 'real' India. Not to be confused with this author). Jay Panda is unambiguous in his belief that there is a seminal change occurring in Indian politics currently—led by a young and economically mobile population. The youth in his constituency are enormously well informed and aware of happenings around India, quite unlike their parents. They are indistinguishable from their urban peers in their impatience, aspirations and expectations.

Young Indians, who are the bulk of our population, have grown up never having to bribe anybody, nor do they buy into the culture of corruption that was endemic in the time of their parents. It is unlikely that these idealistic and impatient youngsters will accept demands of graft with the level of resignation their parents did. As the wheel turns, it's only a matter of time, before these impatient and idealistic young Indians form the voting majority of this country. And they will either force politicians to change, or change them.

THE STEEL FRAME

In January 2015, Barack Obama visited New Delhi to take his place as the Guest of Honour at a rainy Republic Day Parade—the first US President to be accorded this high honour. Speeches were made, agreements were signed and hugs were exchanged (Google images for *Mobama* or *Modi Hug*). But barely 24 hours after President Obama's promising visit ended, the Indian Foreign Secretary was sacked. Her hasty departure became front page news in national dailies, and for days that followed, newspaper columns speculated as to the cause of this unusual step.

This was an especially fascinating topic, as foreign policy is where PM Modi has really excelled. He has taken a very active role in the Ministry of External Affairs (MEA), and to his credit, has been doing a spectacular job—both in optics, and substance.

Normally the bureaucracy gets to share the blame as well as the burden. In the newspapers and the media, three probable causes were speculated[28]: lack of follow-through on business promises with Japan (Mr Modi and Mr Abe share a close friendship); voting against Israel in UN (after deciding to vote for); and, denying a visa to the Danish PM during January for the Vibrant Gujarat Summit (also attended by heads of UN and World Bank).[29]

It is shocking to most Indians as to why we should mind having the Prime Minister of Denmark pay us a visit. To understand why the Danish PM was denied a visa, is to understand the challenges and complexities of the officious Indian system, which is always correct but not always right. Mr Modi is probably the last person to advocate the denial of a visa as a legitimate tool of diplomacy. He too was denied visa to the US in the aftermath of the tragic communal riots in Gujarat in 2002, his first term as CM.

DENMARK AND OTHER UNFRIENDLY NATIONS

We could, however, do better with relations with one European

---

[28] See: http://epaperbeta.timesofindia.com/Article.aspx?eid=31806&articlexml=Govt-had-told-Sujatha-of-her-impending-exit-30012015001028

[29] We have explained elsewhere how different states are competing for FDI. This federal competitiveness, will hopefully, accelerate 'ease of doing business' ahead of the official World Bank rankings. States are no longer being passive, or waiting the centre alone to woo foreign investors.

country. Denmark, curiously, is one of the nations that we do not have overtly cordial ties with. And as with most other things, a useful, if peculiar, example to fathom a subtle issue. We do, by the way, have Most Favoured Nation (MFN) Treaties with Iran and Pakistan.[30]

These bilateral treaties, therefore, serve as an unreliable indicator of business and social ties between India and the world. They do, however, contribute greatly to ease of business for companies operating in that corridor.[31]

Investor Countries in India

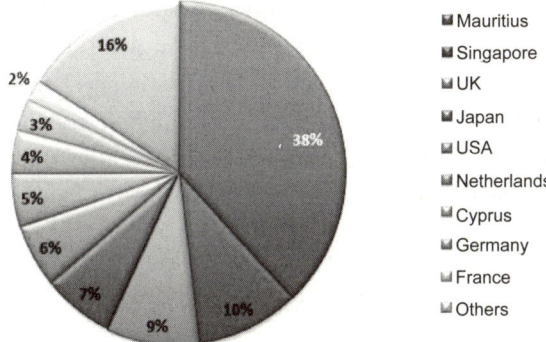

- Mauritius
- Singapore
- UK
- Japan
- USA
- Netherlands
- Cyprus
- Germany
- France
- Others

---

[30]India extended MFN status to Pakistan in 1996. This has not been reciprocated primarily due to how MFN translates into Urdu, suggesting superlative bonhomie. The solution is the proposed NDMA or Non-discriminatory Market Access). It is surely just a coincidence that NDMA also is the abbreviation for India's National Disaster Management Authority.

[31]Tax Avoidance Treaties explain why Mauritius is India's biggest investor. The USA, the EU and China are our largest trading partners, and we do not have operational FTAs with them. While with EU (EU–India FTA) and China (RCEP) FTA negotiations are underway, there is no FTA negotiation happening with the US.

Foreign relations are undeniably the strong suit of the Modi Government's first year in office. With an increasingly confident and buoyant nation, it is expected that national leaders reaffirm India's place in the world, as well as the world's participation in India. Indo-Danish relations illustrate what is known intuitively—that political and executive will faces constant resistance from the 'system' (a word that is used to describe why something cannot be fixed, or why things are the way they are).[32] Ergo, the British built a prolific Indian real estate portfolio in India, and India and Denmark have had formal relations for a long time.

Signs of this heritage continue. Larsen and Toubro (L&T), an Indian multinational engineering firm, was founded by two Danes in 1938; the elephant is the motif of Danish royalty and the Order of the Elephant is the highest civilian honour conferred by Denmark. And most importantly, the elephant has long been the mascot of Carlsberg beer. Indians are yet to

---

[32]Bilateralism consists of the political, economic, or cultural relations between two sovereign states. On the political and economic front, there is evidence of some shared Indo-Danish heritage. Tranquebar, a town in the southern Indian state of Tamil Nadu, was a Danish colony in India from 1620 to 1845. It is spelled Trankebar or Tranquebar in Danish, which comes from the native Tamil, Tarangambadi, meaning 'place of the singing waves'. It was sold, along with the other Danish settlements in mainland India, most notably Serampore (now in West Bengal), to Great Britain in 1845. The Nicobar Islands were also colonized by Denmark, until sold to the British in 1868, who made them part of their colony of British India. After Independence in 1947, Prime Minister Pandit Jawaharlal Nehru's visit to Denmark in 1957 laid the foundation for a friendly relationship between India and Denmark that has endured ever since. The bilateral relations between India and Denmark are cordial and friendly, based on cooperation in political, economic, academic and research fields. There have been periodic high level visits between the two countries. Source: https://en.wikipedia.org/wiki/Denmark%E2%80%93India_relations#cite_note-3

put the picture of an elephant on their beer (though we have the cobra and kingfisher), as the elephant is highly revered, for religious and cultural reasons.

So if bilateralism doesn't quite explain it, what might?

Our official relationship is rather incongruent to the common interest and sentiments shared by business and private citizens of both countries. Most Indians (even in government) are unaware of this official freeze, as probably most Danes are as well.

Though a political pariah during most of his time as CM, Modi used commerce and economic development as his means of deliverance. Under his watch, Gujarat grew to become one of the most prosperous states in the country. Foreign and Indian investors, despite the warnings and scorn of Indian intellectuals, flocked to the coastal state. The astute CM used the biennial Vibrant Gujarat Summit to publicly honour foreign and Indian government officials and businessmen, sign multibillion-dollar memoranda of understanding (MOUs), and publicly receive the approval and accolades of the rich, famous and powerful.

In his Chief Ministerial years, Mr Modi was a pariah for some of the Western world. EU nations, for instance, decided upon an embargo of sorts against the CM and his state government. This meant no formal or diplomatic ties with Gujarat. In his second term as CM, however, a couple of the Nordic member states developed some independent thoughts on the matter. Denmark's new ambassador to India in 2010, Mr Freddy Svane, was invited to Ahmedabad to inaugurate a glittering new factory set up by a Danish company. Breaking rank, Freddy reached out to Modi, asking for, and getting, a private meeting with him on the sidelines of the event.

So the time Freddy reached out to Modi, Denmark was as

embattled as the CM for good reasons or bad. To the credit of both gents, they were able to forge a cordiality that would have possibly culminated in the visit of the Danish PM to the home state of the Indian PM, if not resumption of normal diplomatic ties. But as mentioned earlier, the Danish PM was denied visa to India despite the Prime Minister's Office (PMO) possibly being okay with him leading a Danish business delegation to the flagship Vibrant Gujarat Summit in January 2015.

The MEA is considered one of the big four (the others being the ministries of Defence, Finance and Home), with headquarters located adjacent to the PMO and President's Estate. So it does seem bizarre that political will could be ignored by the bureaucracy (if we may make the distinction within government). To be fair, the MEA was following well-established protocol and guidelines, but of course, failed to adapt swiftly enough to a possible change in foreign strategy.

A bit of a background is probably required here. According to NDTV's website:

> In December 1995 a huge consignment of arms, including hundreds of AK-47s, was air-dropped in West Bengal's Purulia district. The Central Bureau of Investigation (CBI) claims the weapons were meant to arm members of a sect called the Ananda Marg, which wanted to revolt against West Bengal's Communist government.
>
> Peter Bleach, one of the convicted accused in the case, was a retired British Air Force pilot who had been hired by the group who had organized the arms. He informed the British officials who passed on the information to Indian intelligence. The Ministry of Home Affairs (MHA) erroneously sent the alert to Bihar. The alert was, however,

sent back to New Delhi with the note that it should be sent to the West Bengal government. The information finally reached Bengal, but the arms drop had taken place by then. Shockingly, the information was sent through regular postal service.

When the cargo plane flew into Indian air space on its way back from Phuket, it was traced and asked to land. On board was Mr Davy, whose real name is Niel Christian Nielsen, and Mr Bleach. Six people were arrested, including five crew members and Mr Bleach, but Mr Davy managed to escape. Under pressure from Russia, the Latvians were released in 2004. Mr Davy was caught in 2001 in Denmark, based on an Interpol Red Corner Notice, which amounts to an international arrest warrant.

Davy (aka Larsen), the public face of this devious plot, is unwittingly responsible for the souring of diplomatic relations between the two countries.

Fortunately, this problem, like all Indian problems, has multiple possible solutions. Three solutions could be: (i) Davy is extradited (complicated and hasn't happened yet) (ii) the two nations decide that this is water under the bridge, and move on (hope springs eternal) (iii) Davy spends the rest of his natural life in Denmark, unable to even drive his kids to Sweden, under the pain of an Interpol arrest (which is sort of happening at the moment).

Whatever happens, relations between the two elephant-phile nations can only get better.

While one can derive some bittersweet solace from the fact that even the PM of India has to deal with his share of infuriation with the governmental machinery, the real lessons are elsewhere. At some level, even the political or bureaucratic leadership cannot bulldoze the law of the land, and established protocol. Also, regular due diligence and a specialization of the many circulars, notices and legislations that impact your business are critical, if not essential.

Although the senior-most officials of any department (political or executive) are usually accessible, progressive and benign, it is folly to ignore the middle and junior management upon assurances of the top man (or woman). Also, for those of us trying to forecast and plan, things move slower than you might anticipate—even if you're PM! So account for Mr Murphy (or his laws) at every street corner.

Sometimes the fine print, the notations of a junior officer, or complex legacy issues will remain unresolved, but the undeterred continue operating despite these severely limiting constraints. If you understand the legal and practical constraints, it might better prepare you to think of viable solutions, and make headway. The Indian bureaucracy has been described as the steel frame of governance, from the times of the British Raj, and was considered a vital factor in ensuring governance in the early years of India's independence. And true to its promise, the bureaucracy has provided stability and continuity of administration, evolving through Company Raj, Crown Raj and Independent India.

However, the conditions that impact bureaucracy have changed, while the functioning and structure of the bureaucracy have not. The Indian Administrative Service (IAS) remains pre-eminent among the civil services (IAS cadres form the top layer of virtually every governmental department and enterprise), along with the Indian Foreign Service (IFS)—the cadres of which provide India a formidable diplomatic corps.

THE SHIP OF THESEUS

Philosophers such as Plato and Plutarch have debated whether a ship, the wooden parts of which are completely replaced, remains the same or becomes a different ship. Closer to home, there is a Hindi proverb relating to an old razor, the blade and handle of which have been oftentimes replaced over the years. In addressing the daunting need for reform or change, the only solution, some suggest, is the approach of the Ship of Theseus, wherein you change the boat plank by plank, hence retaining the form, while replenishing the structure.

There are those who suggest that policy paralysis has given way to bureaucratic paralysis. Earlier, there was no fear of senior officers being jailed, as no case was approved against joint secretaries and above, (the process required permission from the top), but now serving and even retired IAS officers are arrested, tried and often acquitted after long months of misery and ignominy. The most frightening law for bureaucrats is the sweeping Prevention of Corruption Act, 1988, under which former Secretaries (Coal), a Securities and Exchange Board (SEBI) Chairman, and other senior officers have been investigated by the dreaded Central Bureau of Investigation (CBI).

After three hellish years of investigation and litigation, former Telecom Secretary Shyamal Ghosh was acquitted of criminal conspiracy (under Prevention of Corruption Act) by a special court. The judgment rubbished CBI findings and directed the investigation agency to act against Ghosh's officers. This really is the honest officer's worst-case scenario: a lifetime of work and reputation sullied in the sunset years.

Government employees have penalties for errors of omission or commission, but no reward for good performance. Prithvi

Haldea[33] said, 'Every law requires at least some amount of discretion or interpretation. Discretion can be used in good faith or bad faith. For decisions taken in good faith, officers are aware of a potential risk—the case may be opened in future, and vested interest imputed to action taken or order given—and hence are becoming increasingly hesitant

Haldea wrote, and spoke on TV, that the government must privatize all loss-making PSUs. He received a call from a senior officer who requested him to go slow. When Haldea reiterated his conviction, he was interrupted and told that nobody was willing to do this, for fear of being seen to favour the private sector. Any private buyer of a PSU would do so only expecting a turnaround and success story, if and when that happened allegations of favour and wrongdoing would be raised against the officer (and minister) in charge. One example is of a famous case against a secretary and minister of a government that was in power over a decade ago, for causing undue benefit to the buyer of a floundering government asset.[34]

It's not bold decisions, alone, that are the victim of a diminished risk appetite. Routine decisions often require discretion, and if an officer is hesitant to use discretionary powers, even routine matters are delayed.

Also reform means new laws, and new laws mean interpretation by officers who execute reform through enforcement of new laws.

---

[33]Chairman and Managing Director of Praxis Consulting & Information Services Pvt. Ltd
[34]See: http://timesofindia.indiatimes.com/india/Atal-Bihari-Vajpayee-Arun-Shourie-cleared-hotel-sale-ex-disinvestment-secretary-Pradeep-Baijal-says/articleshow/41235889.cms

REVIEW OF FDI POLICY ON VARIOUS SECTORS

- FDI up to 49 per cent will be under automatic route in defence sector, proposals above 49 per cent will be considered by the Foreign Investment Promotion Board (FIPB).
- FDI policy on the Construction Development sector has been liberalized by relaxing the norms pertaining to minimum area, minimum capitalization and repatriation of funds or exit from the project.
- 100 per cent FDI under automatic route is permitted in completed projects for operation and management of townships, malls/shopping complexes and business centres.
- 100 per cent FDI is permitted in all major plantation sector products—coffee, rubber, cardamom, palm oil tree, olive oil tree. This will be under the automatic route. Until this move only tea plantation was open to FDI.
- Investment by NRIs on non-repatriation basis will be treated as domestic investment.
- Sourcing norms have been relaxed for Single Brand Retail Trading.
- 100 per cent FDI in limited liability partnerships (LLPs) is now permitted under automatic route, in sectors where 100 per cent FDI is allowed. There are no FDI-linked performance conditions.
- The threshold limit for approval by the FIPB has been raised.
- Introduction of Gold Monetization Schemes (GMS) aims to put gold into more productive use.

GOVERNMENTAL INTERFACE

Mr Tulsi Tanti, founder of Suzlon, explains how profoundly

government policies affect his business:

> The policies and actions of the government have always affected the renewable energy sector in general, and Suzlon in particular. Today, for instance, the positive government policy framework is a major contributor to the recent growth of the sector and its increasing opportunities. The government is dedicated to mitigating climate change risks and has set a target of 175GW from renewables by 2022. Government policies are pivotal to shaping the future of this industry.
>
> These policies not only need to be long term focused, but also need to be connected to the ground realities. As a pioneer of the wind industry in India, my input is often solicited when policies are being drafted nationally, and now, even internationally. We, as a company, educated ourselves when there were no practiced policies for wind energy. We could help the policy makers in remaining close to the practical side of the industry and creating more effective policies that looked after sustainable growth. The fact that I can contribute to this is something that delights and humbles me. Suzlon is tackling a world issue—saving our planet through renewable energy. Giving the next generation a green planet is a cause very close to my heart.

Mr Analjit Singh laments the fact that we are a capitalistic country, but our level of empowerment is so low that no one has the courage to allow anything through automatic route. He often sees the government as a problem, not enabler. While eastern European and erstwhile communist countries have realized that capitalism and laissez-faire works, he notes that we still lack 'templates'. 'Why can't I pick up a rule book and know instantaneously if something works or not,' he asks.

Mr Singh concedes that most of the 'licence raj' has gone—referring to his past experiences of applying for industrial and 'capacity' licences, where he would have to convince the government why his plant should be 50 tons (or 100 tons). But he speaks of the phenomenon of regulation, which is increasingly ubiquitous. The Telecom Regulatory Authority of India (TRAI) has long been the regulator of telecoms, but real estate, which needed a regulator, only recently got one.

Mr Singh still sees traces of the 'approval raj+inspector raj', which are self-explanatory,[35] but he contends that approvals are needed for some things even under automatic route.

Good regulation can help the industry, though—SEBI is a great example of regulatory mechanism that works. Capital market efficiency is high, thanks to a mix of good regulation, technology, and enforcement of legislation. Sesame Street works at the state level with government-run crèches till preschool level (called 'anganvadis'), essentially motivating teachers with non-monetary rewards. It has found that recognition goes a long way. This is critical, as at a young level, the training and motivation of teachers trumps technology and teaching tools.

Sesame never participates in bids, as it has no appetite for the tender process. For instance, most bids have manufacture products, such as balls, batons, beads and blocks (accoutrements, playthings that are not educational, really), and hardly ever books (for instance). Also, state governments are more responsive (and less cynical of proposals), when the proposer has obtained the funding, and wants to engage with the government as an implementation or program partner. To be fair, India has its

---

[35] There is a more detailed background in Appendix 1.

fair share of dodgy NGOs and companies. *The Times of India* published an amusing statistic—India has one cop for every 940 people, and one NGO for every 535 Indians. What would you do, as a bureaucrat, if an unknown businessman or NGO came to you with a scheme?

The bureaucracy faces its own problems with transfers, often because they are honest and result-oriented. For instance, a very competent and honest officer was heading a certain organization, was most impressive and issued speaking orders. He was transferred to an unrelated ministry (as is the norm with routine transfers), and soon his new office saw a huge backlog. When asked about the stark difference in his performance, he explained the virtuous cycle that leads to inaction. It takes a senior officer years to understand intricacies of the subject, while the people on other side (private companies, NGOs, etc.) are masters of the subject. His juniors might be as competent, but how far could he trust them to guide him truthfully? If he even tried and learnt, how much time would it take? The officer himself argued that the 'time has come for technocrats in government'. Every subject is getting increasingly complex and technical, so top officers can no longer depend on common sense and understanding of legislation alone.

Members on the Board of the American Markets Regulator, the Securities and Exchange Commission (SEC), require fifteen years of experience in the capital market to be able to deal with the fine print and its nuanccs.

The Indian bureaucracy is widely considered to comprise the most brilliant and seasoned (through their early experience at the district level in quasi-judicial roles) cadres in the world, who could well specialize in different streams after reaching a certain stage in their careers. Many Western governments allow not only induction of the most talented and qualified professionals or academics from the private sector to lead their departments, but also allow their bureaucrats to spend time in the private sector, which help them empathize with the challenges of corporations and share best practices.

In India, discretionary power is also hampered with lack of domain expertise. Mr T.K.A. Nair, former Principal Secretary to Prime Minister, says:

> Reforms in bureaucracy is a continuing process, as it is in other institutions of governance and certainly it should and would continue with focus on different aspects arising out of emerging challenges and opportunities. Many recent developments in our socio-political and economic context have not only added to the complexities of governance, but also to the occupational hazards of those charged with responsibilities of governance, especially at the higher level; those who are known to be exposed to greater occupational risk to justifiably get better compensation. But laying down ratio for the purpose will be a complex exercise. Compensation for higher levels of risk-taking could be in many forms, not necessarily in terms of cash or other monetary incentives. Motivating bureaucracy to give its best is one of the most critical challenges of governance, which to my mind is seldom understood or addressed. Regrettably, many recent developments are indeed disastrous, and need to be squarely addressed for the sake of good governance.

Indian bureaucracy has found a middle path of sorts, that of employing consultants, which is being used to good effect in a few ministries. These domain experts work full-time in ministries on tenures that could stretch up to a couple of years, and are often paid more than their government peers—sans government perks, of course—but take the full satisfaction of meaningful work that impacts a large section of society.

This consultant model could well become a bridge between the need for generalists, who are usually better at sensing and navigating political priorities, and balancing them with practical constraints; and specialists, who understand what needs to be done and how to achieve goals.

Mr Gurcharan Das perceives PM Modi to be effecting reform 'by stealth'. However, the downside of this reform—described by one policy maker as 'creative cumulative incrementalism'—is that it is so stealthy and gradual that it might be imperceptible to the constituencies that it is meant to benefit most: an impatient population that understands little of the nuances of change, but have high expectations. Not only is this population impatient, it is young, highly aspirational, and increasingly educated.

4

DEMOGRAPHIC DIVIDEND
(OR WE THE PEOPLE)

The following is an excerpt from an article about Zomato that appeared in CoolAge (www.coolage.in).

Q. What was the biggest challenge you faced while setting Zomato up and while taking it overseas?

A. Identifying and hiring the right people has been like looking for a white glove in a snowstorm. One of the biggest challenges faced by any fast-growing company is finding the right talent to fuel growth.

At a recent tech conference in Delhi, a few young start-ups were pitching live to a group of investors, in a televised contest. One duo pitched their solution—video CVs that give you a real sense of the candidate, while this company would also do a basic due diligence on the claims made by candidates on areas such as work experience and academic qualifications.

Hiring is a fun exercise in India. It doesn't matter what stage your company is at—start-up, mid-size, or ginormous—you will be revealed the truths of the Indian talent pool. You will find a large number of well-qualified and probably experienced candidates for your vacancy. These promising potential hires will amuse you with their enormous expectations, and the really talented ones will even turn the interview into a sales pitch ('what can the company do for me?').

This process is especially awkward if you're a start-up, or smallish enterprise trying to hire bright young sparks. A friend who did the Ivy League MBA and returned to India to start-up routine, narrated to me what entrepreneurial risk meant for his potential hires. They actually expected a higher salary from the start-up than they currently drew because they were taking a risk joining a start-up. Sweat equity was welcome, but not valued, as they didn't see much value in a company not yet listed.

Most of the job applicants are bound to be mildly disappointing. Not that there's anything wrong with them, but you've already created a mental picture of the candidate from their CV, as you would. But unbeknownst to the trusting new manager, CV embellishment is something of a national sport in India. Some exaggerations are so outrageous, you wonder if the applicant actually expected to ever get away undiscovered.

Diviya Wahi, Director, Samaira Investment, who recently moved back from Silicon Valley to set up an investment fund was amused by the audacious fibs she found on CVs of senior-level candidates:

> They even lie about whom they have worked with. It is hard to find good talent in India, especially at the entry level. I faced myriad issues while hiring a research analyst. Resumes are embellished and strength on paper often does not match the polish. For instance one of the candidates I interviewed, claimed to have a strong boutique private equity background, but it turned out that he had only done project work with the mentioned employer. Moreover, candidates even from some of the top institutes did not appear to have the right skill-set for the role. On a positive

note however, candidates that had attended top institutions and had some work experience thereafter, especially at an MNC or a large corporate, were lot more promising. I think a lot of corporates in India, thus, act as finishing schools, filling gaps that have potentially been created by an outdated curriculum at some of these institutes.

In a relatively small circle, it is unlikely these candidates could claim to work with a big name, and go undiscovered. And when you do make a hire (especially entry level), you realize there's a lot of learning and unlearning to be done before the person can begin to think of performing.[36]

Walk into any MNC in India, and you find virtually all employees are Indian. There's sometimes a senior expat in a key role, but that too is strictly a matter of choice over need. Moreover, Indians in senior management roles of foreign companies—Deutsche Bank (formerly), Berkshire Hathaway, Google, Microsoft, PepsiCo, MasterCard, Nokia, Adobe, Diageo, Cognizant, Vodafone (formerly), etc.—are almost the stuff of legends.

That, and almost ten million new graduates adding to the workforce annually, should make hiring more of a breeze, but the statistics defy logic here. As a rule of thumb, the more senior you hire, the better the quality of hire is likely to be, but don't expect a labour arbitrage here. Top honchos expect (and get) top compensation. C-suite salaries in India are comparable to their Western counterparts.

The same goes for co-founders, or late stage co-founders, and for start-ups too. Expect to part with sweat equity, and prepare

---

[36]Bharat Joshi, 'Is "Trainable" the New "Employable"?' *Wall Street Journal* India blog.

for hard negotiations (usually expected) on pay cheques. You can expect a labour arbitrage, though, at the blue-collar level (unskilled and semi-skilled workforce). However, the quality of workmanship and work ethic can be infuriating.

Large transnational corporations run in-house programmes at an impressive scale to train and retain workforce. The small risk here is that trained machine operators, electricians or mechanics are often poached by competition—abroad! Yep, these hard working, well-trained workers are much in demand internationally, and find employment in places as diverse as Australia and Canada.

Managing industrial relations and labour remains a challenge for other reasons too. Labour unions are notoriously political, and negotiations aren't always as objective as those in some other countries, where unions play a powerful, balancing role, often adding as much value as management to the critical business decisions.

Just recently, my dentist (a gentleman to a fault), was telling me about his brief tryst with manufacturing. He produced a dental medicine, which is precocious in itself, and also set up a small manufacturing facility in Delhi, where he lives. He quickly realized that business wasn't his cup of tea, and had to wind up manufacturing in favour of outsourcing to a modest-sized pharmaceutical company in another town. What did him in wasn't the permits, the inspectors, or the other stringent requirements of the tightly controlled pharmaceutical sector, but rather the labour, which he found to be unmanageable. Despite hiring two 'managers', the good doctor saw the labour hold them hostage. He, of course, had to pay the staff in full before he was able to shut shop, but swore off any business enterprise since, and instead, focuses on his thriving practice.

It hasn't helped that a glut of abusive employers and crooked businessmen have duped, exploited and denied the workforce of even their basic dues. Decades of such practice have created an environment of distrust towards the management, and this has manifested in labour laws that owe their genesis to landmark rulings and attitudes of the courts of law in the early 1980s (and onwards).

This conventionally adversarial relationship is managed admirably by a number of Indian and foreign companies that treat laws and people with equal respect, and witness uninterrupted operations.

Here's what really surprises foreign investors and managers—how easy it is to fire middle management in India. If laws are maternal in protecting labour (to clarify, this is the official, and an inoffensive term in India), they're beyond indifferent towards middle management (and almost hostile towards top management). Middle management has little legal cover against termination on grounds of non-performance.

This perpetuates the hyper competitive, insecure environment that most middle-class Indians have grown up in. School students are under enormous pressure to attain implausible scores in school Board examinations to make it to one of the top colleges (or any college—given the woeful deficit of college seats for the population), failing which they're unlikely to secure a good or government (or any) job. In some regions male college students are under tremendous pressure to crack 'competitive' examinations to get a government job, or score well in college tests to get a good private sector job, failing which they're unlikely to get a bride of their choice (or soon, any bride, given our worsening sex ratio).

Corporate governance laws are becoming increasingly

stringent in India, and after recent ignominious cases of corporate fraud (Satyam was a big one), courts of law are wont to treat senior management and key personnel as 'gold collared criminals' to quote an erudite senior lawyer.

On a macro level, India has a target of training 500 million people by 2022, to make them more employable. There is plenty of scope—800 million Indians are under thirty-five years old. Presently, the unorganized sector comprises 93 per cent of the workforce, and if this target is achieved, the ratio of unorganized to organized could be a healthier 75:25 in 2022.

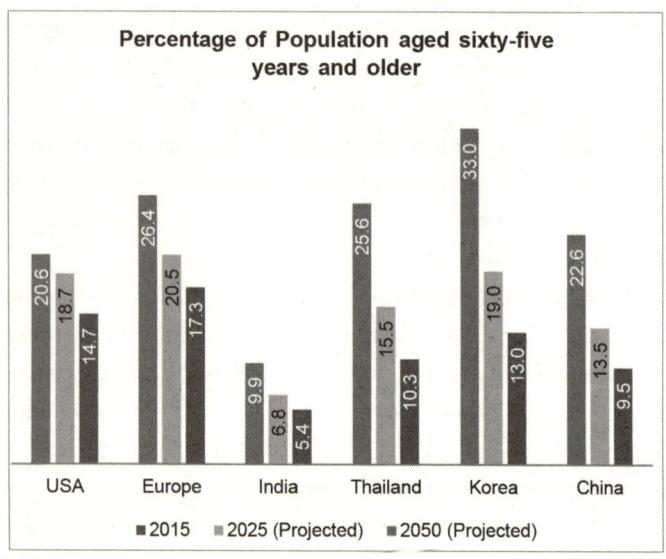

Figure 4.1: India has one of the youngest populations in the world

Source: United Nations, World Population Prospects: 2012 Revision

Further, at the current rate, 10 million new graduates are added to the employment pool annually, and will continue until 2035.

Naturally, the government is rather keen to create these ten million new jobs every year, but realizes that it needs to innovate to address this challenge. Traditionally, the government has been the biggest employer, but the organic churn (new recruits replacing retirees), cannot solve the challenge at the rate at which it used to. These demographics bring us to a fork in the road.

> When I come to a fork in the road, I take it.
> –*Yogi Berra*

We could either become the youngest, most productive and largest workforce on the planet, or this potential workforce could create social unrest at an unprecedented scale (simply because the world has never seen a population as large).

If we fail to provide basic healthcare, education and jobs, the circumstances will create 'haves and have nots' (the latter being the majority), without real hope of crossing over. India simply must become a more egalitarian society, else risk social unrest from poorer people, who are more aspirational than they used to be.

As daunting as this issue seems, the converse is as much of a possibility. The supposed demographic dividend is a negative dividend as people are refusing to do jobs. We tend to think only in industrial terms, but we must also think in agricultural terms—Dalit women working as labour, for instance, are giving up income for dignity. Also, the share of women in the workforce is diminishing almost universally.

This is undeniably a major contributor to the two risks to every business: (i) environmental and social stress (ii) investment based on assumption of predictability and stability. The former applies to virtually every nation with a growing population, and the latter, to every democratic nation.

(i) Risk of environmental and social stress: A growing, prosperous population will create growing demands on finite natural resources, resulting in a socio-environmental crisis (700 million struggling to get by with rising aspirations), between the haves and have nots, the cities and rural areas, and between agriculture and industry. The crisis may create collateral damage, especially for manufacturing-based industry (physical assets—trucks, buildings, shops, cars, etc.).

(ii) Investment based on assumption of predictability and stability: Change of government or change of heart of government can cause serious issues—for instance, Dabhol, where Enron met its Waterloo; and Vodafone, India's most ignominious tax demand.

'It is fiction that governments can create jobs. Economy creates jobs. The reality is that there's a scarcity of labour,' asserts Swaminathan Aiyar. Labour-intensive farming—increasingly giving way to more efficient, mechanized farming—is shrinking as a portion of GDP (refer to Table 4.1).

On the other hand, not all young Indians are best poised for jobs in the large, and growing, services (essentially IT) sector. Over the last twenty years, the sectors that have grown are finance, IT, banking, retail—all settings where you require soft skills. India's surplus labour is in agriculture; unqualified rural youth cannot be productively absorbed in non-manufacturing jobs. Industrial Training Institutes (ITI)-trained people can easily be employed in manufacturing, but not so much in services. Agriculture is highly political, a state subject, and has a long lead time (five years minimum to see results), so reforms are both unlikely and hard to do. With at least a couple of states going to polls every year, media glare on the sector is relentless, and often a deterrent to reform. In recent times, media (mostly television) coverage makes even state elections seem almost like general elections.

Manufacturing boosts job-creation, export revenue, and has a multiplier effect across economic indicators. But for this, issues regarding skill, labour, land, and ease of doing business, need to be resolved. This is where several national programmes converge: Make in India, Skill India, and Startup India.

Warren Buffet notes, 'The most important thing in terms of your circle of competence is not how large the area is, but how well you've defined the perimeter. If you know where the edges are, you're way better off than somebody that's got a circle five times as large but gets very fuzzy at the edges.'

Skill India aims to create a structure of training and tradition of vocational training that beats two extant failings. The first failing is the condescending attitudes towards vocational training and 'diplomas', as against university education and 'degrees'. Male diploma holders are often higher earners than degree graduates from questionable colleges offering obscure courses, but struggle to climb the socio-economic hierarchy or (you should guess this by now), find a suitable bride (marriage marketability of degree holders is higher).

The second failing is the creation of standards and consistent quality around the skills and training imparted at the ITIs or other vocational training centres. A tall order. Swaminathan Aiyar blames a, 'third-rate, ruinous educational system,' for having created a mismatch between expectations and skills, where students pass school and college without really learning the skills expected of them.

Mr Aiyar invested in two social ventures in skill development, but both went bust as employers were unwilling to pay a premium for 'certified' workers, in absence of universal and credible certification (trusted and used by all stakeholders).

The National Skill Development Council (NSDC) was set up as a Public–Private Partnership (PPP) some years ago, to create sector-specific programmes and, through implementation partners, go about addressing this daunting challenge. Fittingly a technocrat, S. Ramadorai, (former CEO of IT major Tata Consultancy Services), heads NSDC and the National Skill Development Agency (NSDA). There is a history of technocrats engaging with the government at both Central and state levels. The better known examples are Sam Pitroda (Telecom, Innovation, etc. from his business in the USA), Nandan Nilekani (Unique Identification Authority of India [home of the Aadhaar Card] from Infosys), Arun Maira (Planning Commission from the Boston Consulting Group), and of course, S. Ramadorai. This is still the exception, rather than the norm, but acceptance is growing. Fairly or unfairly, said technocrats are associated with the ruling party(ies), and their fortunes thereof.

S. Ramadorai deconstructs the problem succinctly:[37]

> The country had no standards of skill development. Every ministry had its own set of schemes. The labour ministry [Ministry of Labour and Employment] had ITIs, MHRD [Ministry of Human Resource Development] has schools and colleges, states have their state board and state skill board. Then you have to build a vocational education system and give a pathway to connect it with the normal education system. Then there is need for outcomes,

---

[37] *Mint* supplement, 4 November 2015.

rationalization of various schemes, etc. There are multiple complexities because of vocational education not getting the centre-stage, formalized mechanism does not exist, and moving unorganized sector workers to organized sector [is a tough task].

For instance, the Indian Plumbing Skills Council, headed by R.K. Somany, Chairman of Hindware (or HSIL), a leading sanitaryware manufacturer, received great interest from the likes of the Danish government, who were more than happy to train selected candidates in Denmark, while benefitting from affordable plumbing services (plumbers in Scandinavia are well-trained and well paid) during the apprenticeship overseas: a win-win for these foreign trained, and gold tinted 'foreign returns' in the Indian plumbing space.

In fact, the problem is so acute in areas like real estate, that lack of skilled/semi-skilled labour is cited as a key inhibiting factor in growth of the sector. There just aren't enough hands to work on large projects. Ironically, a few years ago, large infrastructure and real estate developers resorted to importing construction labour from China. It took official intervention from the Government of India to prohibit this practice, before it was stopped.

The Modi Government augmented these Sector Skill Councils (established earlier) by establishing a new Ministry of Entrepreneurship and Skill Development. The fact that they dovetailed these two subjects is probably recognition of the fact that entrepreneurship really is the best ever jobs programme. And a pretty good skilling programme, too. It is probably no coincidence that the American regulatory framework, to regulate crowdfunding platforms, is called the JOBS Act (Jumpstart Our

Business Startups Act, 2012).

Make in India,[38] another pivotal programme, aims to encourage and effect a revival of the languishing manufacturing sector. The fact is that when the IT sector took off, we let ourselves believe in the popular slogan of the day—China is the factory of the world, Brazil is the farmhouse, and India is the back office. We thought we had arrived, and continued to neglect manufacturing. This was a blunder caused by the belief that services alone would take us all the way.

We are also languishing because at first, we overregulated the sector. As Chairman of the multibillion-dollar Max group, Mr Analjit Singh reminds us—in addition to an industrial licence, businesses would need to procure a 'capacity licence', after having convinced the government why they should be allowed to manufacture as much as they would like.

After we signed an FTA with the Association of South East Asian Nations (ASEAN) in 2009, we soon realized after a couple of years that there was pretty much nothing we could supply to ASEAN, and were instead competing with the manufacturing giants of the region—China, Japan and South Korea. This served as a useful, albeit painful reminder that there's no escaping manufacturing. On services too, only now are we trying to diversify the services sector, moving away from IT to other areas of services—finance, fintech, and hospitality, for instance.

Meanwhile, over the last twenty-five years, the share of agriculture has halved, while the share of services has grown on steroids. Industry, however, has remained unchanged at around 18 per cent of GDP.

---

[38] See Appendix 3 for details about Make in India

TABLE 4.1

Comparative GDP consumption across the three sectors: Agriculture, Industry and Services

	Agriculture	Industry	Services
GDP Consumption 1990–91	32%	27%	41%
GDP Consumption 2013–14	17%	32%	51%

Source: National Accounts

Policymakers now widely accept that manufacturing has perhaps the most enormous potential to absorb manpower, and create prosperity through exports.

Tellingly, the world's largest exporters—China, Germany, Japan and Holland—are also manufacturing giants. A robust manufacturing sector would create jobs while lifting other economic parameters—per capita income, disposable income, balance of trade (and payments), etc.

It is thought that the booming services, and now e-commerce sector, owes its success to a lack of brick and mortar problems, and importantly, lower barriers to entry and lighter regulation. If 'Make in India' could do this for the manufacturing sector, it might just unleash a similar growth in the industry, both in terms of entrepreneurship and scale.

The very fact that we can openly promote and implement the Make in India initiative is remarkable. This programme would have been unthinkable in 1991, the year India undertook reforms to open the economy, for there was still a very palpable fear of the foreigner coming to India, and rendering us a colonial puppet. These fears are almost only expressed by the Left and the unions now. The fear of the foreigner has gone down enormously, leading to an acceptance that Indian companies can be bought by MNCs. For instance, in 2005, Swiss-based

Holcim bought a majority stake in ACC Ltd. from Gujarat Ambuja. Hindustan Motors, which entered into tie-ups with MNCs such as Mitsubishi in 1995 and with General Motors (GM) in 1996, sold off its stake to GM in 1999.

And speaking of entrepreneurship, the Modi Government announced two new programmes in its second year of being—'Startup India' and 'Stand Up India'. These well-conceived and well-meaning programmes are increasingly in the peril of being reduced to, and imprisoned as, slogans.

'The government needs to stop announcing new programmes, and just deliver on what has already been announced,' opines bestselling author Gurcharan Das, advisor to corporations and to the Government of India. While this seems like rather obvious counsel, the current lack of visible change is beginning to create murmurs of discontent amongst the young—the most strident supporters of Mr Modi's 'development' plank to the PMO. However, Indophile Mark Tully feels that MNCs stand to gain with Mr Modi, 'Modi is the strongest PM since Indira Gandhi, and unlike her, his agenda is largely in their (MNC) favour.'

The big issues—labour reform and the hotly debated 'hire and fire' policy—might become moot issues if manufacturing and entrepreneurship cannot create ample opportunity for the youth. Or if companies are unable to pay top dollar for India's very mobile talent that is in demand overseas. Nevertheless, we cannot possibly discuss India's human capital without touching upon caste—so here it is, a brief plunge into a very complex and nuanced issue.

CASTE IN INDIA

> A man is great by deeds, not by birth.
> —*Chanakya (381 B.C.–283 B.C.)*

For professionals and businesses in urban India, caste considerations are unlikely to affect your business (though not entirely impossible).

Noted Dalit commentator, journalist and advisor to the Dalit Indian Chamber of Commerce and Industry (DICCI),[39] Mr Chandrabhan Prasad, has a rational explanation for this phenomenon. 'Business is more important than social roots, except in backward areas,' everywhere else, material markers are replacing social markers.[40]

To elaborate, caste still plays a role depending upon the place of your business (e.g. small 'backward' towns are more sensitive), industry (both upper caste and Dalits are unable to penetrate

---

[39] The Indian Chambers of Commerce, both national and regional are active bodies and engage proactively with industry, government and academia. National chambers include FICCI, CII, Associated Chambers of Commerce and Industry (ASSOCHAM), while regional chambers include Indian Merchant Chambers (IMC), PHD Chambers of Commerce and Industry (PHDCCI), etc. Some chambers are industry or sector-specific, including Automotive Components Manufacturers Association of India (ACMA), Society of Indian Automobile Manufacturers (SIAM) and National Association of Software and Service Companies (NASSCOM).

[40] Occupation and caste are intimately interlinked. Of the four castes, Bania is the mercantile class, and natural businessmen. Mr Prasad narrates a telling tale of a languishing grocery shop in his neighbourhood. The shop owner was advised to convert the shop into a barber's salon, which would be easy to run and have bright prospects. He started the saloon, but after two years reverted to the grocery business. The reason? He was unable to find a match for his eligible granddaughter. Prospective grooms demurred, as it was considered that his caste had become that of a barber.

small retail—the preserve of the Bania caste) and elections (caste remains an unfailingly pertinent issue).

Dalit is the term the traditional lower castes and untouchables have assumed for themselves in India and parts of South Asia. Dalits find it difficult to escape their caste status, even if they change religion. India has communities of 'Dalit Muslims' and Christians and Sikhs have separate churches and Gurudwaras, respectively, for 'Dalit Christians' and 'Dalit Sikhs'. Mr Prasad opines that the only way to transcend caste is for Dalits to change occupation.

For most young urban Indians, however, caste is only ever a consideration when getting married, and that too it is a fast-diminishing concern. This sounds almost ill-informed, considering that Faridabad, a suburb of New Delhi, saw a barbaric act of caste-related violence when two babies of a 'lower caste', were burnt alive in October 2015.

There's no denying the unspeakable treatment of many of the Scheduled Castes (SCs) Dalit communities. In the past, they were deprived of basic dignity, let alone access to education, or mobility of profession, and even where they resided was circumscribed—different areas in the village were assigned to different castes.

Thankfully, though, today there are abundant signs to the contrary. The urban youth routinely marry, befriend, and vote outside of their caste—these were the three big 'no's' of the days of yore, when caste determined these, and more. By all estimates, India of the next couple of decades will be increasingly urban (with small towns 'urbanizing') and young (remember our 'demographic dividend'); so do the math.

On the other hand, a friend who owns a sizeable pharmaceuticals company narrated how provincial sensitivities come to the fore for his field staff of thousands of salespersons. These young men (as they usually are) in central and eastern India, specifically requested that their business cards mention only given names, dropping surnames altogether. Doctors in states like Bihar tend to usually be upper caste, and often refuse to meet salespersons of different castes.

In India, it is still possible to tell the provenance of a person from their full name. In south India, the name can tell you the religion, caste and village. Earlier, you could fairly estimate the profession too!

The DICCI (mentioned earlier)—is a business chamber in the traditions of the Federation of Indian Chambers of Commerce and Industry (FICCI), Confederation of Indian Industry (CII), and other regional chambers and is open only to Dalit entrepreneurs. Established in 2005, the chamber has thirteen Chapters, with 4,000 members. Some members have revenues up to ₹2,000 crore (about USD 300 million), reveals Mr N.K. Chandan, President of the Delhi and NCR Chapter of DICCI.

'Dalits don't succeed in villages,' asserts Mr Prasad. This is because the ecosystem and caste dynamics make economic success virtually impossible. In 'mandis' or traditional markets, Dalits have little chance of success, since they don't have business or community ties with other traders, and are as unlikely to have relatives who are Chartered Accountants or business mentors (especially for those who are in industry, like members of DICCI). 'Non-Dalit businessmen have no ill-will against Dalit businessmen, but the situation evolves with caste playing a conscious role.'

Dalit thinkers like Mr Prasad are keen to see FDI finish off the 'mandi' system, and the black economy that often goes with it, owing to the predominantly cash transactions. Further and much to the horror of the private sector, every few years political parties announce that they are contemplating job quotas in the private sector, along the lines of SC/ST affirmative action in government jobs and education (admissions).[41] This would be both unviable and unwise, explains Mr Prasad—unviable, because even the Municipal Corporation of Delhi (MCD) has been unable to fill the Dalit quota for teaching staff; and unwise, because the private sector plays a big role in the development of Dalits.

Further, Swaminathan Aiyar says private-sector reservations cannot be done, constitutionally, unless these reservations are limited—in duration, area, or both. He postulates that the perceived need for such 'props' arises from an inefficient police-judicial system. He extrapolates the example to explain that caste discrimination is illegal, so a well-functioning enforcement arm would mitigate need for such reservations, and abuse of such schemes might follow—bogus certification for being Dalit, underage, or having income under certain sum favouring the undeserving.

The private sector has played and still plays a very important role in the liberation of the Dalits from the village landlords. The Dalits had roughly three options: (i) opt for education and employment given by the state—but the state only gives

---

[41] A huge topic of discussion around caste is 'reservations', the Indian version of affirmative action. The 'SC/ST' quota, has become so coveted, that even traditionally privileged castes are demanding an SC/ST status. Advantages include preferential terms of admission in colleges and government jobs. The 'general' category left out of this, feel the crunch of ever increasing competition for finite seats (in colleges and jobs). The quota system, implemented in 1989 under the recommendations of the 'Mandal Commission', has been constantly and hotly debated, and remains ever a live issue. It is controversial and confounding, with excellent arguments for, against, and a multitude of 'middle-path' solutions.

jobs to Dalits with some basic education, and most Dalit kids worked alongside their parents (ii) migrate and become an entrepreneur—but, entrepreneurs require capital, which they did not have (iii) become a factory worker in the private sector. Ergo, only this option was open to Dalits who had neither education, nor capital.

This was backed up by the results of 2008 survey Mr Prasad conducted for the Centre for Advanced Study of India (CSAI; University of Pennsylvania), which covered 20,000 households across 300 villages in Uttar Pradesh. They were asked how many government employees a household had, whether serving or retired. The average was 7. When a factory worker was asked the same question, the number shot up to an average 28 per household—an instructive indicator of occupational mobility enabled by the private sector. The role of caste is less pronounced in the private sector, especially in the more professional companies. The bureaucracy is quite secular too, explains Mr Prasad, as there are separate lobbies of all groups—Bania, Thakur, Brahman, Muslim, and Dalit.

I would agree with Mr Prasad that Dalits have a bright future. In a bid to shrug off unfair stereotypes, Dalits go the extra mile to ensure they maintain the most hygienic homes and work spaces, are conscientious, honest, treat employees fairly, and will err on the side of caution. Mr J.J. Irani, former Director, Tata Sons, found in a study that Dalits were least likely to change jobs—an especially valuable virtue in these times on endemic workforce attrition in India. A testimonial from him on the DICCI website states:

> What I have noticed from the influx we are having from various communities, the Dalit community people do have

> a greater sense of loyalty and they work harder to prove themselves. This attitude has been and is very commendable that they are saying that we have been neglected for so long, now you are giving us an opportunity, we will do better. Better than others.

Dalits have a capacity to work in difficult situations, and sustain low-profit margins for sustained periods. Mr Prasad asked thousands of Dalit entrepreneurs how they succeeded. The answer invariably was their belief in high-quality goods. Mr Niraj Shiva, whose company Shiva Enterprises makes fire suits, actually tested his product personally. After hiring the people to test the product, he still worried about the remote possibility of a minor accident bringing disrepute to his company—though evidently he was confident of his product quality, since he tested it himself.

On 16 January 2015, IFCI Venture Capital Funds Ltd, launched a venture capital fund aimed at Dalit entrepreneurs. Prior to this, noted *The Indian Express*, 'Limited access to institutionalized finance ensured that only a few thousand among the 20.13 crore Dalits (according to Census 2011), emerged as businesspersons of any reckoning.' The story covered young Dalit entrepreneurs who have jumped at this opportunity.[42]

Of course, it's illegal and immoral to discriminate on the basis of caste, but affected parties are normally quite good at ascertaining if they're on the receiving end of bias or prejudice. This might bring us to the oft repeated point about law enforcement. If laws were enforced well enough, there would be no caste or gender, religion or other discrimination in India.

---

[42] http://indianexpress.com/article/india/india-news-india/a-new-business-class-dalits-who-turned-first-generation-entrepreneurs/

Different sections of this book might give you a mixed impression of how important a factor caste is in India, and that's because it's a nuanced issue, and we are focusing on the business impact of the said factor.

Incidentally, Dalits, who describe themselves as being outside of the four 'varnas' (segments)—Brahman, Kshatriya, Vaishya, and Shudra—of the Hindu caste system. They generally feel comfortable with foreigners, as foreigners do not have preconceived notions about Dalits, which Indians might.

Caste plays out in other ways too. *The Economic Times* published a study in early 2015 that spoke about how the majority of Indian Boards are occupied by persons from the mercantile castes (Bania, Vaishya, etc.). So there's no denying these mercantile castes have a headstart. India is not unique in having a rigid class system (based on education, race, wealth or religion), but is certainly one of the most complex.

RELIGION

Constitutionally, India is a secular state, and so has no official religion. Despite this official status, religion does continue to impact life and business in India. Even in the most urbane setting, religion remains a large part of individual and communal identity, and is most visible during major festivals—Diwali, Eid, Gurpurab, Buddha Jayanti, Mahavir Jayanti and Christmas.

We have public and bank holidays for every significant day related to almost every religion, instead of no holidays based on religion. The idea is to provide equitable freedom to practice religion, rather than to promote an atheist state.

Some religious minorities have used religious identity and

bonding to great effect in business. A shining example, the Parsis, a miniscule minority who own some of the largest Indian conglomerates—the Tatas, Shapoorji Pallonji and Godrej are households names across the country (and beyond).[43]

Adi Godrej, an alumnus of the Harvard Business School, once said:[44]

> You mentioned the Parsi community. The Parsi community has always been very entrepreneurial, so I think that helped. In fact, my great-uncle was financed by others in the community, and that also helped. The community always paid attention to entrepreneurship, to, of course, professionalism, so overall I think that helped the origins of the business.

The dark side of a strong religious identity in India has over the centuries manifested itself in violent riots that can occur without warning, almost anywhere in the country. The First War of Independence, or the 1857 Mutiny depending on which side you see it from, began in May 1857 and went on till June 1858.

It proved so grievous a challenge to the Company Raj that it almost brought about Indian Independence a century before 1947, and before Mahatma Gandhi and the other giants of the freedom struggle created conditions for an imminent British exit.

---

[43]The total population of Parsis in India is 60,000. A figure so low, that in a nation of 1.2 billion inhabitants, the government has allocated funds to measures to address this trend. Parsis are, by far, the most affluent community in India.

[44]Interview with Adi Godrej, interviewed by Tarun Khanna, 2 May 2013, Creating Emerging Markets Project, Baker Library Historical Collections, Harvard Business School, see: http://www.hbs.edu/businesshistory/emerging-markets/

Demographic Dividend • 137

It was triggered by a bullet or a cartridge. Nobody fired one, the sepoys just had to bite open a greased-paper cartridge before loading it into the new Pattern 1853 Enfield Rifle that had been introduced into the East India Company's army (yes, the Company had its own army in India).

It was alleged that the grease on these cartridges included beef tallow (hugely offensive to Hindus) and pork lard (hugely offensive to Muslims). The soldiers, who were mostly Hindu or Muslim, revolted vehemently; the resulting mutiny spiralled out of control, and caused the end of Maratha, Mughal and Company rule, and paved the way for the British Crown to assume rulership of India.

To be fair, the British were sensitive to local sensibilities, but they still failed to realize the mayhem pork lard and beef tallow could cause. Even today, personal or material disputes are given a religious tinge by villains to attract more support to their cause. Religion can be both, an adversary of business, as the British East India Company found out, or a solution to dilemmas, as acquaintance of a friend's friend discovered. We will call him Mr Kumar.

Mr Kumar established a business school in a tier-two city, and right across a highly respected, government-backed business school (B-school). The plot he was able to purchase was about a hundred metres off the main road, hence access was through a dirt road, unlike the larger B-school, the gates of which opened onto the main road to welcome students and visitors.

Mr Kumar's burning ambition was to also have access from the main road, legitimizing his claim as a worthy younger challenger to the incumbent institution of learning. His problem was a greedy land owner, who refused to sell land to Singh at a fair price. The land owner knew how important direct road access was to Kumar's school, and demanded several times the market price for his coveted piece of land. Predictably, all talks broke down.

A pensive Mr Kumar was driving around his greedy (or savvy, depending on whether you're on the sell side or buy side) neighbour's property to get to his school, when he spotted a peepal tree (also known as the Sacred Fig or *Ficus Religiosa*). The peepal is a remarkable tree, widely revered by Hindus. Singh had a Machiavellian brainwave, pivoted around the peepal.

He placed an idol of worship at the base of the peepal tree, and hired a priest to receive devotees. Over time, the size of the following grew, and in the space of a year a small temple had been built near the tree. Kumar, thereafter, wrote to the local authorities informing them of this ancient temple, which attracted pilgrims from all corners of the country. There was no direct access to this temple (which bordered his boundary), and as a good Samaritan, he would be willing to fund construction of a road to the shrine.

The authorities agreed, and built the road at his expense. I am told that the greedy neighbour now chases after Mr Kumar offering him his (the neighbour's) plot of land at a discount, which Mr Kumar clearly has no use for any longer.

The moral of this story is certainly not to manipulate religious sentiments for personal gain, but to appreciate how formidable a force religion still is in this country. Religion has brought down empires in India and still retains the might to do so.

Genuine respect for religious sentiments is a necessity, and is reciprocated in equal measure by those you demonstrate sincere respect for. The moral of the story is perhaps also this—to not hold out so long that you lose an opportunity. Perhaps a bit like sitting on the fence a little too long before entering India.

The Reserve Bank of India (RBI) classifies centres into six tiers based on population.[45]

TABLE 4.2
Classification of centres (tier-wise)

Population classification	Population (2001 Census)
Tier-1	100,000 and above
Tier-2	50,000 to 99,999
Tier-3	20,000 to 49,999
Tier-4	10,000 to 19,999
Tier-5	5,000 to 9,999
Tier-6	less than 5000

TABLE 4.3
Population-group wise classification of centres

Population classification	Population (2001 Census)
Rural centre	up to 9,999
Semi-urban centre	10,000 to 99,999
Urban centre	100,000 to 999,999
Metropolitan centre	1,000,000 and above

In an ambitious bid to transform rural areas to economically, socially and physically sustainable spaces, the government adopted the Shyama Prasad Mukherji Rurban (rural-urban) Mission (SPMRM) with an outlay of over ₹5000 crores.

The Mission aims at development of rural growth clusters (by promoting economic activity, skilling and local entrepreneurship and infrastructure), to trigger overall development in the region.

---

[45]https://en.wikipedia.org/wiki/Classification_of_Indian_cities#cite_note-10

The Rurban Mission will thus develop a cluster of Smart Villages.

The Government of India under Prime Minister Narendra Modi has a vision of developing 100 smart cities as satellite towns of larger cities and by modernizing the existing mid-sized cities. A total of ₹98,000 crore (US$ 15 billion) has been approved by the Indian Cabinet for development of 100 smart cities and rejuvenation of 500 others. For the smart cities mission, ₹48,000 crore (US$ 7.2 billion), and for the Atal Mission for Rejuvenation and Urban Transformation (AMRUT), total funding of ₹50,000 crore (US$ 7.5 billion) has been approved by the Cabinet.

5
EASE OF DOING BUSINESS IN INDIA

The World Bank's Ease of Doing Business rankings, benchmarked to June 2014 placed India 142nd out of 189 countries—below Sri Lanka and Pakistan.

The World Bank ranks economies on ten parameters: Starting a Business, Dealing with Construction Permits, Getting Electricity, Registering Property, Getting Credit, Protecting Minority Investors, Paying Taxes, Trading Across Borders, Enforcing Contracts, and Resolving Insolvency.

In other words, ease of doing business essentially is three things in the lifecycle of an enterprise—incorporation, running thereof, and closure. The World Bank's annual *Doing Business* report has come to be the gold standard on measuring how easy, or hard, economies make it for businesses; and to measure progress or deterioration on a series on metrics or parameters.

Let's start with the most morbid of the three: winding up a company, which the World Bank rates as and terms 'Insolvency Laws'. World Bank ranks India 136 out of 189 countries on the 'resolving insolvency' parameter. Distressingly, India was also ranked at the bottom of league tables on *Quality of Death* in a 2015 study by *The Economist* on palliative care, marking it among the world's worst countries to die in.

Add to this the irony that the Indian philosophy of forgiveness seldom translates into second chances for failed entrepreneurs, and consequently, bankruptcy laws. So there's hardly any thought given to the afterlife of a company. Insolvency in India is an expensive (9 per cent of estate), time consuming (takes 4.3 years compared to 1.7 years in China) and inefficient (recovery rate of 25.7 cents on the dollar) business.

Companies are routinely wound up, though, and with efficient handling of matters, most bona fide cases aren't the horror stories that pull down the rankings. The big risks to watch out for are rather obvious—pending litigation, labour disputes, or creditors (banks, vendors, and the ilk).

You're, hopefully, not reading this book to figure out how to wind down your India business (the subject of another volume, deservedly), and much of this book deals with the business of doing business in India, so in the next couple of pages, we'll focus on setting up and running a business in the country.[46]

The official view of capitalism, though gradually changing, has been thus—government firms (PSUs) are better than the private sector; and if private, Indian is better than foreign owned.

So, the incorporation phase might require a couple of extra steps, if your business will largely be foreign owned. This is not as big a deal as it used to be, and going forward, will become even more relaxed—the notable exceptions (and likely to remain so) are defence, legal services, accounting services and the print media.

---

[46] However, if you remain concerned about the corporate afterlife, there's good news too. With an eye on the EODB rankings, the *Insolvency and Bankruptcy Code 2016* replaced the Presidency Towns Insolvency Act 1909 (among others), introducing a *time limit* on the bankruptcy process (broadly 180, extendable by 90 days); a bankruptcy and insolvency adjudicator each; and regulator to oversee information companies and professionals in the area. There will be a time lag, though, till a pool of licensed insolvency professionals are able to carry this through for all companies, but it's a significant step in the right direction.

Regardless of your provenance though, twenty-six clearances are required from about twenty departments/authorities and then some, to get a business/factory going. For instance, if you were to set up a power plant, you'd need another twenty-four clearances, giving you fifty clearances to allow you to start off, and then you would need to obtain periodic clearances (annual, quarterly, 'as per need', etc.).

But there's hope. The Government of India is 'seized of the matter' (officialese), and in late 2014 set a target for India to make it to the top fifty countries in the Ease of Doing Business Index of the World Bank from the 142nd rank in three years—a ninety-two rung jump!

As daunting as it sounds, the Department of Industrial Policy and Promotion (DIPP) in the Ministry of Commerce, tasked with the Make in India programme, contends that if we were to adopt best practices of all Indian states at the Central level, we would already make it to the top fifty.

An Expert Committee to 'examine the possibility of replacing multiple prior permissions with pre-existing regulatory mechanism,' was promptly constituted upon the Budget Speech of Finance Minister Arun Jaitley. Committees (or even Commissions) are a sure fire way of finding solutions to the seemingly insurmountable, so this would surely augment the efforts of the larger programmes.

The Government of India has taken strong steps in the following areas.

- More openness to foreign investments: FDI limit in the defence and insurance sector was enhanced to 49 per cent from 26 per cent previously, and 100 per cent FDI was allowed in railway infrastructure and medical devices sector. Real estate benefited from easing FDI norms in

the construction sector. Also, a composite cap has been implemented on FDI and the distinction between FII's, NRI's and other FDI has been done away with.
- Re-capitalization of PSU banks: The government decided to infuse PSU banks with ₹70,000 crore, over a span of four years, for their capitalization and to help them meet the Basel III norms. The banks will receive ₹25,000 crore each in FY16 and FY17, and ₹10,000 crore each in FY18 and FY19.
- Non-adversarial and investor friendly tax system: the Goods and Services Tax (GST) is rolled out and General Anti-Avoidance Rules (GAAR) have been deferred by another two years. The government has also proposed lower corporate tax rate from 30 per cent to 25 per cent and exempted Foreign Portfolio Investors (FPIs) from paying the minimum alternative tax (MAT).
- Easing the regulatory environment for doing business: The government has recently launched an e-biz portal which provides approvals for fourteen regulatory permissions at one source. Also, to improve business environment, government has set a timeline for clearing applications, enabled online application for industrial licence and IEMs (Industrial Entrepreneurs' Memorandum), and has proposed setting up a comprehensive bankruptcy code, corporatization of ports and replacing the system of multiple prior permissions with a pre-existing regulatory mechanism.
- Also, by making auctions the sole method for granting mineral concessions and mining leases, the government has been able to take a step towards inculcating transparency into the system.

VISION 2019

'The vision of ease of doing business in India is to transform the business environment by providing efficient, convenient, transparent and integrated electronics services to investors, industries, and business throughout the business lifecycle. India has to create a business and investor-friendly ecosystem by making all business and investment-related regulatory service across Central, State and local governments available on a single portal.

'The purpose is to make the environment enabling for the prospective investor and existing businesses, to avoid making them visit multiple offices or a plethora of websites. The ease of doing business should cover the entire life cycle of a business—right from its establishment, through its ongoing operations, to even its possible closure.

'The Vision of India is to be customer-centric whereby a single application submitted by a customer, for a number of permissions, clearances, approvals and registrations will be routed automatically across multiple governmental agencies in a logical manner. An inbuilt payment gateway will also add value by allowing all payments to be collected at one point and then apportioned, split and routed to the respective heads of account of Central and State Government along with generation of Challans and MIS reports.'

The main objective of ease of doing business is to 'First Develop India'; then, 'Make in India'; then 'Make for India'; and finally, 'Make for Rest of the World'.

Programmes like 'Make in India' and 'Digital India', amongst others, have been undertaken to primarily address issues around ease of doing business, breaking down the larger picture by industry (Make in India, run by DIPP, focuses on twenty-five sectors), and leveraging technology to overcome systemic red tape (Digital India, run by the Department of Electronics and Information Technology or DeITy, under the Ministry of Communication and IT, has a huge focus around e-governance and transforming India into a 'digitally empowered society').

A little over a year after the launch of the high octane 'Make in India' programme, we did rise twelve ranks to finish at 130 on the World Bank's *Doing Business Report 2016*, in October 2015. However, we would do well to remember, that a high ease of doing business ranking does not necessarily translate into a benign business climate till the enforcement of law is in spirit of the legislation.

India is ranked seventh in comparison to Singapore, which ranks third in the World Bank's 'Protecting Minority Investors' indicator. This indicator measures the strength of minority shareholder protections against misuse of corporate assets by directors for personal gain; and shareholder rights, governance safeguards and corporate transparency requirements that mitigate the risk of abuse. India's strong corporate laws including very detailed Companies Act 2013 ensure a vaulted rating, but these regulations often act as a bottleneck for faster growth.

As impressive as this improvement is, it is easy to forget that the World Bank study measures only two cities in each country that it ranks. For India, these are Mumbai and Delhi. As important as they might be, India is not Mumbai and Delhi alone; and Delhi/Mumbai is not India.

And even Mumbai and Delhi are quite different.

The cost incurred to start a business in Delhi is 10.4 per cent (of income per capita), while it's a steeper 17 per cent in

Mumbai, and it takes about fourteen procedures in Mumbai, compared to twelve in Delhi, though both take the same amount of time—twenty-nine days.

If this seems like hair splitting, consider the more telling parameter of 'dealing with construction permits'. Getting a construction permit takes forty procedures and 147 days in Mumbai, and twenty-eight procedures and 231 days in Delhi. Little surprise, then, that India still ranks 183 of 189 countries on this measure, having climbed up one spot from the year before.

Many companies have come a cropper at the State level. Ease of doing business at the State level is, in some ways, more important than that at the Central level. To be sure, physical infrastructural constraints are as critical as the metrics measured by World Bank under its ease of doing business parameter.

In early 2016, Chennai (formerly Madras), one of India's largest metropolises, was reeling under the aftermath of flooding that would be associated with only the remotest and least developed Indian villages. Supplies had to be air-dropped, large-hearted inhabitants opened up their homes, offices and hotels to provide food and shelter to affected parties, and there was a shortage of essential commodities. In the post-crisis analysis, it was thought that poor governance caused three or four of Chennai's major drains to be blocked, causing the problem. To add to the calamity, over-building on the city's flood plains—an IT park among other projects—ensured there was no place for the water to run off to.

SEVENTH-TIME LUCKY

For those who still are unsure of the Indian belief in rebirth,

Mr Tanti's career path offers compelling evidence. After six unsuccessful attempts, his seventh, Suzlon, grew to become a global force in the renewable energy segment. 'Failures are part of every success story. I don't ever see my failures in a negative connotation, I see them as an opportunity to start over again and do it better,' says Tulsi Tanti candidly.

'It is true that I have set up multiple businesses and not all of them have been great successes,' he admits. 'When I started some of these businesses, India used to be a very different economy, it was not easy to start and sustain a successful venture.'

The son of a farmer, Mr Tanti's 'dreams and aspirations were big but my resources and environment to scale up were weak'. Along with his three brothers, Mr Tanti decided to diversify from farming by starting small ventures such as an ice factory, a cold storage facility, and later a more successful textile business. He attributes his business acumen and entrepreneurial spirit to these early ventures, which he calls the 'founding pillars' for the fabulous success that would later come his way:

> From all these ventures, we got many learnings that we later implemented in Suzlon. From our ice business, we learned the significance of inventory management and JIT systems. The cold storage business taught us the importance of buying right: at the right time, at the right price. The textiles business taught us three very fundamental lessons. Firstly, the importance of technology. In an industry like textiles, technology is the key differentiating factor. It is through technology that a player in the industry could get margins by having a competitive edge.
>
> Secondly, to be established in the industry, one has to

be consistent in quality delivered to the customer. Over time, this is what builds the credibility of the brand and establishes trust in the consumers' minds.

And lastly, it was in the textiles industry that we realized how high the power costs were and how inconsistent the power supply was. To reduce this cost factor, we installed two small turbines. And thus began our journey towards the founding of Suzlon.

Perhaps most importantly, they learnt that they could only be followers, and not market leaders in established industries. Mr Tanti continues:

The other biggest learning was to always dream big and aim to be amongst the top three in the industry. This can only be done by thinking outside the box and being able to see what the society will need over the next few decades. Combined, these two learnings ensure scale and sustainability. In the previous experiences, we were part of established industries where we would always be a follower, not the market leader. I learned that to be truly successful in any venture, we needed to have a core competence which would give us a competitive edge in a market that we could potentially lead.

When Suzlon was founded, the wind segment was still a virgin industry with no players in India and only a few globally. And despite the evident need, there was little awareness about wind energy. Mr Tanti realized that a market could be created in India by focussing on technology and quality. He had a clear vision, 'to be one of the top wind turbine manufacturers globally.'

To begin with, Suzlon established its R&D facility in the

Netherlands, which gave the company an in-depth grasp and command on the technology front. Soon after, they started manufacturing blades for their turbines, the most critical component of a wind turbine. After a few years of operation, Suzlon began to vertically integrate into other components, to address the shortage in supply of key components which were very specialized. The next push, however, was on the legislation and policy front for the renewable energy industry in India. Suzlon started working with government bodies to design policies that would encourage the renewable energy sector in India. Simultanously, Mr Tanti continued to focus on improving efficiency in manufacturing operations, constantly ensuring that quality was best in class.

Suzlon succeeded in creating a market that had barely existed, and were finally where they wanted to be—in the position of market creator instead of market follower.

Increasingly, Indian companies are displaying signs of confidence of going global. What is the biggest challenge Indian companies face in doing so vis-à-vis foreign peers?

Mr Tanti sees Indian entrepreneurs itching to spread their wings and explore new opportunities globally. 'Constantly evolving technology and information transfers are shrinking the world and making geographical boundaries obsolete,' he states. Suzlon had a high profile foreign presence from its early days, so Mr Tanti can speak from experience.

One of the biggest challenges to Indian companies becoming successful globally, he feels, is adaptability to local market conditions and demands. Also, Indian companies are more owner-driven, whereas internationally companies are professional and process-driven. Indian companies aiming to make it big globally must evolve in this direction. A very strong understanding of the local legal framework is also equally important. Addressing these issues Mr Tanti says:

> My first advice to the younger generation would be to have a clear focus and goal in life. Many times, we get caught up in trying to do too many things in the hope that one will succeed. However, success requires a very clear determined focus.
>
> The second advice would be to have the perseverance to go through the ups and downs of the business. All ventures will have their own cycles of boom and bust, and entrepreneurs must be unwavering and consistent in their drive. They must inculcate a 'never-say-die' attitude in everything they do; and embrace their challenges and difficulties with positivity and enthusiasm, for these are the times that will shape character and determine the altitude their life goes to. Look for innovative solutions, think outside the box, and never ever give up. Keep sight of your destination and keep going.
>
> The third piece of advice would be to build your business on very strong principled and ethical grounds. Sustainable growth and success can only come when the company stands on a strong foundation of principles.
>
> The fourth piece of advice would be to realize that success is never about personal achievements, but rather in ensuring the satisfaction of all the various stakeholders involved in the business, i.e., customers, vendors, employees, lenders, etc.
>
> And lastly, I would advise entrepreneurs to build a very strong team with execution capabilities. Many a time, an entrepreneur has a strong vision, but lacks in execution

skills. Hence, it is very important to build a team that can translate the entrepreneur's dream into a reality.

TAX TERRORISM

Paying taxes helps you in your ease of doing business in the long term. Intriguingly, the 2015 ranking was not led by a unanimous improvement. India actually did worse on two parameters—getting loans and paying taxes. To use the example of the lifecycle that we started with, it has become easier to start a business, but not to run one (at least if you need to access funds, or pay taxes). And taxation can be a contentious issue in India. The Vodafone case is the best known and worst feared example of a foreign investor's run in with the government.

The simplified version is that Vodafone acquired Hutchison Telecom's India business (licences, operations and the rest), and was sent a bill by the taxman for dues payable for the transaction, had it occurred on Indian soil. This is alternatively known as the 'retrospective taxation case', which appropriately causes anxiety to existing and would-be investors.

Then there is the official version. Vodafone acquired an Indian company through its holding company in a tax haven, knowing full well that it would have to pay taxes on the transaction. Vodafone, however, demurred and chose to litigate and won in court. The Government of India, having lost the case possibly due to ambiguity in tax laws, went on to clarify these laws with retrospective effect, and hence the heartburn and headlines.

The only version I can reliably vouch for, is that both parties are seeking an amiable settlement via arbitration. The Government of India is aware of the damage the said case has done to 'Brand India', and is keen to put the matter to bed.

Ease of Doing Business in India • 153

There's a need to address the issue of Tax Terrorism (retrospective or retroactive tax laws and aggressive tax scrutiny), as it appears to be the most discussed and feared, especially amongst foreign investors. Other than the well-publicized Vodafone dispute, the tax authorities have also issued notices to companies like Cairn India (owned by UK's Vedanta Resources). The Finance Minister has explicitly stated that no retrospective taxation will be pursued, but Tax still endures as a source of concern for Indian and foreign investors alike; as do measures like the deferring of GAAR.[47]

The regulation allows tax officials to deny tax benefits, if a deal is found without any commercial purpose other than tax avoidance. It allows tax officials to target participatory notes. Under GAAR, the investor has to prove that the participatory note was not set to avoid taxes. It also allows officials to deny double taxation avoidance benefits, if deals made in tax havens like Mauritius were found to be avoiding taxes.

Prithvi Haldea offers a counter point, 'tax terrorism' is only for top 2 per cent of companies, but as this top percentile consists of big companies, it makes it to the news.'

It is hard to empathize ever with the taxman, but Indian companies have historically been loath to pay taxes—first because of incredibly high rates, and then because of reasons that really have no justification. Hence, it is important to distinguish between cases of tax terrorism and tax extraction.

Failure to comply with covenants of the Companies Act may

---

[47] General Anti-Avoidance Rule (GAAR) is an anti-tax avoidance regulation of India. It was introduced by then Finance Minister, Pranab Mukherjee, on 16 March 2012 during the Budget session. It was considered controversial because it had provisions to seek taxes from past overseas deals involving local assets in retrospect. During the 2015 Budget presentation Finance Minister Arun Jaitley announced that its implementation would be delayed by two years.

lead to imprisonment at alarming speed. As a result, companies find it difficult to get worthy independent directors outside of their known circle. Directors will not assume Board positions with companies they do not have complete financial oversight of, as the risk-reward equation just doesn't make sense. Private equity firms and venture capitalists have found a solution to this by taking 'non-participatory observer seats' (instead of Board seats) in investee companies.

I cannot resist mentioning a less nuanced, nay incredulous, law that rather directly impacts the ease of doing business and the sanity of the entrepreneur. An entrepreneur who does not want to be named, so let's call him Mr Khan, recently received a judicial summons, because he had allegedly not answered the Indian Statistical Bureau. This bureau essentially collects information such as the number of workers on rolls over a period of time, wages, and other such measurements. These are distinct measurements that involve income tax, excise and so forth. These are a more puritan statistical exercise.

Intriguingly, if you do not give this information, it is a jailable offence. Because this is a Central government department, any failure to answer can be referred to a judge, who can put the offender behind bars. To Mr Khan's fury, the request for information was not addressed to anyone in particular. It just had the name of the company in question, so where it could end up, would be anybody's guess.

Evidently, I caught Mr Khan on a particularly bad day. 'Have you ever been in a country outside India where police encourage you to close your office?'

It took me a moment to realize this was a rhetorical question, so thankfully he continued to answer, 'Whenever there is a general call for a strike, especially if it's a big union like the ones supporting Congress or other big parties, rather than maintain law and order, the easiest way for them is to "convince" factories to shut down. The fact that a business suffers is irrelevant...', and I left out before writers became the object of his ire.

Perceptibly, the major source of frustration stems from a complex and intertwined relationship between the body politic and the bureaucracy which seemingly impedes activity, however well-intentioned, with seemingly pointless road blocks. The real risk here is of investors voting with their feet, ergo the current raft of reforms to address this impression.

Ease of doing business is really at the heart of a couple of larger issues—legislative reform and corruption. Both we explore in subsequent chapters.

Sir Mark Tully has found in his decades of residing in and covering India for the BBC that 'even though it is difficult to do business here, in the end it is worthwhile.'

Tax courts need to be streamlined. The Companies Act, for instance, which was rewritten in 2013 (after some sixty years), is already being revised on account of feedback received from companies and stakeholders. This is both an acknowledgement of a law that could be better and an intent to make things better for business.

Law-making, however, is particularly perplexing in India, as some members of the various committees for revision of Companies Act explain. Not only is the process laborious, the miscreants always seem one step ahead of the law. Like every well-meaning law, there's been some misuse and alternative interpretation of these as well.

A case in point is the Amway case of May 2014, wherein Amway India's Chairman and CEO, William S. Pinckney (an American) and two other directors of the company, Sanjay

Malhotra and Anshu Budhraja (both Indian), were subjected to arrest and judicial custody on charges of unethical circulation of money through Amway operations.[48]

---

[48]Elaborated later in the book, on p. 164.

6
INDIA HAS LAW, CHINA HAS ORDER

INDIA, WITH its independent and active press and judiciary, has always (with the notable exception of the Emergency) found a natural balance to the jeopardy of excesses of the Executive or Legislature. In fact, the four pillars of Legislature, Executive, Judiciary and Press do provide a balanced, robust base for a stable democracy.

However, being democratic in all things also means dealing with a plethora of divergent views, being patient with the length of time it takes to get things done, and complying with processes that might appear to outgrow the purpose.

As management guru Gurcharan Das adroitly says, 'India has law, China has order'.

To be fair, India has been fortunate to have excellent laws and policies. Sadly, we talk of the more egregious legislations, as they are instructive as they are cautionary. For business affairs, legalese is largely well defined and followed. Until a dispute arises. Intriguingly, our laws (and often policy) are written in English. That and the heritage of common law, often create added comfort, not concern for foreign and 'international' businesses.

From his decades in India, Sir Mark Tully points out the flip side of a fair and well defined legal system. 'Courts take a long time, and that gives India a bad name,' and drafting can also be contorted. 'There are all these provisos in laws,' so you have one understanding of law, but the provision gives another complexion, 'bureaucracy seems to always seem to retain some discretion,' Sir Mark surmises.

And as we all know, from discretion rises the dual challenge—scope for inaction from upright officers, and potential for malfeasance by crooked administrators.

Legally enforcing a contract is hard to say the least. It is expensive in terms of time and effort, if not money. Entrepreneurs who lead unlisted, or small to mid-sized enterprises are typically time and money poor, so litigation is a luxury they can ill afford. 'The prospect of waiting twenty or thirty years before getting redressal is discouraging for even the most litigious of businessmen,' concludes Dhruv Shringi of yatra.com, from personal experience. A well-wisher from the police told him that economic offences are simply not a priority for the police.

That is, until the economic office is treated like a criminal offence. And we discuss some of those horror stories in the book. But Swaminathan Aiyar contends, 'you're lucky if even crime is priority!' During a particularly trying time, the chief of police of a small North Indian town bemoaned how fully stretched he was trying to prevent riots, and had no time for attending to crime.

Nobody disputes that police-judicial reform is urgently required. It is commendable that the system does, for the most part, work. On one hand, while the system cannot convict, it can certainly harass. In the past, those with political clout would often get away with wrongdoing, but with increased media pressure and active judiciary, this is becoming increasingly rare. Sadly, there's little will to reform the police. Mr N.C. Saxena was head of the Police Reforms Commission in the 1970s. He said the four main reasons were that the police were caught up with the following:

1. Harass their opponents
2. Protect their own crooks
3. Organize VIP 'bandobast'
4. If you still have time, attend to law and order

A similar study today might come to comparable conclusions.

A couple of German investors have experienced, first hand, the functioning of law enforcement. In Hyderabad, a BMW dealer, whose dealership was not extended by the luxury carmaker, went on to sue BMW for cheating him. BMW stated that the contract had expired, which it had no intent of extending.

The influential former-dealer managed to get an arrest warrant against the senior-most officer of BMW in India, who, incidentally, was not even in the country (not posted here) when the dispute first arose. He was arrested from the BMW garage in Gurgaon and flown to another city ('like a kidnapping, almost') and produced before a judge. He was, of course, released shortly after, but the incident created a negative image of the legal system, and how it might be misused by the influential. The clear (even if unfair) impression BMW took away, was that the, 'dealer managed to get this done'.

A similar business spat arose between a Porsche dealer and a principal, when they terminated a dealership on grounds of wrongdoing. What followed was an arrest warrant against the whole Board of Porsche in Germany. Bernard Steinruecke, President of the Indo-German Chambers of Commerce says that these and cases like Amway or Nokia are not good for India. He does stress though, that these are truly exceptional cases. For the most part, state (or other) courts do not liberally hand out arrest warrants.

These are rare exceptions, but India needs to be very careful here, or an incorrect reputation might be built.

THE BEST DEFENCE: A FORTRESS OF GOODWILL

Venkatesh Kini, the President of Coke in the subcontinent, postulates that in India, the government doesn't offer right to operate—instead, local communities grant you privilege to operate. So obtaining licences, acquiring land, benefiting local communities, and following law of land is not enough. 'Companies need to build a fortress of goodwill to guard themselves from attacks from various quarters—socialist, political, religious,' says Mr Kini. Coke, Pepsi and McDonalds have often been the most visible targets of all kinds of protest and ire, so the fortress in these cases needs to be especially robust.

One of the noisiest places to do business, but once you figure it out, India is a great place to do business.

State and local governments also determine your business. The Central government has little control over day-to-day operations of manufacturing-related businesses. The state government and the local MP or MLA are more crucial in day-to-day affairs like ensuring law and order, non-politicization of the labour union, and ensuring water and power supply. Conversely, if an inspector issues a negative order (for instance, a negative order issued by an Inspector of the Pollution Control Board), you can be shut down—Nokia was shut down by a tax case. In essence, a single order can shut you down, while you need around forty permissions to start up. Coke has suffered in instances when bottling plants have been shut for an year or two before they were acquitted by junior and then higher courts (authorities may appeal if they lose in lower courts).

AMWAY'S WOES[49]

Amway suffered a civil suit which was treated almost like a criminal plaint. Amway obtained FIPB (Foreign Investment Promotion Board) approval in 1995, but commenced its operations only in 1998. It engaged in direct selling of consumer products through a strategy often referred to as MLM, or multi-level marketing.

Indian laws, like those of many western jurisdictions, permit direct selling, but seek to curb defraudment of the public through pyramid schemes of various stripes, which are known to emerge with remorseless frequency. Amway, in this case, had to establish that they weren't running a 'pyramid scheme', besides facing charges of cheating as well as extortion under relevant sections of the Indian Penal Code (IPC).

The Prize Chits and Money Circulation Schemes (Banning) Act, imposed curbs on various money-circulation schemes (a type of pyramid scheme in which money is paid to the enroller for recruiting members) and prize chit-fund schemes. This Act gave the power to the police to seize, seal and arrest on the basis of a complaint.

So, Indian laws allow direct selling, but forbid business models built around recruiting new members or distributors.

Amway's India woes started in the states of Andhra Pradesh, Telangana and Kerala, following which authorities shut down all corporate offices, conducted raids against distributors, and arrested managers, in response to public complaints.

In 2013, Crime Branch officials of Kerala Police arrested

---

[49] See:http://cribmc.blogspot.in/2014/05/founding-amway-amway-japan-head-office.html

American William S. Pinckney, Managing Director and CEO of Amway India Enterprises, along with two Indian directors of the company on charges of running a pyramid scheme. They were granted bail the following day.

Amway, to be clear, has faced multiple legal challenges in countries around the world, regarding its operations and business models, not to forget the various political controversies it has courted in the USA, UK, Canada and Poland, to name a few.

In hindsight, the company, with its track record of consistently running afoul of laws of many lands, could perhaps have made greater attempts to engage with stakeholders in India, explaining their model.

Amway has paid enormous amounts of money for settlements in the USA, for instance. For a fraction of the amount, they might have ensured compliance—and if they couldn't comply, they could have found a different India model, as many companies have successfully and transparently done.

Epilogue: Amway's India website features a cheerful Bollywood star (Farhan Akhtar) promoting a health supplement, so it would seem all is well with the world. Perhaps they have found their India model (in this case, a Bollywood model).

A THINNING CROWD

In these times of crowd funding and crowd sourcing (and other such democratic phenomena like flash mobs), Indian laws have been slow to adapt to the needs of the fast growing start-up ecosystem.

Until recently, Indian tech prowess has been largely confined to writing code for large Silicon Valley type employers or customers. It is an unfortunate stereotype, but the huge concern has been that while Indians have excelled in senior management roles abroad (and still do—among others, Nadella heads Microsoft, Nooyi heads PepsiCo and Pichai heads Google), a comparable proliferation of Indian entrepreneurs in the valley (or other start-up hubs).

A self-confessed Indophile, Prof. Steven Rogers at Harvard Business School reveals that The Indus Entrepreneurs (TiE) was set up in Silicon Valley some two decades ago to address this very problem, that of creating more Indian entrepreneurs.[50]

To be fair, there are examples of Indian entrepreneurial genius in the likes of Vinod Dham, Vinod Khosla, Ramesh Wadhwani (Symphony Technology Group), Kavitark Ram Shriram, and Bharat Desai (Syntel), to confine ourselves to tech billionaires. And closer to home almost weekly a new tech billionaire is minted with constantly climbing valuations, and a seemingly infinite supply of venture capital funding.

The Government of India seems to have realized that the best jobs programme is to foster a start-up ecosystem. When employment is to be created for almost a million new jobs a month, for many months (another ten or so years), there is only so much the conventional means of job creation can do.

If the Prime Minister's Independence Day Speech, 2014, was about 'Make in India', the 2015 edition spoke of the 'Startup India' and 'Stand-Up India' campaigns. While the DIPP consulted rockstars of the entrepreneurship space, including Nikesh Arora (Soft Bank), Kunal Behl (Snapdeal), Ritesh Agarwal (Oyo Rooms) and Mohandas Pai (Infosys), there is some distance to be covered to enable start-ups to well, start up.

---

[50] An interesting play on words, is TiE. Indus, of course, refers to the river that spawned Indic civilizations; but it also is 'Ind' and 'US'.

Like all angels, Business Angels are around (if you believe in them), but be wary. Venture capital funds are growing in appetite and number. Crowd funding is nascent and without precedent of scale. If you're looking at scale, it still is pretty much hard-nosed banks, and the equity markets. The finance industry is rapidly growing, but has its challenges. Whilst the bond market is virtually absent, a healthy stock market has, for decades, rewarded Indian subsidiaries of foreign companies for performance and good governance.

The two major exchanges remain the National Stock Exchange (NSE) and the Bombay Stock Exchange (BSE), in that order. Some cities, other than Mumbai, run their own exchanges, which are either comatose, dormant or somnambulant.

Prithvi Haldea tells all entrepreneurs who list, to stop taking money out of the company, as, 'virtually all companies are doing this to some degree.' If you don't, markets reward through higher PE, better terms from bank, and each rupee you leave in the company is multiplied manifold via PE multiples.

A big Mumbai investor does not invest in companies where the owner has unmarried daughters. 'If there are two or three (daughters), ₹15–20 crores might be siphoned off,' he postulates in a cynical mix of fiduciary prudence and cultural insight. As a father of two unmarried girls (they're both under a year old), I hope you will avoid such chauvinistic brokers like the plague. Or persuade him to set up a philanthropic fund for fathers of 'two to three unmarried daughters'.

Mercifully, the new breed of entrepreneurs are not thinking that way. I'm talking business ethics now. Young entrepreneurs are quite satisfied to cover living expenses and do the 'wealth creation in company', i.e. keep their fingers out of the till.

This is a seminal change, if it gains momentum. Traditionally,

Indian laws have been written from a position of suspicion and distrust. Initially so, due to the colonial legacy centred around control, and later endured with the help of instances of wrongdoing that fed into the cliché of the crooked businessman, who had to be kept in line under pain of legal penalty or imprisonment.

Newer laws are experimenting with very new concepts like self-certification—essentially a trust-based compliance, where only the offenders are penalized, and even they are initially trusted to do the right thing. This one stroke upsides both, the fundamental logic of law-making (or at least writing compliance guidelines), and mitigates the need for visits to government offices and inspectors.

Delays in incorporation of companies, lack of early stage (essentially seed or angel) funding, limited options around employee stock options, insolvency laws, lack of access to external commercial borrowing, and the cumbersome Foreign Exchange Management Act (FEMA) are only some of the constraints budding start-ups encounter. And the numerous governmental compliances are serious deterrents and distractions to aspiring entrepreneurs. But despite these constraints, the Indian start-up ecosystem is estimated to be among the top five, globally.

So here we are—one of the world's busiest start-up scenes, and an enormous appetite and ability to fund the better ventures. Nevertheless, it is estimated that in 2014, 56 per cent of all funded start-ups (of a certain scale and stage) moved headquarters and listed/are listing on the Singapore exchange. By mid-2015, this share was three quarters of all start-ups of this demographic. This flight of our best and brightest arises from the lack of opportunity for these companies to grow financially through Indian markets and instruments. The stock markets, and stock market regulator (SEBI), have been trying to enact laws to arrest this exodus, but reform is still awaited.

Because of the constantly evolving structure, rapidly increasing speed and unprecedented growth of these new-age firms, the laws haven't quite kept up with them. Old concepts like 'promoter' and 'promoter family' need to be reviewed or jettisoned, whereas new ideas of 'phantom equity' and 'crowd sourcing' need to be squarely addressed. The Government of India (DIPP again) has been working on giving the 'Startup India' programme more teeth. There are many promising ideas being floated, and after due iterations it will be interesting to see which version finally makes it to legislation. There's obviously a lot to be done. The case for easier access to capital has been made in this chapter, as also the challenges caused by our culture (accepting failure); the chapter on labour and talent pool outlines challenges that insecurity causes (hyper competitiveness, and mutual distrust); the need for enabling infrastructure (Chapter 3 speaks of prohibitive real estate prices) and ecosystems need to be created if start-ups are to have a chance at all.

Uber, for instance, faced teething trouble after commencing operations, as the law didn't exactly cover this novel concept. Some interest groups alleged that the payment system (via credit cards) contravened regulations. The solution was to accommodate a two-factor authentication process, or effect transactions through a payment gateway (homegrown Paytm, for instance).

This is an emergent matter far from over though, so watch out. As often is the case with India, local challengers have appeared (and secured significant funding), the frontrunner being as well Ola, which has a 75 per cent share of market, after acquiring competitor TaxiForSure. Uber, like the other taxi aggregators, has also incorporated autorickshaws (tuk-tuks) into its offerings, where you still need to pay the auto-wallah cash, but you never know, before long e-payments might become viable for small ticket transactions as well (Ola already does).

The next wave is likely to be the Indian start-up that takes on the world. Freshdesk, for instance, is an Indian challenger to Zendesk, the cloud-based customer service platform. Zendesk is listed on NYSE, with revenues in excess of US$100 million, but if Freshdesk proves to be a legitimate challenger for the top spot, it will create a new type of Indian start-up: engaging with the global customer, not confined to playing the 'India story', alone.

Zomato was founded as FoodieBay in Gurugram (formerly Gurgaon), the famous NCR suburb in 2008, before it was rechristened Zomato in November 2010. Backed heavily by InfoEdge and other investors, the company has raised about US$ 113 million over time, with a valuation of about US$ 660 million. In 2012, it spread wings globally and acquired as many as five low-key restaurant listing companies in emerging markets, before buying out UrbanSpoon to mark its entry into the biggest of all markets—the US. Zomato is now present in 22 countries with a listing of over a million restaurants globally.

Ola towers over Uber (in market share and geographical presence) in India, and fuelled with further venture capital or PE funding, might even expand abroad to compete with Uber, if things go well. A young venture capital investor's eyes light up at the prospect of Indian companies chasing competition around the globe. 'Just imagine,' he says, 'what Indian companies could achieve if they weren't distracted by the local regulatory environment, and managing the non-business part of their existence.' The inherent disadvantage for all Indian companies is the high cost of capital compared to competitors and poor infrastructure. However, industry is more focused on keeping duty structure high, whereas lower cost of capital, for instance, would give greater benefit.

Onerous laws, however, are not necessarily the end of your India plans. When Sesame Street first came to India, the laws did not reconcile NGO with surplus (NGOs are, after all, meant to be 'not for profit'). As a solution, Sesame set up a dual entity; the NGO is 'Sesame Workshop India Trust', and the company is 'Sesame Workshop India Initiative Pvt. Ltd'. Later a third entity, 'Sesame Schoolhouse Pvt. Ltd' was created to run the pre-schools.

'The India operation is for-profit and a not-for-profit,' explains Sashwati Banerjee, Managing Director of Sesame Street in India. Laws can seem constraining, but as the thriving economic ecosystem demonstrates, the constraints are not entirely incapacitating to companies (or non-companies, in this case).

INTELLECTUAL PROPERTY (IP)

'One generation ago,' explains one of India's leading legal luminaries, 'Indians were loath to pay a lawyer or doctor for their time. They would be happy to pay for the medicine, or court cases, but not counsel.' While this tremendously successful lawyer notes a change of heart among his present clientele, the older trend sadly continues to this day for some management consultants.

Evidence of the earlier era is still manifest at social gatherings and parties, doctors and lawyers will routinely be subjected to the gory details of woes of other merrymakers, who will think nothing of expecting specialist advice on their concerns. Culturally, we are coming to accept why IP of any kind—a brand, a song (even books, I hope), or a patent should accrue earnings to its maker. This change is likely to have two interesting outcomes:

a. the incidence of insensitive infringement will reduce. For instance, seeing the likeness of Hollywood (or Indian) stars, or international brands, on firecrackers, though wilful offenders will continue undeterred.
b. IP laws will become even more effective in letter and enforcement than the current standards.

There are more pragmatic reasons for continued reform here. Foreign investors would be reluctant to invest or 'Make in India' if their hard won IP is not adequately protected in this land of infinite opportunity. There's been some public chatter about a new IP Policy (and stronger laws, one supposes), which clearly say they will protect IP and encourage manufacturing and business due to IP—hopefully say how—perhaps through new laws and mechanisms.

Indian IP laws are strong and fair, but do take resources to be assertable.[51] Here's a quick reckoner of what to expect: copyrights don't mandate registration, but aren't as critical in the business sense, so they see little attention here in courts or in corporations.

For businesses that invest in huge amounts to build a brand, trademarks become more important, and therefore see more action. An interesting suit filed by TT Garments against Audi, resulted in courts restraining Audi from selling the trendy 'TT' sports car in Delhi. On appeal, however, the order was reversed and the ban over the sale of Audi TT cars was lifted. The

---

[51]To be clear, copyright covers very generally, the expression of ideas. So, everything in relation to a movie, for example, a script once written, the music, the movie itself becomes copyrightable. So, in the corporate sense, copyrights have not so much of an impact, but copyright is what is believed to be the creative backbone of IP.

plaintiff, who has been selling TT branded underwear since 1968, has legally prevailed over map maker TT and kitchenware maker TTK in the past.[52]

The courts weigh 'Freedom of Speech' heavier on the balance against IP rights. Half a decade ago, Greenpeace created an online game 'Turtle vs TATA' which shows a Tata logo scaring away a turtle. The Tata group sued for infringement of their trademark but failed as the Delhi High Court held that the use of the mark by Greenpeace was parody and not an infringement. This decision follows the strong parody defence set out in the US trademark laws and aims to establish a level playing field in the attempt to assert IP rights—conglomerates or the so-called underdog, notwithstanding.[53]

Patents, or protection granted to something you 'create', (provided it's novel, has an inventive step and is capable of industrial application), is especially big in high R&D areas like pharmaceuticals and advanced engineering. Obviously big and gaining more importance, given the demand for patented goods, a richer economy is bound to see.

We will steer clear of moral dilemmas exploring whether life-saving drugs should be sold cheap to the poor (go ahead and read the Novartis judgement passed by the Supreme Court which created a huge stir in the First world), or whether the very Indian Basmati rice can be patented by precocious foreigners (and I'm told that there are attempts underway to patent yoga, though I'm not really sure how that works).

---

[52] http://www.legallyindia.com/Bar-Bench-Litigation/saikrishna-wins-permission-to-use-audi-tt-name-on-audi-cars-after-delhi-hc-outright-ban

[53] http://timesofindia.indiatimes.com/home/environment/developmental-issues/No-legal-reprieve-for-Tata-Sons-in-battle-with-Greenpeace/articleshow/7380296.cms

As IP laws are very new, compared to penal code and other laws, lack of precedent and the alarming speed of technological development make them relatively easier to circumvent. But in practice, the enthusiasm in law enforcement (and shortened timelines), makes up for this and increasingly dissuades would be poseurs.

Coming back to our initial point, most IP violators in India are not aware of the IP rights they infringe upon (and no, that's not a valid defence), and they are pretty small potatoes, as compared to their more organized Asian counterparts who are usually richer and know full well about the laws they violate. However, the hope is that the incidence of compliance will increase via altruism or deterring laws.

Three quarters of patents in India are reportedly filed by foreign companies. A senior officer of a leading German MNC explains, 'IP is also what is in the heads of employees. Due to the IP intensive nature of our business, we're happy due to the loyal workforce in India.'

Caveat: one of the bright IP lawyers I consulted for the book, admitted to using Torrents to download e-books and movies, rather that fork out hard-earned money to Amazon and Netflix.

MEDIA TRIALS

In mid-2015, there was an outbreak of truly sensational news. Maggi noodles, a favourite (even staple) of Indians across generation and demographic, contained traces of lead. This outrageous discovery spread like wildfire, and televised 'Media trials' ensued, where eight or ten so-called experts started debating the case, and pronounced snap judgment on Nestle (which has been in India since 1912, and owns the Maggi brand). Courts, of course, take longer to decide and follow a due process, but the immeasurable harm is often done to companies or individuals in the reportage of a story.

For Coke, 'trial by media' has certainly been a consideration in shutting down plants. Mr Kini explains how opposition was not from local population as much as from various quarters using them to gain national and international fame, especially 'in absence of strong libel laws to take care of wrong or biased reporting'.

Like anywhere else in the world, irresponsible journalism is really the preserve of less professional news outfits. And unlike many places in the world, the Indian public expects news channels and papers to actively keep the powerful on the straight and narrow path. In fact, journalists enjoy a huge amount of trust and influence in India.

Coke had a particularly rough time in 2006, when it was accused for the second time in three years, of having unacceptable levels of pesticides in beverages (of several brands, including Coke and PepsiCo) by an NGO (Centre for Science and Environment or CSE), which went public with its findings.

The same NGO had been clamouring for years about pesticide in the food chain (through polluted water, soil, air, etc.), but Coke and PepsiCo got headlines. The ensuing furore was possibly a sense of betrayal of consumers' trust, and resulted in a drop in business that took Coke three years to recover from. 'That incident set industry back by 3–5 years,' says Venkatesh Kini.

Coke is wiser from the experience, though. The first accusations in 2003 were ridiculed by the leadership of Coke, and portrayed the NGO (CSE) in poor light. Media lost interest, but the case didn't go away, but simmered. The second time around, Coke engaged with the government, media (through factory visits and sharing of test reports from international labs), testified before government, and the NGO itself. 'The Supreme Court gave us a clean chit after six years (which also included joint Parliamentary Committees),' says Kini.

BBC veteran Sir Mark warns of how easy it is to float stories, and instances of unscrupulous journalists using the power of a media trial for extortion. But regulations might lead to censorship—so the media needs to introspect. There's also a risk of crooks getting away due to strong libel laws.

'The guilt of a famous brand or person is more newsworthy than their innocence,' philosophizes Mr Kini, adding, 'Go on defensive with courts, tribunals, etc. rarely litigate proactively. PILs [Public Interest Litigations] are often misused, causing difficulty and expense. People go after the deepest pockets.'

Also, the world loves the underdog, so it is hard for large corporations to pursue a case of defamation against an individual or small organization, without seeming heavy handed. The best defence is a bank of goodwill, rather than legal route. Even Coke thinks that the situation is turning for the better. There's a maturing in last five or so years, and the media is no longer as brazen in accusations.

Social media, however, trumps organized media in what might constitute libel in non-extraordinary circumstances. Both sides of any debate are found equally guilty of mean spirited attacks, and 'trolling' to raise the din to an online shouting match, before mainstream media is forced to acknowledge and report the issue. The rise of social media in India, as in the world, might make the excesses of conventional media seem trifling.

DISAPPEARING DAUGHTERS/WORKMEN ONLY

> Maa chahiye, behen chahiye, biwi chahiye.
> Phir beti kyu nahi chahiye?
> —*Written outside a school in Rohtak, Haryana*

Translation—
> Need a mother, need a sister, need a wife.
> Then why not a daughter?

The scale of India's demographic dividend (as with some corporations: projected, but yet to be paid) would imply a near universal growth of working age population. However, the numbers are sadly skewed. While our workforce grows rapidly, the participation of women in the workforce has fallen from 30 per cent to 22.5 per cent by some estimates. But as worrying as this statistic is, the true figure might be half of that.

'That's the figure which also includes unpaid workers. If you consider the paid workforce, women account for a mere 13 per cent,' rues Gautam Bhardwaj, co-founder of microPension Foundation. The reasons for this distressing decline are both socio-economic and legislative.

Dalit women, for instance, have stopped working in fields of upper-caste landowners in rural India. Socially, this is a great development, as these women put dignity before income; but this also translates into problems for agriculture and industry—a shortage of skilled/semi-skilled workforce. Also cultural biases being what they are, working Dalit women cannot get good husbands. We, therefore, need adequate educational and physical infrastructure to create mobility in skills and employability.

MicroPension Foundation's research reveals that women routinely drop out of the workforce: temporarily to bear children, and permanently, in their late forties. This is a particularly grave problem, because they normally have greater longevity than men, and lesser rights (e.g. inheritance, unequal pay and unpaid work). This means the government has a vested interest in keeping them in the workforce, and financially secure (while ensuring India's demographic dividend does pay off).

Fortunately, the government has framed laws especially to address this concern. Unfortunately, some of the laws have exacerbated the problem. In a country where gender related crime seems to continue unabated, and routinely hits the headlines, there is ever increasing public pressure for stronger laws to protect women, especially against gender-related crimes. This is universally demanded. And while we got what we wished for, the results have been mixed.

Traditionally, a widespread preference for the male child, and a (mostly) patriarchal society led to India's infamous ignominy—female foeticide and dowry deaths. Mercifully, we have already seen some success in checking female foeticide and dowry-related crimes (even murder), owing to strong laws and publicity educating masses on these social evils and crimes. However, on the flip side there are women who exploit these laws. Cases have been reported where accusations of dowry demands and abuse have been wrongly made against the estranged husband's family during an ugly divorce lawsuit. The beginning of Amway's legal woes (Chapter 5) also began with a dowry complaint in Kerala.

A senior IPS officer, who does not wish to be named, reveals that a large number of all dowry-related plaints are false, being essentially used as pressure tactics in marital spats or divorce settlements. However, he does admit that genuine dowry-related harassment cases are particularly vile.

In the 1980s and 1990s, the homestead was the theatre of

abuse of women—domestic violence and dowry-related murders. This has now moved to crimes against women at the hands of strangers. The Nirbhaya case, a brutal rape of a college girl in Delhi, who would later succumb to grievous injuries, shook the nation to its core and brought the debate to the fore. A déjà vu of when dowry deaths became the predominant cultural (movies and art), social, and political issue of the previous decade—a social evil that needed to be eliminated. Today, young Indian women are encouraged by the police, family and friends to install SOS mobile apps, should they ever—God forbid—need help in a difficult situation.

It is important to put gender-related legislation and social mores into context, else it may be easy to make a false snap judgment of the new laws on Sexual Harassment in the Workplace.

The head of a leading European MNC overcame his initial fright when he witnessed six cases of sexual harassment being reported in the first six weeks of his India stint. While this is an alarming statistic by any standards, he was further vexed by the fact that all six complainants filed plaints after being terminated from their jobs. Furthermore, his predecessor (an Indian), battled with charges of sexual harassment from an employee who had been fired, and just before he was transferred out, the plaintiff withdrew her accusation, accepting it to be false.

I brought to his notice the many less scrupulous companies with dodgy HR practices, that witness abuse of employees with little or no protection, other than this law, but for a recent inhabitant, his personal experiences were a greater influence of his world view, than my 'see the larger picture' advice.

The somewhat cynical advice from the lawyers of this European MNC suggested installing CCTV cameras in offices to, among other reasons, determine veracity and enable swift investigation of future cases, if they were to arise.

Again, these are early days for the law and application thereof, and the prevention or redress of even one genuine case of abuse more than makes up for potential misuse of this provision. Like all laws, there will be some iteration and precedents that will shape a version that is accepted and fair to most. Remember, it's the greater common good that needs to be the overarching objective of these laws.

However, it is the reality that Indian laws meant to protect the weak and vulnerable, err on the side of caution. And in doing so, often hurt the constituency they are meant to protect. Labour laws and courts function in a manner that seeks to protect workers from the clout of employers that might extend to courtrooms in the form of a battery of senior lawyers. But this translates into an inordinately large number of 'contract employees (vs those on payrolls). Similarly, the law that deals with sexual harassment is not quite gender neutral; as the name suggests, it is the Sexual Harassment of Women in the Workplace (Prevention, Prohibition and Redressal) Act, 2013. Sairee Chahal, CEO of Sheroes, laments the adverse impact the law has had in the hiring of women by even respected companies.

Sheroes specializes in enabling young mothers to rejoin the workforce (after a temporary drop out, as discussed above), as full or part-time professionals, but the laws have given many prospective employers cold feet. Many companies have become hesitant hiring women. Sairee has been conducting workshops to explain the letter and application of the law to companies, and help them build a framework (mandated by law) within their companies to deal with complaints.

The law is new, but the constraint is familiar. The more urban BPO industry learnt to deal with well-intentioned, albeit egregious rules, which caused challenges, especially if they were to work late (which was just about every BPO operation). Libel laws impact both these subjects (wrongful plaints and media trials, explained earlier), and while this is not a silver bullet for these challenges, stronger laws, and enforcement thereof would certainly help filter out frivolous and false cases from genuine grievances.

Rarefied levels of company boards are not impervious to this either. According to Dr (Ms) Reena Ramachandran who has over forty years of industry experience, men are hesitant to speak out on women-related laws that are egregious, for fear of appearing prejudiced. However, men comprise the majority on selection committees, and seldom pick women for the top job (though there is usually one woman on the committee). The reasons stated are—lack of experience, insufficient qualifications, etc. even if other candidates are comparable.

Public sector units, meant to be model corporate citizens, have taken the new Company Act (which mandates minimum one woman director on a Board) as a cap of one woman per Board—so, both the independent, and woman are complied with by the appointment of a woman. These women are usually IAS officers in the department or ministry that oversees the concerned PSU.

Dr Ramachandran was the only woman Chairperson among all 258 PSUs when she retired in 2000. For next ten years, there were no women at the helm of PSU's. Even today there are just about three women at the helm of (PSU) affairs. Banking and financial services, however, have been a beacon of light: women routinely hold the top job in private and government-owned banks—HSBC, SBI, ICICI, Central Bank, etc.

'These laws have made corporations doubtful about employing women in general, and also reluctant when it comes to top positions. There seems to be a glass ceiling imposed by onerous legislation,' Dr Ramachandran[54] asserts.

Libel laws are a subset of a larger issue—the law enforcement-judicial system. 'You basically have a dysfunctional state,' says an outspoken Swaminathan Aiyar. 'When murder, rape, and loot are major problems, how can libel be addressed?' He explains how the police and judiciary have mutual contempt for each other. The police blames the judiciary for letting perpetrators get away. The judiciary blames the police for not knowing the law, for conducting shoddy investigations and then blaming hostile witnesses (beating confession out of persons) for cases getting thrown out.

Pascal, in *Pensées*, phrased the sentiment in different words, 'Justice without force is impotent; force without justice is tyranny.'

Weak law enforcement has created a sense of impunity among criminals who consider themselves above the law. These villainous characters are spurred on by:

1. No sense of guilt
2. No public shame
3. No fear of law

In contrast to the lack of shame and guilt prevailing in general, I was told of an instance in the 1960s, when a government employee was suspended for corruption (submitting false medical bill), and was virtually made an outcast for this outrageous crime. Admittedly, today we are more forgiving. The formerly jailed,

---

[54]Former CMD, Hindustan Organic Chemicals; member, Task Force, Performance Management Division, Cabinet Secretariat; Independent Director in the Board of 'United Phosphorus Ltd.' (now UPL Ltd) and Indian Additives Ltd.

or recently raided by Income Tax Department go about their social lives as before, and people will, for example, unflinchingly partake in parties and celebrations of the publicly indicted.

The evaporation of fear of law stems from a (rather cynical) sequence of widely accepted assumptions as follows: you won't be caught; if caught, will bribe; if can't bribe, will use influence; if can't use influence and jailed, will get bail; and when out on bail, will drag the case on for fifteen to twenty years in the courts.

A friend involved with financial markets and legislation routinely monitors SEBI orders, and on occasion, finds an acquaintance mentioned as an accused. When confronted with this public information, the accused remorselessly says (as if in defence): 'I took every precaution, but still got caught. But now you "know" SEBI, so please help (let me off).' The implication being that the crime is being caught red-handed, not the offence itself.

Bear in mind, you would have to be a sociopath to do the above, like anywhere in the world, but this ties in with the sense of VIP entitlement we discussed in Chapter 2.

'Laws are always reactive,' muses Prithvi Haldea, 'while markets (or criminals) are ingenious and far ahead of regulatory wisdom.' This truism is further exacerbated by the speed at which Indian business and society are moving, which is much ahead of laws and even legal definition (especially true of tech-heavy sectors). Laws will have to ensure that they keep up with innovation in business and technology, keep introspecting and tweaking, till we reach a balance between control and trust.

Arresting expatriate (or Indian) executives, treating co-workers as guilty (of sexual harassment) till proven innocent, extortionate PILs, or allowing the Press to make dramatic accusations without fear of consequence are only some of the larger concerns that vex the potential investor. Each of these concerns, singularly, has the ability to derail the India story as the retrospective taxation case (Chapter 4) almost did.

Some of these laws seem remorseless in their treatment of misdeeds, and this understandably causes some anguish. But this is partly because the degree of violence and heinousness demonstrated in recent acts of criminality are unprecedented in the country. Thankfully, there is stronger and more profound evidence to the contrary. Laws and compliance based on trust, and assuming that the private, or corporate, citizen is not a criminal as a starting point, is extraordinary.

For instance, acceptance of 'self-certification' from businesses is telling of the shift from a formerly colonial mindset of control and mistrust, where private and corporate citizens were suspect, until proven otherwise.

7

THE ELEPHANT IN THE ROOM

The UN (United Nations) estimates that worldwide almost a trillion dollars is paid annually in bribes. This increases the cost of doing business in developing countries by at least 20 per cent. And yet, companies are mostly silent on the subject.

A major concern for investors—Indian and foreign—remains the perceived risk of being drawn into a web of corrupt and unsavoury practices that are considered a part of doing business in the developing world.

While this is a real possibility, it is not a prerequisite to doing business in India. In terms of perception, too, India is not considered the most crooked emerging market. Far from it—Transparency International's annual *Corruption Perception Index 2014*, ranks India 85th (improving over 2013 by 9 spots), better than China (100th) and Russia (136th), but lags Brazil (69th) and South Africa (65th) on the study that covers 174 countries (Denmark is ranked 1st).

CORRUPTION IN BUSINESS, GOVERNMENT AND LIFE IN INDIA

'Indians have an appetite to accept malfeasance,' stated Mr Vinod Rai, dryly. Mr Rai, for the unacquainted, is best known for his role is bringing ginormous government scams to light in his role as the former Comptroller Auditor General of India (CAG).

In a telling manifestation of this tolerance for corruption, it is not unusual to enquire of eligible junior officers during pre-nuptial discussions, '*Upar ka kitna kama lete hain?*' (how much income does he earn over and above his salary?). But often, this information will be volunteered when soliciting a match. Mr Rai admits that the numbers and scale of the scams were an exaggeration, but that exaggeration was required to shake people out of this acceptance of corruption as the norm.

Graft is classified into three boxes: (i) facilitation (ii) harassment, (iii) deriving undue advantage.

How do the most public and scrupulous corporations—both Indian and transnational—navigate this minefield and keep their noses clean, and tackle the government's new legislative attempts at addressing this menace and the disrepute past baggage has brought.

Petty corruption does not account for all malfeasance, which can also be top-down. Thankfully, no scams have come to light in the recent past, but hardnosed auditors also warn that there's a lag in discovering the same, as audit is post facto. So fingers crossed, and hope there's a less cynical reason—a lesser instance of venality.

As lower-level discretion is minimized through e-governance and single-window clearance, petty bureaucracy will be diluted. The labour inspector, customs inspector, health inspector, factory boiler inspector will have fewer opportunities to indulge in corruption where the human interface is mitigated.

Often junior or middling officers are billionaires (at least in rupee terms), while the heads of departments and ministries subsist on modest incomes. The attitudes of the government, bureaucracy and officials in States and the Centre are the same—often worse in states. So, not much difference in small government and big government.

SOLUTIONS

Mr Vinod Rai established a Code of Ethics for the Audit Party. Auditors had to show this to the Auditee before they began. This brought down the benefits, gifts, car, sightseeing, etc., that PSUs routinely provided auditors. It became awkward and uncomfortable for both sides to accept or offer these frills that had become the norm. If all inspectors have to show a similar Code to the business being inspected, this might help bring about a slow change.

Prof. Ashish Nanda notes, 'Corruption is extremely debilitating, it is the grease for getting business done, but leads to people exerting power, exerting extra authority to hold back decisions, to take non-market-optimal decisions, and so leads to business dilemma.'

HONESTY IS EXPENSIVE

For this book, I had the occasion to lunch with an upright mid-career bureaucrat (who insisted on splitting the bill, which is uncommon). In an act of disarming candour, he disclosed his personal finances to me and mentioned how rewarding foreign postings were, not only because of a more generous compensation package, but also because the many official dinners meant a lower cost of running the home kitchen.

He explained how fortunate he was not having to solely depend on his modest government salary to survive in a city as expensive as Delhi (remember Dhruv Shringi's sticker shock?), as he came from an affluent family, who paid for certain expenses. For instance, his kid's annual school fees are equivalent to a three-month salary. Now, imagine yourself as a parent of three on that very salary, and wishing to send your children to a good school.

For those who are not exceptionally austere, there are but three ways to survive in expensive Indian cities on a frugal government salary:

a) have a double income, where both parents work to eke out a respectable living
b) be lucky enough to have support from family, assuming your family can offer fiscal assistance
c) opt for graft, where opportunity and morals allow

So for those caught in this situation where official income is meagre, but opportunity for wrongful enrichment is massive, it is something of a luxury to be principled. As a senior officer told my friend, 'to be honest is expensive'. Not all government servants are subjected to unfair economic conditions, though. And thankfully don't have to resort to graft for sustenance.

According to Swaminathan Aiyar, real estate, minerals or government contracts cause most instances of corruption. 'When your own ministers (or coalition partners) are involved in making money, you cannot disown them. If a civil servant is involved, you can take action (suspend, etc.) and distance yourself.'

The government has issued the Smart Card and uses biometrics to plug leakage in the public distribution system (PDS).

COKE

Large companies employ an army of people on the legal side, and to comply with government paperwork.

Due to FCPA (Foreign Corrupt Practices Act) and other internal and external regulations, compliance takes much longer for Coke. All expenses and suppliers are audited, vendors must sign supplier guiding principles, and Coke can use no intermediaries, explains Kini. This often translates to a higher cost of doing business, but that's acceptable to Coca-Cola. They are, for instance, one of highest payers of traffic fines, because when stopped by cops, truck drivers are not even allowed to give a free coke (let alone a bribe), but pay the fine instead.

Kini elaborates how his company has established a culture within the organization that they would rather shut down business than violate ethics and integrity, and made it clear across the organization that you can be fired on integrity, but not on account of loss of business suffered for not compromising on ethics.

'People will go after softer targets,' opines Kini, hence demands will dwindle when they realize you won't pay. However, 'Till the reputation is built, you will experience problems, as there is a constant churn (of officers in corporations and government) at lower levels', he warns.

Coke faces this more, as the company functions across widespread locations. Single location companies develop deep local ties over time. When one of Coke's fifty-six plants is in the news, it seems as though Coke is constantly in the news. On the other hand, companies with smaller footprint are more vulnerable.

Intriguingly, the top leadership—bureaucracy or political—is receptive and accessible. Good leadership, is good leadership regardless of who is in power. Such leadership is positively inclined to industry and encouraging on a one-on-one basis.

ELEPHANT FODDER: THE PARALLEL ECONOMY

The size of the Indian economy is estimated to be about US$ 2 trillion (in GDP terms, and almost US$ 7 trillion in PPP terms). The size of the unregulated, untaxed 'black economy' is estimated at US$ 700 billion, almost a third of the size of the formal economy. This economy is fuelled by the smallest actions in our everyday lives as much as the large-scale scams Mr Vinod Rai speaks about.

A trip to any (non-retail chain) shop is revealing in how mass participation adds to this economy every day. A price is quoted for even branded products (governed by MRP or Maximum Retail Price), and no bill is given. If at all, an informal, handwritten bill is scribbled on an anonymous looking piece of paper. Should you request for a formal invoice, the shopkeeper informs you that the price of the product will go up by the prevailing rate of VAT of taxes (say 10 per cent). To avoid this unnecessary inflation on a small purchase (say a box of eggs), which doesn't require warranty, you eschew the invoice. The shopkeeper has clearly not registered the sale, so does not owe the tax man the VAT, nor tax on income.

This story plays out in varying degrees across a range of financial transactions. Unscrupulous employers will attempt to pay part of their managers' wages off the books, in 'cash', which they have generated by dodging the taxman. Some businessmen have complained to me about how they have to resort to 'converting from white to black', since their business offers little opportunity to generate 'cash', or they just want to run a clean business. A Harvard-educated Chartered Accountant complained of how he is invariably asked if he does 'conversions', when he tells people at parties that he's a CA.

The usual compulsions of needing cash are purchase of real estate from the secondary market (new developments are all-cheque), and bribes. When a demand is made of a business, the payoff is obviously to be made off the books, and so unaccounted funds are required.

Let's be clear, though: the vast majority of tax evaders and bribe payers are not victims. They do so voluntarily and wilfully. Black money is a major political issue[55] as well. It is required for fighting elections, bringing black money back into circulation, etc.

Mr S.Y. Quraishi, former Chief Election Commissioner (CEC) of India, has seen the brute might of money power in elections. Mr Quraishi deems electoral fundraising to be one of the few remaining large scale sources of corruption. Even reluctant politicians (or political workers) will routinely ask (or be offered by unctuous businessmen) individuals or organizations to contribute to the 'party fund'. The implication being that no wrongdoing has been suggested or conducted, however the gratification itself cannot be denied.

His job, essentially, is keeping elections free and fair. Free from influence of muscle, intimidation, booze and other immoral and illegal means of campaigning. The Election Commission of

---

[55]The BJP government was voted to power, having promised along with development, progress and economic growth, that undisclosed 'black money' would be brought back to India from overseas banks. Two years after these electoral promises, FM Arun Jaitley claims that there's been a 'sizeable dip' in illegal assets stashed abroad by Indians due to his government's 'activism', 'technological intervention' and action initiated by G-20 countries.

India has done a first-rate job in securing the periodic making of our democracy, and even greatly improving the process in many areas. In the not too distant past, 'booth capturing' was a real possibility, and even occurrence. Armed goons would annex voting booths and cast votes on behalf of the local populace.

Fear and greed, the time-honoured tools of persuasion, were used liberally in elections of the past, especially if the election was held in more backward and/or remote areas. Sir Mark Tully says there's been no radical change (improvement) in red tape. It has become worse in cases, as they are so afraid of corruption accusations, they are afraid to do anything. 'One problem is that you don't know if you will get what you paid for. In China, for instance, it's done neatly, and once you pay, the whole thing goes through. India is inefficient corruption, China is efficient corruption.'

One way of addressing this is to appoint an agent and pay the official 'fee'.

DEMONETIZATION

In early November 2016, all that every media house was covering was the 'world election': Trump vs Clinton. Indians, however, started counting notes, not votes as PM Modi announced on national television the policy to demonetize the old currency denomination of five hundred and one thousand rupee notes (then the largest notes) from the midnight of 8 November 2016 to curb the menace of black money in the economy.

As Indians scrambled to spend, or deposit as much of these bank notes as they could, and rumours of large cash transactions, thought to be black money, for purchase of gold and foreign currency emerged. Limits were imposed on the amount of cash that each individual could withdraw in a month, and deposits over a defined (modest) limit had to be explained, under pain of tax scrutiny and penalty. However, new banknotes (two thousand rupee notes were introduced, and the earlier notes would be replenished over time) were trickling in slower than demand, causing infuriation and challenges to individuals and businesses.

India's addiction to cash is further complicated by the instance of black money—generated through tax evasion, counterfeit currency, criminal activity and corruption. For example, India's Tax to GDP ratio remains a joke, with only some two and a half million taxpayers admitting annual income over INR 1 million (US$ 15,000), while government data indicates that only about 1 per cent of the population pays tax.

The demonetization policy was initiated to address these challenges, and optimistic observers point out that the formalizing of the hitherto black economy alone adds growth to GDP, and tax rupees to the government.

The many upsides of the initiative, including better tax compliance and wider tax base are; increased formalization of the economy; lower inflation and interest rates; stronger investor confidence; and a greater acceptance of digital payments leading to higher productivity. However, it is expected that GDP growth in the short term (say, two quarters) will decline before taking off again, possibly a hockey stick curve to higher growth numbers than those when demonization was introduced.

On the downside, cash withdrawal limits caused temporary pain to SMEs, as petty cash expenses such as local transportation, entry taxes and paying daily wage contract workers were incurred on a daily basis. The rural economy remains largely agrarian, and very much a cash ecosystem.

All economists have unanimously lowered their short term

GDP growth forecasts from the 7.5 per cent region to a hair below 7 per cent. Though some believe there might be a sharp upward revival when money supply normalizes.

This is understandable, as uncertainty towards cash supply, land prices, etc. has dulled consumer sentiment and consequently industrial spending, but there might be a J-Curve of consumer spending due to deferred and latent demand.

However, this is a great opportunity for the country to start a cashless revolution, provided users don't revert to cash, once currency supply normalizes. A wide government base of RuPay cards, particularly with Unified Payment Interface (UPI), together with mobile connectivity will help. Prime Minister Narendra Modi launched the BHIM (Bharat Interface for Money), an Aadhaar-based mobile payment application that targets the poor by working in cheap phones without internet connectivity, in addition to smartphones.

Developed by National Payment Corporation of India (NPCI), BHIM witnessed 3 million downloads and half a million transactions just three days after launch. Contrast this with Paytm who leads the e-wallet market with 150 million users. If sustained, this momentum could take India closer to a less-cash, if not a cash-less economy.

The finance sector (including fintech stalwarts and startups, alike) would stand to gain from necessity and the many government initiatives to encourage non-cash transactions. Payment banks and others in the ecosystem have witnessed such phenomenal and unexpected growth post-demonetization, that they are now thinking of cash, not other online payment gateways, as their competitor.

It is expected that the digital push will also tie in well with the new GST regime, administrated through the GSTN (General Goods and Services Network), enhancing tax collections and plugging leakage e.g. wholesalers who would transact in cash, would now have a single GST number to determine input credit and output (tax). Increased tax compliance and transparency, and consequent ease of doing business, will make India less of a black box in minds of foreign investors, and might encourage investment decisions.

There are those who theorize that demonetization is congruous with the 'Jan Dhan Yojana' to bank the unbanked, amnesty schemes for black money, getting banks to invest in digital banking, and programmes such as Digital India, and these collectively are driving the shift to digital economy.

There are infinite imponderables, but experts feel the short term slowdown will be wiped out by significant structural benefits in the longer run.

There is a real possibility of reversing India's skewed tax and cash to GDP ratios: Cash to GDP is among the highest in the world, whereas tax to GDP is among the lowest. If able to address this, India would have pulled off a systemic shift that will yield results for years to come.

We will know only in hindsight whether this tough experiment has yielded expected results, or even if programmes such as the Jan Dhan Yojana, which could potentially see a multiplier effect if coupled with Aadhar (remember: the first Aadhar-enabled ATM withdrawals were enabled well before this policy). But the general populace endured personal hardship in the hope that the future outcome will far outweigh temporary discomfort, and in the schadenfreude of the corrupt rich getting their comeuppance.

There are those who cynically believe that governments only undertake real action when faced with crisis. If so, that's the silver lining if this move leads India into a crisis.

PULLING TEETH (OR THE COST OF DOING BUSINESS IN INDIA)

'I have a budget for the cost of operating in India,' explained Amar Singh, Canadian CEO of Clove Dental. Amar is no stranger to India, having grown up here, before he moved to North America to study and work, and it was two decades before he finally took the call to move back with family, armed with a Harvard MBA and a faint impression of what India used to be in the nineties.

His brushes with petty corruption have been numerous, on account of running a business that's part retail (i.e. high visibility) and part medical (Clove is a chain of dental clinics in North India). Amar has remained steadfast in his approach of denying any demands for graft, no matter how small or commonplace.

The reason, initially, for resisting graft was fiduciary and compliance-led. Not only would they be breaking the law, their foreign investors would not accept any instance, no matter how innocuous. This is increasingly, the case with many professionally run companies, both big and small.

Predictably, such altruism created crippling short-term problems for Clove. For instance, import of medical equipment that should routinely have taken a few days, ended up taking a few months—all because they wouldn't relent to the small amount of 'speed money' that was to be paid to relevant officials. In the worst cases, the official concerned might consider the denial of demands as a personal affront—the perceived slight of a company taking the moral (or legal) high ground, and denying graft can easily descend into a battle of egos that gets messier if the officer in-charge is especially spiteful.

It takes time to build a reputation of being a truly no-graft establishment, but once that's achieved, the demands for bribes go down drastically. Like all efficient markets, here too, the operators go after soft targets with a higher chance of success with minimal effort.

In his experiments with truth, Amar found a novel way of dealing with one particular challenge. Road signs are fairly erratic in India in cities, and the numbering and layout of colonies, equally confounding. So, to help customers find their way, Clove would put up its own signage in the routes leading up to their premises. Usually, these road signs are permitted for medical establishments, and not retailers. As we've already covered, Clove is part retail and part clinic, so depending on the interpretation the local officials choose to take, they would either allow the road signs, or remove them.

In one area, the local municipal officials demanded a bribe to allow the signs to stay up, and when denied, promptly took down the signage. It was a small amount (less than US$ 100 per month), but Amar refused to relent, and found another way. In different areas, they adopted upkeep of the neighbourhood park, or garbage dump, in exchange for signage rights. Market and resident welfare associations were only too happy to agree, and thus began an alternative solution.

Now, this won't necessarily save Clove much money, but is certainly a legal tax-deductible way of tackling a vexing situation.

I find a couple of intriguing lessons from Amar's experience. The first is that it is possible for a small business with limited governmental leverage to operate without succumbing to graft. In three years, Clove has grown to a network of sixty clinics in three states. But this is painful. A bit like pulling teeth, as they would do in Amar's line of work.

The second is that not paying bribes might not necessarily

save you much money in the short term, but there are potential long-term payoffs (in the non-altruistic sense).

But more on this at the end of this chapter.

YOUR INDIA GUY (OR PRIVATE SECTOR CORRUPTION)

Lest you believe corruption is confined to the public sector, examples abound of malfeasance in transactions among private corporations, and even internal corruption in some cases.

A leading corporate honcho, who serves on the boards of several companies, chose to speak anonymously about 'damning forensic reports of two very large', listed Indian companies. Corporate fraud is widespread, he warns, with 'virtually everyone running a little scam'. By way of specifics, he readily rolls out several instances. Those in charge of hiring are taking kickbacks. In cases where a headhunter is mandated, the HR department may recruit directly, but name a certain headhunter, who is to be paid a commission and receive kickbacks. The purchase or procurement department has historically been maligned, and owing to the moral hazards, this is also usually under control of the owner or top management, and ironically the least corrupt department (probably).

And then there are cases of impropriety that are not department-specific. For example, employees in one firm are allowed to order dinner if they stay beyond 9.30 p.m. (Indians eat dinner late), so many would stay on to avail free food and free conveyance. This, in itself is not entirely ethical, if the stay back is to only avail these perquisites. But a greater evil is this—there was one bill of 120 rotis (bread), which was essentially the digits 1 and 0 added on either side of 2 (the original number). Correspondingly, the rupee amount was duly manipulated and inflated sixtyfold. This is relatively small-scale corruption, but it was surprisingly attempted by a respectable executive (so not quite petty corruption).

As elsewhere in the world, festivities and social occasions have spawned innovation in malfeasance. Festivals like Diwali or Christmas constantly challenge the limits of what may be considered bonafide gifting. In this country, gifting and gratification can often be tough to distinguish, but there are some rather easy to tell. One leading industrialist sent a special set of wedding cards to a select few. The invite was a gold statue of the Buddha, with a small drawer at the base, containing the customary invitation card and sweets.

A leading investment banker reflects that the 'erosion of value systems' might be a risk factor to the India story. He knows of multiple companies that are professionally run, profitable and ripe for an IPO. However, these companies are loath to list on the markets for reasons of compliance. Rules mandate a retrospective scrutiny to determine origin of promoter's capital (SEBI requirement to study capital structure from day one), and this causes many a promoter to shy away from opening that can of worms.

This is an intriguing notion—considering this challenge akin to the risk factors investment bankers examine in a red herring prospectus (offer document). Mr Analjit Singh, Chairman Emeritus of the Max Group, has no doubt that India will continue to grow economically, 'in spite of and despite the government', 'but will India grow in a balanced manner?', he asks. The citizenry of India, the social fabric and its deterioration is his big concern, stemming in part from the growth that can cause further imbalance in the way wealth is distributed. 'Influences in us have not been positive,' he explains, 'and have vitiated the quality of our social fabric through erosion of virtues like truthfulness and self righteousness.'

ADIDAS-REEBOK

The Adidas-Reebok scam that was unearthed in 2012 is a story of not only how unscrupulous practices, internal politics, inter-management hostilities, and 'success at any cost', led to a great dent on the brand and trustworthiness of the company, but it also exemplifies the fact that if greed takes over ethics, then the price to be paid by those responsible is their career and personal integrity (apart from legal proceedings). Adidas' takeover of Reebok in 2005, was a move that was poised to change the competitive dynamics of the sports goods market, but as it turns out, it became a story of short-term 'ghost' profits and long-term shame. To those watching from outside, the story of Reebok from 2005 onward for the next six years, unfolded as a fairy tale. From hardly 100 stores in 2003, Reebok had around 1,000 stores in 325 cities by 2012. There was a major expansion of Reebok stores in India thanks to the aggressive strategy adopted by its MD, Subhinder Singh Prem and COO, Vishnu Bhagat. But the rosy picture, exemplifying the triumph and vision of the top management was, in truth, a hollow edifice built on greed, irresponsibility and reckless practices that were as unethical as they were criminal.

In 2012, in a bi-annual meeting in Phoenix, Arizona, Subhinder Singh Prem presented the company's business plan wherein Reebok's India businesses were to be downsized. This was the moment when Pandora's box opened for Mr Prem. The Adidas management asked him to step down. Since then, though time has passed and the legal process is taking its course, the case has engraved a lesson in the book of corporate governance and ethics. Today, Reebok is struggling with two successive quarters of declining sales and reduction in its sales target for 2015.

To understand the case, one needs to go back to 2005, the year when the German Sports goods firm, Adidas bought the British firm, Reebok for US$ 3.8 billion (£2.9 billion) in an attempt to take on its rival, Nike. Though Reebok was acquired by Adidas, initially both these firms operated as different entities. Both had a different style of operating and management. Reebok culture was more aggressive while Adidas operated in a more disciplined manner.

To increase the market share of Reebok, its management employed the Minimum Guarantee model for distribution/franchisees, a concept pioneered by Benetton in India. Adidas too, was using the same model but with proper checks, safeguards and parameters, which were to be followed while negotiating a deal. The Minimum Guarantee model insisted that the turnover from a store must be at least three times the money paid and that the loss-making stores were to be shutdown. Moreover, permission would be required from the Headquarters (HQ) for sealing any deal.

Reebok followed no such practice that could act as a cover for the brazen risk it was taking, which sacrificed margins and thereby, profitability. Reebok under Mr Prem, billed more goods than the franchisee had the capacity to sell, with an assurance that unsold inventory would be taken back by the company. The sham could have been checked had internal politics in the management not split it all wide open. Andreas Geller, MD of Adidas India raised concerns regarding these proceedings but the Adidas HQ didn't consider the complaints as serious, as it was seen as a product of the tussle between individuals in the management.

The kettle began boiling over when franchisees, unable to sell their inventory, demanded unsold inventory be taken back. When the company was unable to do so, these franchisees stopped payments. Disputes with distributors and franchisees, lack of funds to pay to the vendors/suppliers, unrecovered money and accumulating inventories were the hallmarks of the situation on the ground. The lid was blown and it was for the world to see the mess.

Adidas appointed Shahin Padath as the CFO of the combined entity. An internal examination by him made it clear that things were not right in Reebok's India Operations. Mr Prem was sacked in March 2012 along with COO Vishnu Bhagat who was accused of financial irregularities.

In May 2012, Reebok India filed an FIR against Subhinder Singh Prem and Vishnu Bhagat, accusing them of a financial fraud of up to US$ 233 million (₹870 crore). The charges included running a false franchisee referral programme, diverting/stealing goods to supply 4 private warehouses, inflating sales revenue through fake invoices (₹530 crore), and misappropriation of funds, though the amount estimated by the company is believed to be exaggerated, according to the investigating authorities. This led to the arrest of the two protagonists along with twelve other employees associated with the scam.

The scam was investigated by an audit firm, E&Y (and previously KPMG) employed by Adidas. The government and regulatory authorities such as the Income Tax department under the Ministry of Finance, the Serious Fraud Investigation Office under the Ministry of Corporate Affairs, and the Economic Offences wing of the Gurgaon Police, undertook their own

> official investigations and started legal proceedings against the duo and their associates. The Institute of Chartered Accountants of India (ICAI), the body that regulates auditors and accountants in the country, also undertook its own investigation to ascertain any negligence by the auditors of the company.
>
> The case is still in the legal process and one can expect a result in times to come, but the woes of the principal players—Subhinder Singh Prem and Vishnu Bhagat—are endless. Not only are they implicated by the legal ramifications of the case, but they have also lost their integrity and careers. Adidas, on the other hand had to write off €265 million (£231 million) from its financial books. Moreover, it shut one-third of its stores as part of its restructuring, apart from cleaning the mess related to inventories and receivables. The sales for Reebok had been declining, which can be ascertained from the quarterly financial reports (2014) of the company with humble targets for 2015.
>
> All in all, the case underlies the fundamental need for proper control mechanisms, ethical practices in management along with a sense of responsibility in an individual, amidst competition and the need for survival, both for the company and oneself.

Prof. Ashish Nanda agrees with the view that standing up to corruption is the best strategy for dealing with the menace. Prof. Nanda advises companies to not accede to demands from unscrupulous officials (private or government), if they are to play the long game, 'but be prepared for friction in short run,' he warns. 'In the short run you won't win every contract, or get great results,' cautions Prof. Nanda, 'but India is a long-term play.' And while, admittedly, it is easier for foreign companies to say 'no', increasingly Indian companies are developing a resistance to demands for graft.

There are friends, who confide that they have neither the wherewithal, nor the appetite to resist demands. And the most honest are rather sanguine about the two forms of corruption (facilitation and opportunism) that are not extortionate. But in the fight against corruption for those who aim to fight the good fight, they have some strong players in their corner. Diverse and influential stakeholders are simultaneously countering corruption in a multitude of ways.

Active institutions like the Election Commission, the CAG, the Chief Vigilance Commissioner, and the Lokayukta (state-level anti-corruption ombudsman), are becoming ever more bold in the actors and scale of scams they take head on. Several NGOs have been instrumental in raising the profile of corruption as a public interest issue and a political/electoral issue. India Against Corruption (IAC) was probably the most visible of these, and spawned the Aam Aadmi Party, when Mr Kejriwal broke away from the mother ship.

Media trials and sting operations tend to be sensational more often than not, but are instrumental in keeping public opinion charged against major issues of the day. Corruption is seen as a major evil (and story) by all major media houses, hence, the heat is on those caught in the crosshairs.

Legislation, too, provides further tools to those seeking to combat corruption. Public interest litigations allow a third party (individual, NGO or even the court suo motu), rather than the aggrieved party, to file a suit in a court of law. Relatively new laws like the Right to Information (RTI) Act have been put to good use by sophisticated professionals in India's megacities, and farmers in rural India. As it turns out, just asking why there's an inordinate delay (to take an easy example) through RTI is adequate to spur the concerned officer into action.

Mr Vinod Rai and Mr S.Y. Quraishi, who know more about this subject than most Indians, caution that it is unrealistic to expect malfeasance to completely be eliminated in any country, but the trends are encouraging. And hopefully before long, the scourge of petty corruption that is manifest in harassment of the common man, and of small business, will diminish.

8
THE END

> You can see a lot by looking.
> —*Yogi Berra*

The documentary, *I am 20* was produced by Films Division in 1967 to mark twenty years of independence, and to capture the rather poignant mood of the nation.[56] They interviewed several twenty-year-olds (allegedly born on the day of Indian Independence—15 August 1947), and asked their views. This is a charming film with some telling moments—when asked which Indian each of the interviewees admired, one mentioned, 'an Indian you wouldn't have heard of, Zubin Mehta, the only Indian conductor.'

The Economist (quoted in *Intelligent Life*), recently did a story that found that the young kids who were most patriotic and optimistic, were the ones to migrate (to USA etc.) while those who saw little hope for India actually stayed on, formed NGOs and undertook other worthy initiatives to improve the areas they were most despondent about. Betraying a scepticism beyond his years, one kid described the prevailing mood of the nation during the last general elections, 'frustration is in fashion

---

[56] The Films Division (Ministry of Information and Broadcasting) website states, 'Those born on Independence Day in 1947 were selected from different parts of India and interviewed to know their hopes and desires, ambitions, hobbies, fears and frustrations, and the result is this unique film.'

today.' This is uncannily similar to something the young Indians of *I am 20* had to say. One interviewee said: 'Well, it seems to me the fashion today is to denigrate the country, and when two people meet, they get into a sort of competition about who can abuse the government better.'

The young cast of this documentary often alluded to the 'brain drain', when speaking of their future plans. Brain drain was a much discussed phenomenon in the eighties, when my generation was raised on the deeply cynical theory that the best and the brightest would leave for foreign lands, leaving the fate of the country to their less illustrious peers. Today, this seems almost unbelievable, given the multitude of Indians and PIOs coming to India for the business opportunities.

This widely felt dissatisfaction with the status quo evidently helped create conditions for Mr Modi's spectacular victory, but it also created heightened expectations. This again has the potential to spur young Indians to rise to the challenge, or create another 'brain drain'. However, dissatisfaction is a prerequisite for any improvement in the status quo, and so desirable to some degree.

For the left brained reader, here's Harvard Business School's formula for change. Change happens when:

$D*M*P > Rc + Cc$
D: Desire to change
M: Model for change
P: Process of change
Rc: Resistance to change
Cc: Cost of change
Or
Amount of Change = [Dissatisfaction × Vision × Process] > Cost of Change

We still do have a fading colonial hangover. Indians hate the fact that we were ruled, and for so long, by the British, but still have the fixation that foreigners are better at many things than Indians are, or have a distinct headstart. A constantly embarrassing reminder of this is the high sales of 'skin whitening' creams sold across the country. Traditionally (or since the Raj), fairness was associated with beauty, and an indicator of elevated socio-economic standing.

It was not just physically that the British ruled. There was a sense of inferiority instilled in Indians. In my grandfather's age, most Indians would meet a British officer as a superior. In my father's time, there still was a gap, which narrowed to equity. For many Indians, a foreigner (especially Caucasian) continues to instinctively appear as a superior, but to those too young, urbane or flippant, this association will not be as natural. An indication of an increasing sense of self-importance, nouveau riche Indians are inventing insignias for themselves.

When I was growing up in Mumbai (then Bombay), my brothers and I would trail behind our mother to sales of 'export reject' or 'export-surplus' goods that had providentially made their way to domestic markets. The belief was that even something that was 'almost good enough' for foreign markets would be superior to what was typically available.

Indian companies also tempered their world view and ambitions accordingly. Initially, even our impressive IT growth came from doing cheaper what the foreign worker was doing. This then led to confidence of doing things better, and daring to dream beyond the back office.

A new generation is impervious to previous baggage that kept Indians from dreaming big. Also, the evolution of technology and legislative framework has enabled meritocracy in new sectors, where there really haven't been any large incumbents. Pugnacious Indian start-ups are now seeking to punch above their weight, often expanding overseas early in their life cycle and even acquiring much larger foreign competitors—for instance, Zomato.

Probably for the first time since Pandit Nehru, every professional (including filmmakers, artists and doctors) considers himself or herself to be engaged in 'Nation Building'. If Nehru was building the 'temples of modern India', in the form of steel mills, dams, power plants and heavy industry, our temples today are built in cyberspace, on foreign lands and by private enterprise, more than by the government.

The confidence and the ambition is to take on the world and win.

Mr V.S.S. Mani of JustDial was one of the keynote speakers at TechSparks 2011 Round Table, Pune. He described himself as, 'I am a Tam-Bram (Tamil Brahmin), so probably there has not been an entrepreneur in my family for 100 generations. Here are, according to me, some key pointers from his speech:

- The growing middle class is demanding as consumers, and huge consumers of information. They will shape, make and define the nation, its polity, business and public life.
- Your business needs to cater to them, and understand them as employees, customers or stakeholders.
- The emergence of a growing middle class and a younger, richer and better-informed population is causing a tectonic shift in every sphere of life in India: professional, social, structural, political, legislative and economic.
- Because of increased probity, and because Indians are

increasingly large consumers of information, business based on governmental patronage will become increasingly complex, which is a good thing, as it will be more transparent and meritorious.
- On the flip side, the bureaucracy will be ever more tentative about taking bold decisions—former secretaries arrested and investigated, RTI, etc.
- Politics will get cleaner, as the middle class demands good governance, not doles and freebies. People are actually voting out parties tainted by corruption, which is unprecedented; not following the time-honoured cash-for-votes practice (as pointed out by S.Y. Quraishi), this and a more active Election Commission is mitigating money power in elections.
- This however, will not be an enduring feature because, quite honestly, this is unsustainable. Iterations between legal reform and courageous action will build a new kind of system of public administration (which may be subtle, not conspicuous).
- Technology will also help further accelerate the mobility from poor to middle class for the remote and unbanked.
- Technology in business and governance, through e-governance, m-governance (through mobile devices), is helping administrators and entrepreneurs overcome infrastructural constraints.

RISKS AND POTENTIAL SPOILERS

In a morbidly unstable and intolerant region, India has remained an oasis of relative harmony. Social and political stability, and law and order are essential to sentiment and running of business in any economy. Management guru Gurcharan Das likes to say, 'India has Law, China has Order'.

Right-wing vigilantes, masquerading as the 'activist' arm of political parties cause alarm and heartburn to said parties and investors who harbour great aversion to acts of violence of any kind.

Diverse nations need to go the extra mile to reassure minorities. I again revert to Singapore, as a great example of explaining most concepts quickly (and yes, it's not the same size or complexity as India). The two large minorities (Malay and Indian) have been well-cared-for, and actively integrated into the mainstream, averting ghettoization and disproportionate success among races.

India is very diverse, and a subcontinent, and hence, needs a system of decentralized decision-making, and degree of freedom for people from diverse backgrounds to flourish. Perhaps this model will be able to reconcile social conservatism and economic opportunism on a sustained basis.

Swings in democracy are to be expected, where one party dominates and then the other. However, in the last quarter of a century, we have seen consistency in the economic agenda of India, regardless of the government and coalitions in power. The model of market-welfarism has truly been accepted by voter and elected, alike.

The central and the state governments have made explicit (GST, GAAR, retrospective taxation, ease of doing business) and implicit promises to investors and entrepreneurs. If we now don't deliver on promises, the trust investors have placed will run out. Of more perilous consequences are the high expectations of India's vast youth. The young have seen their peers transcend the confines of socio-economic class with unprecedented mobility.

We are blessed with a young population, at a scale unprecedented in the history of the world—a single nation with 800 million people, who are yet to celebrate their thirty-fifth birthday! But this demographic dividend might as easily become a demographic time bomb. Young, impatient and aspirational youth might easily stray to the wrong side of the law, if they fail to find employment or brides. This brings us to the problem of an alarmingly skewed sex ratio in many parts of India. Among worst offenders are the more prosperous states of Haryana (at 903 women per 1,000 men according to the 2015 census), Punjab at 893 and Delhi at 866.

There are 'red corridors' in parts of India, where naxals (of Maoist ideology) hold sway, often through organized violence. The solution to most such issues has been to incorporate them into the mainstream of Indian democracy. Decades old, the bitter issue with cessationists in Nagaland was resolved in mid-2015, through the signing of a peace accord between the Naga stakeholders and the Indian Union.

Swaminathan Aiyar noted:

> Naxal affected states are all doing 10 per cent growth. They are growing the fastest in history, in exactly the same period they are receiving maximum publicity—Madhya Pradesh, Jharkhand, Odisha, Bihar, Chattisgarh, Andhra. Naxalism is an impediment in relative areas; the state 'doesn't exist in certain areas'. Andhra used the police in a military-style operation, but always backed by civilian programmes for local people to regain confidence in the State (and then people turn informers and support the state administration). It's vital that the state is present in its myriad forms in all districts: a police station, NREGA, ration shop, school, etc.

The State 'fled' in many of these areas, only then did it become a problem, and was so-called liberated territory. The Northeast is different, as in central areas the tribals are in minority and non-tribals control everything and dominate non-tribals. Ethnic tribals make up 30 per cent of the population in Jharkhand.

Swaminathan Aiyar's brother Mani Shankar Aiyar said it doesn't matter how many quotas you create, the only people who speak at meetings will be non-tribals—they have the knowledge, literacy and ideas. In the Northeast, the locals are the majority and control everything. The cessationist movement in the Northeast is not ideological (unlike the Maoist movement elsewhere). The average income of hill tribals is higher than the national average, while that of Central Indian tribals lower than national average.

'All of us came out of forests very recently—we, came just a couple of hundred years before them.'—said Swaminathan Aiyar

The rising forces of economics have forced Maoists to yield areas hitherto under their control. In Bihar, for instance, the Maoists helped the labouring classes (Dalits, Other Backward Classes or the OBCs as classified by the Constitution) fight against landowners for minimum wage through violent clashes with the Ranvir Sena (landowners muscle). Today, labour shortage has sent the daily or 'dihari' wage rate above the minimum wage, so the Maoist monopoly (the notion that they alone could ensure minimum wage) is broken. Bihar was a supplier of labour to other states, but now faces labour shortages of its own.

While the larger risks—both economic and terrorist—of an increasingly interlinked world holds true for India, as for any large economy, we have a bit of a head start, being one of the early victims of terrorism and the later beneficiaries of globalization. Broadly:

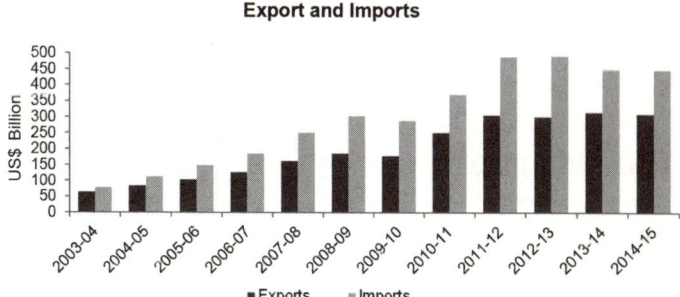

Export and Imports

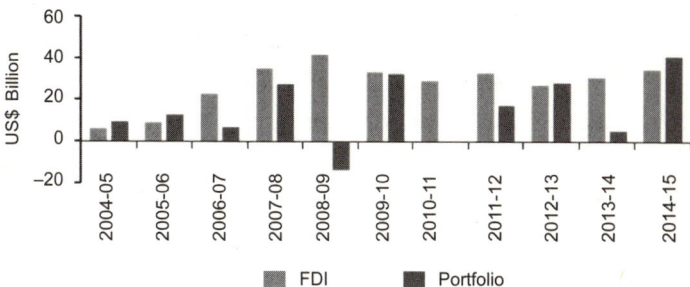

FDI and Portfolio Inflows

Source: RBI

- India's external trade situation is yet to recover completely as global demand remains subdued on account of continued weakness in some major economies around the world.
- Portfolio inflows have now stabilized after considerable volatility in 2013–14, impacted by uncertainties in the global economic environment and expected monetary tightening by the US Federal Reserve.
- Strong FDI inflows continue at $34.7 billion in 2014–15.

While these are real risks, the benefits of India's model of market welfarism is already being felt by the previously aggrieved. And of course, there are no guarantees. It is crazy to think that our past challenges are like small pox—eradicated, never to return.

UNFORCED ERRORS

There are blunders that you may commit:

- turning your Country Manager into a glorified sales head
- importing your emerging 'market strategy' here
- walking out at the end of your 'deadline', regardless of how much time and resources you have committed into India. Or, sitting on the fence too long till the conditions are ideal for you to invest/reinvest
- excessive reliance upon, or distrust of, your Indian partner

BIGGEST MYTHS

- India is a single market
- You can transplant your existing 'China business model' to India
- Indian Standard Time implies inefficiencies and indefinite delays
- You can be opportunistic about your India strategy
- You have to compromise on ethical practice

We have seen encouraging examples of what has worked even in the present times, and that is reason for hope. Not just hope for the future, but also the present, for those of meagre means or influence, and those unwilling or unable to 'work the system'.

With all the contrasts, it's sometimes easy to forget how much India is like other countries—a competitive marketplace with demanding and discerning customers, fickle suppliers, and conscientious employees.

The big risk is mistaking success in India to hinge on one thing alone: 'managing the environment' or government relations. After spending many a page explaining why government, big and small, is vital, this might seem contrarian, but the lesson is that you need both—an understanding of the market and the regulatory framework.

THE SUBCONTINENT: PEACE, PROMISE AND BEYOND

> Who are destitute of sight?
> Those who do not perceive the future world.
> —*A Sanskrit proverb*

India alone probably has greater ethnic, linguistic and racial diversity than all the EU nations put together. And while relations are often hairy, the EU fought two dreadful wars (the last some seventy years ago), which were multilateral.

Clearly, all SAARC countries (save India) have fewer dissimilarities among themselves and vis à vis India has between all its twenty-nine states. A fact that was much discussed in the bonhomie that resulted from Mr Modi's oath-taking ceremony at the President's Estate in mid-2014.

Breaking from convention (and despite domestic opposition), Modi invited all heads of SAARC states to his swearing-in ceremony.[57] Graciously, all obliged, including Mr Nawaz Sharif,

---

[57]Politicians from Tamil Nadu, mindful of their constituency, have consistently opposed any cooperation or relations with Sri Lanka. Predictably, there was vehement opposition to an invitation to Sri Lankan PM. The invites were sent on a somewhat short notice, so the Speaker of Bangladeshi Parliament attended,

Pakistan's Prime Minister, despite some domestic opposition of his own, it is thought.

So for marketers, a market the size of the USA is waiting to be tapped.[58] This might seem a distant dream today, but time will tell how the region matures and develops. If we were able to create reliable transport infrastructure in the subcontinent—essentially railways and waterways—that would be an immense enabler of trade. And freight transport would also be less contentious than people transport, which remains stiflingly controlled between India and Pakistan, for instance.

Trade has the potential of leading formal diplomacy in creating the conditions for stability and relative prosperity in the SAARC region. And if this does happen, the Indian state and industry will have a large role.

In the EU most countries are of similar economic standing. The process of uniting them economically started in 1952 and continued till 1999, when they adopted the Euro. It took fifty years to achieve economic union. SAARC, on the other hand, though culturally and geographically contiguous, is not economically homogenous. India's aspirations cannot be fulfilled by neighbours, but for Pakistan, Bhutan, Nepal and Sri Lanka—if they are able to access India, that's enough! Here is a market of 1.2 billion people, and really the only market most companies need (or will even be able to serve). But India perforce needs to look beyond SAARC. India can fulfil investment needs of neighbours, but they cannot fulfil India's investment needs,

---

instead of President Hasina, who spent years in India in self-exile.

[58]Population in the region: Pakistan (190 million), Afghanistan (33 million), Sri Lanka (21 million), Bangladesh (164 million), Bhutan (0.7 million), Maldives (0.3 million) and Nepal (29 million)—an additional population of 438 million on top of India's 1.3 billion.

so India will need to look beyond SAARC. Pakistan, with its immense tracts of fertile land, has the potential of contributing substantially to the food security of the region.

Foreign policy is of course an ongoing process, but the role of India has changed on the world stage. India is today sitting on all high tables of the world, including WTO, G20, UN, WB, IMF, BRICS and IBSA.

While India Inc. must leverage the growing global role of India, it must accept that leadership has a cost (e.g. US is a large aid donor). Industry and tax payers must pay for this leadership. We are largest in South Asia (India has an 80 per cent share, and Pakistan a 10 per cent share of regional GDP). In some cases we cannot expect reciprocity. For example, Bangladesh has highly competitive readymade garments industry (internationally), but we have given zero per cent duty market access, which even the US has not. Indian industry was opposed to this, but we need to do so as it is a least developed country (LDC).

I'm not, of course, suggesting that a reunification on German lines is on the anvil, but an economic union (the European Economic and Monetary Union) just might be feasible. Many countries (as far east as Indonesia) already call their currencies the Rupee, so we won't even have to think of a new name, if common currency were a consideration.

But on a serious note, when a younger and well-travelled population meets in different parts of the world, and is able to relate with regional and interpersonal dynamics, it does give reason for hope. As they say, it's hard to fight with a country where you have friends.

As Jack Welch says, 'Jump the extreme jump'.

Benefits to the economy would be immense, if fewer resources could be spent on defence. Not to mention the enormous benefit to the stability of the region and the world at large. Afghanistan–Pakistan are on top of Asia's 'fragile states index' of fund for peace. Could SAARC be the next EU?

ENLIGHTENED SELF-INTEREST

A rising tide lifts all boats.

Absolutely all companies in India have the truest opportunity of 'doing well by doing good'. Whether by providing livelihood to employees, a benign work environment, or equal opportunity, companies can create positive impact before delving into the more serious CSR-esque programmes. Structural gaps and systemic constraints reward corporations that pro-actively tackle challenges their businesses face.

We've discussed many challenges in the various conversations and confabulations through the book. Here's a quick recap of some.

- Hiring is difficult. So hire for aptitude (not qualification), and train your own people. Treat them well so they don't leave, but be prepared for attrition.
- Millennials want to work for more ethical and balanced companies.
- Media or courtroom trials? Create that 'fortress of goodwill'. Engage with communities, near and far, so you'll have friends in the common people, before you need them.
- No market for your product? Create it. By awareness, disposable income levels, or innovations.
- If you're overpriced, try frugal innovation.
- If you have no POC (Proof of Concept), try it in a

developmental context (maybe a free pilot in a rural setting). Thereafter, iterate, improve and find a paying customer.
- And here's the kicker—you could (possibly) incorporate your CSR spend in some of these—skilling, R&D, rural development, health and sanitation are all CSR compliant activities as per the new Companies Act. Ergo, you might even get your hardnosed CFO on your side for this.

LEAPFROGGING EXCESS

> Everything is theoretically impossible, until it is done.
> —*Robert Heinlein*

In the 1990s, India famously went from low landline telephony penetration to mobile telephony. The conventional wisdom was that we would be left out of the internet revolution, because you needed landlines and modems in those days to 'dial up' to the Internet.

Could we go from rising income levels to shared economy, completely avoiding the evils of aspirational overconsumption that have plagued the West? Friends in Europe are eschewing non-vegetarian diets for ecological reasons. Indians have been low meat eaters (even non-vegetarians would not eat meat every day). Now, eating meat is part aspiration, part status symbol.

So, could we exercise moderation here?

Cities are choked (also literally, given Delhi's pollution levels), could car-pooling, public transport, community living and a shared economy be the 'smart' answer to India's urbanization? We need to educate the young that there is a middle path between conspicuous consumption and destitution. That they can enjoy their success responsibly—which sounds like a way of saying 'feel guilty' or 'don't have too much fun'—but isn't.

The more developed and evolved Western economies now question the notion of consumption and ownership we take for granted. For instance, do we really need to own a car (when we can Uber), or cook own meals (Dutch apps allow you to sell what you cook in excess at home), rent office space (when you can use a co-working space) or even buy a television set.

Shared economy is the way of sustainable and progressive economies. And frankly, a necessity for Indian cities that witness rural migration in the millions each year. The Barclay bike in posh London, car-sharing (Zipcar, Flinkster, car2go and BMW's DriveNow) in Germany, where car ownership is a part of identity, have shown how the young and ambitious are up-siding traditional mores to find solutions to yesterday's problems.

That could be a beacon of light for the world—economy, ecology, society. And honestly, seems like the only means of sustainability.

There's recent evidence of this. A prepaid-card based micro-payment solution developed with VISA was accepted and adopted by primitive tribal communities in rural India to make periodic contributions to the Government of India's new National Pension Scheme (NPS).

Three of India's most primitive tribes are in the Nilgiri mountains—Pania, Karumba and Kattunayakan. They have meagre incomes and near-zero access to banking or savings. They struggle for two square meals a day, surviving off daily wages.

Invited by the government's Centre for Tribal Research and Development (CTRD), Invest India Micro Pension Services (IIMPS) initially failed to implement the programme due to unbanked population (and challenges of collecting, reconciling and transmitting without risk of fraud or error) Use a low-cost card swiping device and basic mobile phone.[59]

These tribals have gone from no formal banking or savings options to electronic money (the other extreme of saving for long-term saving horizon), in the last few months. This in many ways is a more profound kind of leapfrogging than the technical leapfrog of telecom (which had cascading effects that continue). In all, 80 per cent of tribals who join are women. Solutions may not work equally well for men and women.

Intuitively, Indians (or South Asians, for that matter) have ever placed metaphysical evolution before material success.[60] Even in the debatable caste system, Brahmins (teachers, doctors, seers and priests) were placed above other privileged castes Kshatriya (warriors, and usually rulers) and Vaishya (businessmen, and sometimes even rulers), in the scheme of things.

There is a great possibility that the adoption of 'progressive' ways of the West will bring both, benefits and emancipation, but also familiar problems of an eroded social (and family) structure, hyper consumerism, and upsiding the old ethos—where greater common good prevailed over individual aspirations and needs.

Gurcharan Das discerns the 'guru' culture is huge in India. A huge amount of millionaires, bureaucrats and middle-class people go to spiritual gurus of their choosing. This is true,

---

[59] See: https://goo.gl/Qlxj6o

[60] Even the rich and famous aspire to raise their children with these traditional values. Conservationist and writer Aman Nath narrates how Amitabh Bachhan (among India's biggest stars) revealed that 'the most difficult thing is to give your children a middle-class upbringing'. An example of middle-class values could be Mr Nath's memory from age five, when the family bought a fan for their Pusa Road home, and it was an 'event' for the family of refugees from Pakistan.

as seen in cases of gurus like Baba Ramdev and Sadhguru, who are still heard by the middle-class youth, and they are cautioned and pre-warned not to arrive at the top of the ladder without any spiritual oxygen (detachment) from the result of their karma. Inspirationally, they may still be ruthless and still find the vacuum above.

This might prove as a limiting factor—a constant reminder of the evils of covetousness. On the other hand, Patanjali, India's fastest-growing FMCG brand (already at US$ 2 billion) is founded by Baba Ramdev's organization.

Observers are convinced that 'India will not become one big mall'. Nor does it need to. India can achieve double-digit growth in the medium term, by focusing on bringing millions from poverty to middle class.

APPENDIX 1

HOW WE GOT HERE

The history of modern India is fascinating by all accounts. And depending on how you define 'modern', we could start a few hundred years ago. This book, however, is constrained to focus on only the business aspects of this fascinating country and, as far as possible we'll try and keep all references as contemporary as possible.

THE RAJ (1858-1947)

The 'Raj' or 'rule' refers to colonial India, which essentially means British rule (we don't much talk about the smaller Dutch, Danish, French or Portugese colonies) in undivided India (i.e. India+Pakistan+Bangladesh).

We have mostly conquered our fear and wariness of foreign corporations, which arose from the fact that India was ruled by a foreign enterprise (The British East India Company, 1757 onwards), before the British crown formally took over the Raj. The company faced a serious existential crisis during the First War of Independence in 1857, and hence submitted to the transition of power.

The British Crown took over in 1857 and moved the political capital from Kolkata (then Calcutta) in the east, to the more central Delhi (by decimating the capital of the last figurehead

Mughal ruler, and building 'New' Delhi in 1911).

In the two centuries of the Raj, virtually all sizeable enterprise existed due to the encouragement, patronage, or lack of British hostility. This period created resilient companies, many of which endure to this day. Often these companies were established and run by enterprising Anglo-Indian, Parsi, Marwari, Chettiar and Bania businessmen. Technology, specifications, standards and trade flows had large British influence.

British rule ended in 1947, leaving India a legacy of administration (through the Civil Services), the English language, public and private enterprises and reasonable physical infrastructure (in areas such as the railways and post).

The partition of India and creation of Pakistan (Bangladesh was then East Pakistan), caused great disruption in the business model and supply chains of corporations. An acrimonious and bloody partition ensured that subsidiaries, vendors or partners could no longer transact business across new political boundaries.

This was the turning point for many, with fortunes and lives lost and created anew.

THE LICENCE RAJ (1947–91)

Post independence, British patronage was replaced with an almost identical form of governmental patronage. Pandit Nehru, as first prime minister, reputedly had a deep dislike for private enterprise, coupled with a fondness for socialist policies, such as Five Year Plans. Until recently, the Planning Commission continued to use Five Year Plans as the principal device of a planned economy.

Despite accusations of Fabian Socialism, possibly associated with his upper crust Oxbridge grooming, PM Nehru did create some very important institutions for a young India with an unwavering focus on self-reliance (import by choice, not need), the Non-Aligned Movement (he was one of the architects of NAM), and primary industry (steel mills, power plants, et al. the 'temples of modern India').

To his credit, despite Pandit Nehru's well-known emphasis on planned economy, under his watch India saw the provision of capital (to industry), a market (consumers), and machines (modernizing industry).

When the British left, there was hardly any Indian industry worth note. Notable exceptions being the cotton industry, that fed the war demand. The formidable Indian railways and army and just about all departments were equipped and furnished with as many British imports as possible. Indian-owned business was mostly tolerated in the realm of trading, or as vendors/agents to British enterprise.

Opinion Editor of *The Economic Times,* T.K. Arun, explains how this stunted, malnourished Indian industry was too small to build infrastructure or essentials such as machine tools, steel or agricultural implements for the young nation. As government created PSUs to fulfil this demand, it created purchasing power in the hands of people. And with high tariffs, demand was also created for Indian products. Companies like HMT that simultaneously manufactured industrial machinery, tractors and wrist watches, provided much needed mechanization to Indian industry.

A spate of national banks and insurance companies encouraged savings through the public (deposits) and banks (via bonds), which were routed to industry as capital in the form of debt. The tax regime, however was catastrophic. Rates in the 1950s and 1960s remained high, but the 1970s took the cake.

In 1970-71, the maximum marginal rate for individuals was a mind-boggling 93.50 per cent, and in 1973-74 the highest tax rate applicable to an individual could have gone up to 97.50 per cent.

With unreasonable rates, tax planning and evasion was the norm, and the image of the crooked businessman fortified in the public Indian conscience. Thankfully, from 1985, tax rates began being rationalized.

After Nehru, his daughter Indira Gandhi, persisted with similar policies, even nationalizing (government acquiring on its own terms) large private banks and corporations and requiring permissions for establishing business—even determining how much you were allowed to produce.

Very much an iron lady, akin to her British counterpart, Margaret Thatcher, Mrs Gandhi's time in office is remembered more for her political actions (the ignominious 'Emergency', and the heroic military action to liberate Bangladesh—then East Pakistan—from Pakistan), than her economic achievements.[61]

Indira Gandhi's nationalization phase was briefly followed by the socialist phase of the Janata Party (1977-79, not to be confused with the Bhartiya Janata Party or BJP), which was again a trying time for foreign-owned businesses in particular. This was the period when the likes of IBM and Coke opted to exit India, rather than dilute their ownership to under 50

---

[61] Using an Orwellian constitutional provision, Mrs Gandhi's government imposed a state of Emergency (1975–77), wherein all democratic rights and provisions were suspended. Giving Indians a taste of what a totalitarian state would be like, government bodies had absolute power. 'In the time of Mussolini trains ran on time.' A large number of political prisoners were taken, without due process (which wasn't needed under the Emergency), public demonstrations and protests were outlawed, and even wedding celebrations were limited (the 'guest control' that mandated no more than fifty invitees per wedding).

per cent of shareholding. The country veered completely to the left. Licensing became a bureaucratic nightmare (from capital allocation process).

The Congress was again voted into power in January 1980. Upon Indira Gandhi's tragic assassination, her son Rajiv was elected chief of the Congress (I) party, and Prime Minister of India in 1984. He initiated a raft of reforms that fostered economic green shoots ahead of the economic turnaround of the nineties. This period saw introduction of computers to government offices, thawing of ties with the USA, easing of the licence raj, restrictions on foreign travel, imports, foreign currency and even foreign investment (PepsiCo entered India in this period). Notably, this period saw the development of India's space programme, telecommunications industry, and beginning of the IT and software industry. These measures would set the stage for his successor in 1991. But more on that later.[62]

Largely, this period—1947 to around 1991—was a peculiar period for Indian businesses. The main skill required of business leaders was navigating the government for, among other things, to secure permissions to manufacture! Indian industry was heavily protectionist, and consequently devoid of the need for innovation or improvement. We couldn't import partly due to protectionist laws, but mostly because we had no foreign reserves.

We could hardly export, as there was little demand for Indian made products, and almost everything was in short supply (internally). So inferior were Indian products that flash sales (aka 'exhibition-cum-sale') of 'export reject' or 'export-surplus' goods

---

[62]India had other PMs who served short terms: Morarji Desai, Choudhary Charan Singh, HD Deve Gowda, I.K. Gujral. There was optimism when Rajiv Gandhi assumed office, similar to that when Modi became PM in 2014. BJP must not get derailed, the way Rajiv Gandhi (youngest PM at forty) was.

were in high demand—not quite as premium as imported, but not as pricey either.

Former Prime Minister P.V. Narsimha Rao and his Finance Minister (and future PM), Dr Manmohan Singh, announced drastic reforms in 1991, allowing foreign companies to invest, operate and trade more openly in India, which was until now essentially a closed economy.

LIBERALIZATION (1991–CIRCA 2001)

Liberalization was greeted with very mixed reactions. Socialists were alarmed, capitalists were alarmed, and politicians were alarmed. So unmixed reactions, really, except if you were a pre-teen (like this author and friends), waiting to be able to buy real jeans, sneakers and other trappings of western success we only saw on cable TV that started beaming into Indian homes. Little did we realize the profound impact mobile telephony would 'leapfrog' the fixed-line telephony problem, or how the IT sector would explode onto the world stage.

Economically, India's back was to the wall in the period right after the Gulf War. All economic indicators were in the red—fiscal deficit in double digits, industrial growth, etc. Foreign reserves infamously were at US$ 1.2 billion, barely enough to cover three weeks of essential imports. The nation was only weeks way from defaulting on its external balance of payment obligations. Disgracefully, the RBI had to airlift 47 tonnes of gold to the Bank of England, and 20 tonnes to the Union Bank of Switzerland to raise US$ 600 million to raise an emergency loan of US$ 2.2 billion.

As part of the conditions for loaning the money to India for overcoming the crisis, IMF mandated opening up of the hitherto closed economy. The government that flew out the gold and negotiated the deal didn't survive beyond a few months of the act (though India averted default and overcame crisis). The team of Prime Minister P.V. Narsimha Rao and Finance Minister Manmohan Singh signalled intent from the word go, and began implementing economic reform.

Indian business houses/businessmen/women that had created a successful business against great odds were anxious about the effect free competition would have upon their businesses. And so 'The Bombay Club' was formed by eight doyens of Indian Industry—Rahul Bajaj (Bajaj motorcycles), Jamshyd Godrej (Godrej), Lala Bharat Ram, Lalit Mohan Thapar, Hari Shankar Singhania (Raymond), M.V. Arunachalam, B.K. Modi and C.K. Birla.

Circa 1993, this influential pressure group lobbied for a 'level playing field' against foreign competitors who were light years ahead in financial muscle, marketing stratagem, technological prowess and global economies of scale (productivity was achieving newer heights in the early days of globalization).

The Bombay (now Mumbai) Club delivered a note to then Finance Minister Manmohan Singh (who would go on to become Prime Minister of India for two consecutive terms in the next decade), urging the government to enable Indian industry to play a 'rightful role in the industrial development of the country'. The government, of course, took this note seriously, and the mid-nineties saw a slew of protectionist measures in pursuit of this 'level playing field'.

To deter foreign companies from discarding local partners they no longer needed (earlier restrictions on FDI required majority and/ or mandatory Indian ownership), foreign partners were required to obtain a 'no objection certificate' from Indian partners before they could fly solo. Indian companies were able to access further capital, as they were permitted to raise preference (non-voting) shares up to 25 per cent of their issued capital.

Ironically, the companies (not restricted to the few in the Bombay Club) who feared the invasion of foreign companies, and their own impending ruin, have been the most to gain from the liberalization and economic reform process that began in 1991. In scale, geographical spread, brand power and technology, these companies are truly world leaders.

'DISINVESTMENT' (1999-2004)

The BJP dominated NDA (National Democratic Alliance) formed the government and continued with the previous government's economic reforms. In a courageous move, the government began divesting state-owned companies, under the disinvestment programme and even formed a Ministry of Disinvestment.

These PSU's were often sick units that resourceful entrepreneurs bought into and turned around. And the profit-making units brought in much needed cash to government coffers. And the government began to move out of the business of doing business.

This period also saw a large infrastructure push—mostly roads, ports and telecom. The IT momentum was carried on from the mid-nineties, the burst of the first dot com bubble, and Y2K fears notwithstanding.

As Prime Minister, the stately Atal Bihari Vajpayee created ties with Japan, which have since blossomed into mega projects and investments. India also surprised the world with tests of nuclear bombs made with indigenous technology. Inevitable economic sanctions followed, which the economy weathered, till the climate improved. Dr A.P.J. Abdul Kalam, the father of the Indian nuclear programme, also went on to serve as the President of the Republic of India later.

Pakistan, not entirely surprisingly, followed up with tests of nuclear bombs made with dubious technology. Dr A.Q. Khan, the father of the Pakistani nuclear programme, later went on to become an international fugitive, on charges of selling nuclear technology to rogue states.

UPA 1 AND 2 (2004-2014)

UPA 1, or the first five-year run of the Congress party led United Progressive Alliance (UPA) was exceptionally favourable.

Almost all asset classes and sectors did well, Prime Minister Manmohan Singh, the cerebral economist further reshaped India's foreign policy, and continued to bring India out of nuclear apartheid with the signing of the 1-2-3 deal with the support of the US administration. This gave India access to nuclear fuel and parts, and essentially lifted all direct or indirect concerns and sanctions arising from this issue.

This was seminal in other ways too. For one, it was a bit of a departure from Nehru's NAM, and deep ties with, and aid from, the Soviet Union (and later Russia). Declassified files on Nixon's appalling comments on Mrs Indira Gandhi describe frosty Indo-American relations that prevailed in preceding years.

The big change is that even until the 1980s and mid-90s, it was not considered great to be seen as close to business/industry. Today, politicians are happy to be photographed with captains of industry.

India has said no to aid. It recognizes developmental

challenges such as child labour, and malnutrition, but says it will address these internally. Private sector has led the charge—investment-led growth, not aid-led growth!

Presently, and in the immediate future, UPA 2 will be best remembered for scams and graft at an unprecedented scale. Politically, these incidents spawned a mass movement against political graft and excess, and consequently led to the creation of the Aam Aadmi Party (Hindi for 'common man party').

Economically, this couldn't have come at a worse time, as business sentiment was hit just as global markets were seeing a meltdown.

Among other developments, a number of 'rights' bills were enacted by Parliament—Right to Food (National Food Security Act), Right to Employment (NREGA National Rural Employment Guarantee Act 2005), Right to Information Act (2005), Right to Education Act (2009); modern new airports were operationalized (UPA 1 onwards) and the US$ 100 billion DMIC (Delhi Mumbai Industrial Corridor) was established with Japanese support.

Heightened public sensitivity and rights bills mitigated graft, but also mitigated the will of civil servants to act. There was no reward for good performance, whereas a potentially questionable decision taken in good faith could be scrutinized retrospectively. There were instances of retired secretaries to the government of India being arrested and sued for suspected graft. Only recently, have a couple of them won the case after much anguish and infamy.

Sir Mark Tully summed up the mood by quoting a cynical City banker in the UK, who told him how the only way things got done in India was through pay-offs, and since no one was accepting bribes now, nothing got done. 'This (anti-corruption movement) is very bad news.'

On a more serious note, though, India received an inordinate amount of bad press, both at home and abroad for three failings—crimes against women, graft, and economic slide. The mood changed after the watershed elections of 2014, when Narendra Modi was elected the prime minister in a campaign akin to a personality-led US presidential poll, a far cry from the usual elections of our Westminster-style elections, where final choice of prime minister is subject to many a back-room negotiation.

Most observers agree that the finance budgets of the Modi government, seen as a report card of performance and barometer of the government's mood vis à vis industry, have been in the right direction, but devoid of a wow factor. The economy is turning, slowly but surely. Economic reform lost two years with Prime Ministers Gowda and Gujral at the helm for one year each, but Vajpayee was able to bring the economy on to stable ground—despite the Kargil war (in Jammu and Kashmir) and nuclear tests (in Pokhran, Rajasthan), which put the strain of economic embargoes on India.

Compared to his BJP predecessor, Modi takes over in a better position. With a full majority in Lok Sabha, no Kargil, Pokhran, or looming economic crisis, a 10 per cent growth seems within grasp to economists. The big risks are, as always, a diminished political appetite to see economic reform through, and monsoon, which still determines the fate of agriculture, and hence India's rural economy.

Modi is seen as a no-nonsense and clean leader, but so was Manmohan Singh, who nevertheless had a stormy second term. Investors are watching closely which way BJP's politics will go after a couple of decisive defeats in state elections (notably, Delhi and Bihar). With state elections a perennial feature (between 2 and 4 Indian states go to polls every year), investors are hopeful that BJP will not move away from its inclusive and development agenda, to a narrow identity-based appeal (which is the mainstay of most political parties and elections). As a great communicator, the PM has so far managed to keep the Indian brand attractive to foreign audiences, but as a political analyst commented, 'Modi has to travel the world and also take care of the common man.'

The 2014 election was also noteworthy for bringing a party into power with simple majority, after over three decades of coalition politics. The NDA is a coalition, but only nominally.[63]

---

[63]Simple majority is winning over half the 545 seats in Lok Sabha, the lower house of Parliament. The 245 members of the Rajya Sabha, or Upper House, are nominated by parties from a state-wide quota (hence, state elections are crucial in the federal structure). Unless a government attains absolute majority (two-thirds of seats in the Lok Sabha, bills need to be ratified by Rajya Sabha, after having been passed by the lower house.

APPENDIX 2

CHRONICLE OF A PPP

A SUMMARY
(As submitted by Neemrana Hotels Private Limited)

Ten-year sequence of (non) events from the Tender bid to our single-handed work in this PPP Project at Tijara Fort!

Month	Particulars
September 2003	In September 2003, at the pre-bid meet—the thirty years lease period was found too short, so the matter went up to Cabinet Secretariat for appraisal and Tijara was approved for sixty years.
	Pre-bid Meeting. Thirty years lease period extended to sixty years as bidders complain of this being a high cost, low-return project.
November 2003	Submission of Tender.
March 2004	Technical bid.
	They required additional information which was submitted.
May 2004	Financial bid.
July 2004	Received letter that road to be made by state government. But later the government

decided that it would be done by the bidder. Neemrana Hotels Pvt. Ltd. agreed to build the hill road but permission for the road was to be taken by Government of Rajasthan as also the connectivity from the village to the hill. This road was finally undertaken ten years later.

September 2004 We informed the Rajasthan Government that access to the hill where the Fort stands belongs to the forest department. This fact had been informed earlier at the pre-bid meet before 14 potential bidders but was denied by the Rajasthan Government. Later, this turned out to be true.

August 2006 Sudden letter from Forest Department to Government of Rajasthan for reversion of 7.22 hectares of forest land, also saying that environment sanction is required.

October 2006 Correspondence between Jaipur and Forest Department Lucknow begins regarding Tijara. Rajasthan Government makes 3 attempts to barter its land with forest, first offering land that didn't belong to them, then a second attempt with land and a third which the Forest Department refused. Three years had passed!

January 2007 Government of Rajasthan then demands from us ₹1,25,87,294.00 to be paid to the forest department.

December 2007 Submission of EIA Report to PDCOR.

April 2008 Government of Rajasthan demanded ₹1.47 crores i.e.

Chronicle of a PPP • 235

	₹1,25,87, 294/- for the Forest Department ₹15 lakh for Project Success Fee and ₹6,17,980/- towards EIA Report.
June 2008	Payment of ₹1.47 crore made to Government of Rajasthan.
February 2009	In a seven-hour meeting PDCOR informs Tourism and Neemrana that forest land can actually be used for the purpose for which it was allocated!
	We had already stated earlier that it would be used for car parking, staff quarters, drilling water, building a generator room and the Director, Tourism, conveyed to us that land could be used for the above-mentioned purposes and that they have already got the approval. In a PPP lease, shouldn't this land be given by the government, since it will revert to it?.
March 2009	It was finally settled that the agreement will be signed within the financial year of 2009. Therefore, 31 March was fixed for signing. On this day, on our arrival, the Government of Rajasthan requested three more days from the Tourism Department.
April 2009	On Rajasthan Day we were called again and the same matter was discussed and we were then told that the agreement would be signed immediately after the elections were over.
April 2009	H.E. the Governor of Rajasthan intervened in this impasse and spoke to Minister, Tourism, and CM of Rajasthan. Things began to move.

May 2009	After the election results, the Government of Rajasthan re-requested the Tourism Department for two weeks and a likely date for the signing was to be after 10 June 2009.
June 2009	11 June was fixed, but once again on our arrival in Jaipur, they asked for one more week. It was exactly five years after the selection of the final party that the papers had yet to be cleared and the project started.
22th June 2009	The papers were signed and one RTDC officer was sent to Tijara.
15th Dec 2009	Till this date, no one of any governing authority from the Government of Rajasthan or from Rajasthan Tourism had even entered the tendered property, leave aside visit us to try and understand or solve any problems. We had no electricity and no proper link road to the hill base from where the road we have cut in the rocks takes us up. Suppliers were not willing to send their trucks. Yet, it was expected that this mammoth heritage project that no one else in India was willing to do, should be completed within 30 months—or we would be penalized! We had said that a large part would be reasonably ready for use. Was this true Public Private Partnership, or old wine in a new bottle as the Private Person's Problem?
August 2011	The first visit from the PWD was made to address our road access problems, thanks to

the instructions of Minister Jitendra Singh of Alwar.

May 2012 There was a first meeting of all the departments at Tijara Fort where the Principal Secretary Tourism, Government of Rajasthan along with the General Manager RTDC and all connected government departments were present and a plan was made to settle all the pending matters.

October 2012 NHPL paid the annual License fees of ₹10,00,000 to the Government of Rajasthan. Then again approximately ₹18,12,000 was paid under duress to the Sub-Registrar as Stamp duty charges and interest so that the Stamp duty matter could be settled.

After all these delays and the injustice of making us pay for all that was never mentioned in the original Tender, the Forest and Rajasthan Tourism Departments again started a pointless debate on whether Tijara should have been tendered to a private party!

February 2013 A District Forest Officer visited the site for a few minutes and issued a notice that we were constructing the pool on government land. We had to stop construction at the site for a few months and there was no meeting to resolve this matter.

March 2013 RTDC in an internal meeting decided that the agreement would not be valid, as NHPL did not form a Special Purpose Company, did not complete the work in the timeframe

	given in the agreement that was executed between the parties and they did not get the ratification which the Department of Tourism was supposed to take from the Ministry of Environment and Forests (MoEF).
November 2014	A meeting was held under the Chairmanship of the Chief Secretary wherein it was decided for Neemrana Hotels Private Limited that land from another area be surrendered in lieu of the area where the construction of the pool was done.

DOT will get ex post facto approval from the MoEF and give to the RTDC and ask to ensure that the agreement remains in force and further extend the time frame so that the Neemrana Hotels Private Limited could commence the project.

APPENDIX 3

KEY FEATURES OF 'MAKE IN INDIA'

Launched in September 2014 as part of a wider set of nation-building initiatives, and devised to transform India into a global design and manufacturing hub. A timely response to a critical situation. The manufacturing sector in India had witnessed a downward trend with growth rates of 1.1 per cent and -0.7 per cent during 2012–13 and 2013–14 respectively.

This global initiative was launched to invite both domestic and foreign investors to invest in India. The Make in India initiative is based on four pillars, which have been identified to give boost to entrepreneurship in India, in not only the manufacturing but also other sectors. The four pillars are listed below.

New Processes: Recognizes 'ease of doing business' as the single most important factor to promote entrepreneurship.

New Infrastructure: Government intends to develop industrial corridors and smart cities, create world-class infrastructure with state-of-the-art technology and high-speed communication. Improved infrastructure for IPR registration and requirement of skills for industry are to be identified and accordingly development of workforce to be taken up.

New Sectors: FDI has been opened up in Defence Production, Insurance, Medical Devices, Construction, and Railway infrastructure in a big way. Similarly, FDI has been allowed in Insurance and Medical Devices.

New Mindset: In order to partner with industry in economic development of the country, Government shall act as a facilitator and not a regulator.

ACKNOWLEDGMENTS

This book is the result of the greatest support received from many friends, as well as those I barely knew when we first communicated. Some of these extraordinary individuals find mention in the book, while others have chosen to remain anonymous.

Like any worthwhile endeavour of mine, visible and invisible well-wishers are responsible for any good that may be achieved. The faults and failings, however, remain mine alone.

Everybody involved in shaping this book has been exceptionally generous with their time and candid in sharing experiences. For this acknowledgment, I seek indulgence of friends and supporters in my choosing not to list the names, as any such list would be inexhaustible and verbose.

INDEX

2G Spectrum licence allocation scam, 23, *See also* Raja, A.
1857 Mutiny, 136

Aadhar-enabled ATM withdrawals, 192
Aam Aadmi (common man) Party (AAP), 97–98
Abe, Shinzo, 57
Adidas-Reebok scam, 197–200
Adobe, 117
Adversarial relationship, 119
Agarwal, Ritesh, 163
Airport City Real Estate, 81
Aiyar, Mani Shankar, 210
Aiyar, Swaminathan, 60, 66, 89, 122–123, 132, 158, 179, 185, 209–210
  semi feudal system by, 66
Akhtar, Farhan, 162
Ambuja, 128
American regulatory framework, 125
Amma kitchen, by Jayalalithaa, 66
Amway, 161–162, 175
Anand, G.R., 44
Ananda Marg, 104
Anganvadis, 111
Anti-tax avoidance regulation, 153
Approval raj+inspector raj, 111
Arab Spring, 66
Arora, Nikesh, 163
Arun Icecreams, 44
Arun, T.K., 223

Arunachalam, M.V., 227
Arvind Mills, 78
Associated Chambers of Commerce and Industry (ASSOCHAM), 129
Association of South East Asian Nations (ASEAN), 126
Assumption of predictability and stability, 121–122
Atal Mission for Rejuvenation and Urban Transformation (AMRUT), 140
Automotive Components Manufacturers Association of India (ACMA), 129
Average Revenue Per User (ARPU), 57

Bachchan, Amitabh, 219
Bajaj Allianz Insurance, 83
Bajaj, Rahul, 227
Bandra-Worli sealink, 80
Banerjee, Sashwati, 168
Bangalore, 64
Bankruptcy and insolvency adjudicator, 142
BASF, 81
BBC, 50, 155, 173
Behl, Kunal, 163
Berkshire Hathaway, 117
Berra, Yogi, 121, 203
Bhardwaj, Gautam, 174
Bhartiya Janata Party (BJP), 95, 97–98, 188, 224–225, 228,

231–232
BHIM (Bharat Interface for Money), 191
Bilateral treaties, 101
Bilateralism, 103
Birla, 35, 227
Birla, C.K., 227
BKC (Bandra-Kurla Complex), 80
Black economy, 131, 187, 190
Black money, 188–190, 192
Bleach, Peter, 104
Blue-collar workforce, 46
BMW, 63, 83, 159, 218
Bombay Club, 86, 227–228
Bombay Stock Exchange (BSE), 164
Booth capturing, 189
BPO industry, 177
Brain drain, 204
Brand conscious, 44
Brand India, 153
Brexit, ix
BRIC nations, 2–3, 12, 25, 215
  agricultural profile of, 24
British East India Company, 137, 221
British Raj, 60, 106
Budhraja, Anshu, 156
Business Angels, 164
Business automation, 45
Business, ease of doing, 9, 22–23, 31, 35, 54, 82, 90–91, 100–101, 123, 141–156, 192, 208, 239
Business-friendly laws, 15

Capital market efficiency, 111
Capitalism, 19, 55, 66, 96, 110, 142
Capitalist consumerist, 56
Carlsberg beer, 102
Car-sharing, 218
Cash, Johnny, 86
Cash-less economy, 191
Cash-on-delivery (COD) sales, 41
Caste in India, 129–135
  dalit Christians, 130
  dalit Muslims, 130
  dalit Sikhs, 130
  SC/ST quota, 132
CavinKare, 44
CEC, 188
Central Bureau of Investigation (CBI), 23, 104, 107
Centre for Advanced Study of India (CSAI), 133
Centre for Tribal Research and Development (CTRD), 218
Cessationist movement, 210
Chahal, Sairee, 177
Chappell, Ian, 13
China business model, 212
China Model, 17–27
  agricultural reform, 19
  denouncing wealth policy, 19
  dual currency, 20
  economic growth, 18
  economic reform, 18–19
  exports, 18
  FDI, 19, 22
  financial governance, 22
  GDP, 17
  governmental spending, 21
  growth drivers, 21
  'Made in China' worries, 18
  'Management Responsibility' system, 20
  'One Child' policy, 20
  swathe of reforms, 21
  trading partners, 18
Clinton, Hillary, 96
Clove Dental, 34, 193–194
Coca-Cola, 49, 55–56, 186
Code of Ethics for the Audit Party, 184

Cognizant, 117
Coke, 55–58, 85, 160, 172–173, 186–187, 224
Cola Wars, 55–58
Companies Act, 66, 69, 146, 154–155, 178, 217
Company Raj, 106, 136
Compound Annual Growth Rate (CAGR), 9
Comptroller Auditor General of India (CAG), 183
Confederation of Indian Industry (CII), 129, 131
Consultant model, 114
Contract employees (vs those on payrolls), 177
CoolAge (www.coolage.com), 115
Copyrights, 169
Corporate Governance, 76, 119, 198
Corporate Social Responsibility (CSR), 48, 66–69, 216–217
   -esque programmes, 216
   legislation, 67
   projects, 48
Corruption in Business, 182–184
Corruption Perception Index 2014, 182
Corruption, 182–184
   petty, 183, 193, 196, 202
Creative cumulative incrementalism, 114
Credit Rating and Intelligence Systems India Limited (CRISIL), 50
Crimes against women, 4, 175, 231
Crony Capitalism, 96
Crown Raj, 106
C-suite salaries, 117

Dalit Indian Chamber of Commerce and Industry (DICCI), 129, 131, 133

Dalit women, 121, 174
Danish royalty, 102
Darwinian Indian conditions, 48
Das, Gurcharan, 17, 114, 128, 157, 208, 219
DAX, 81
Decollectivization, 20
Deferred gratification, 65
Delhi Metro Rail Corporation (DMRC), 54
Delhi–Mumbai Industrial Corridor (DMIC), 5, 7, 230
Democracy, swings in, 208
Demographic
Demographic, 3–4, 9, 20, 22, 66, 115, 121, 130–131, 133, 135, 139, 165, 171, 174–175, 209
   dividend, 9, 20, 22, 115–140, 174–175, 209
   favourable demographics, 13
   of the G7, 4
   and rising labour rates, 21
   worry of the 'inverted pyramid, 20
Demonetization, 189–192
   addiction to cash, 190
   downside, 190
   upsides of, 190
Denmark, 101–106
Department of Industrial Policy and Promotion (DIPP), 143, 146, 163, 166
Desai, Bharat, 163
Desai, Morarji, 225
Deutsche Bank, 81, 84, 117
Dham, Vinod, 163
Diageo, 117
Digital India, 9–10, 146, 192
Disinvestment (1999–2004), 228–229
Doing Business Report, 141, 146
Domestic violence, 175
Double-digit growth, 12, 220

Dowry-related murders, 175

E&Y, 199
Early adapters, 44
Ease of Doing Business Index, 143
East India Company, 137, 221
e-biz portal, 144
e-booker, 39
e-commerce, 36, 42, 45–46, 127
  potential, 46
Economic crisis, 22, 231
Economic indicators, 16, 23, 30, 123, 226
Economics, 97, 210
Economist, The, 141, 203

Egalitarian society, 121
e-governance, 207
Electronic Credit Ledger System (ECLS), 89
Electronic money, 219
Elephant Fodder, 187–189
Emerging economy, 3
Emerging market, 3, 91, 136, 167, 182, 212
Environmental and social stress, 121–122
EODB rankings, 142
EOU, x
Ergo, 95, 102, 133, 155, 217
EU, ix, 8, 18
European Economic and Monetary Union, 215
Eurovision, 79–85
Eurozone, 90
e-wallet, 191
Export reject, 205, 225
Export-surplus goods, 205, 225

Fabian Socialism, 222
FDI, 54, 82, 86, 90, 100, 109, 131, 143–144, 211, 227, 239–240
  license, 30
  limit in the defence and insurance sector, 143
  policy, review of, 109
Federation of Indian Chambers of Commerce and Industry (FICCI), 129, 131
FII, ix, 144
First War of Independence, *see* 1857 Mutiny
First-generation expatriate entrepreneurs, proliferation of, 35
Five Year Plans, 222
Flash mobs, 162
Flowtex, 84
Foreign business model, 50
Foreign Corrupt Practices Act (FCPA), 186
Foreign Exchange Management Act (FEMA), 165
Foreign Investment Promotion Board (FIPB), 30, 109, 161
Foreign Policy, 100, 215, 229
Foreign Portfolio Investors (FPIs), 144
Foreign-owned corporations, 84
Fortune magazine, 70
Foxification, 95–97
Free Trade Agreement (FTA), 78, 94, 101
FRRO, xii

G-20 countries, 188, 215
Gandhi, Indira, 128, 224–225, 229
  nationalization phase, 224
Gandhi, Mahatma, 136
Garden of Eden, 1
Gender-related legislation, 176
General Anti Avoidance Rules

(GAAR), 144, 153, 208
General Motors (GM), 128
Generalized System of Preferences (GSP), 77–78
Germany, 2, 12, 61, 62, 63, 84, 101, 127, 159, 218
Ghosh, Shyamal, 107
Gilded Age, 96
Global Gender Gap Report 2016, 90
Global growth rates, 29, 28
GMR Group, 81
Godrej, Adi, 136
Godrej, Jamshyd, 227
Gold Monetization Schemes (GMS), 109
Goods and Services Tax (GST), 86–95, 144, 191–192, 208
  Bill, 87
  Council, 87, 90
  Constitution Amendment, 87, 94
  final shape, 88, 90
  implementation of, 87, 90–91, 93–94
  mitigating tax inefficiency, 92
Google, 5, 99, 117, 163
Governmental Interface, 109–114
Gowda, H.D. Deve, 225, 231
Goyal, Kamesh, 83
Green cities, 7
Green energy, 7
Green revolution, 20
Greenpeace, 170
Gross Domestic Product (GDP), 2, 80, 88, 91, 93, 122, 126–127, 187, 190–192, 215
Gross National Income (GNI), 28
GRT Group, 44
GSTN, 89, 191–192
Gujarat, communal riots, 100, *See also* Modi, Narendra
Gujral, I.K., 225, 231

Gulf War, 226

Haldea, Prithvi, 108, 153, 164, 180
Hardymon, Felda, 3, 50
Harvard Business School, 3, 4, 34, 35, 50, 78, 136, 163, 204
Hazare, Anna, 4
Hindu rate of growth, 4
Hindu, The, 9, 23, 44, 135
Hindustan Motors, 128
Hindware (HSIL), 125
Hire and fire policy, 128
Honesty, 184–185
Hyderabad, 6, 70, 81, 84, 159
Hyper competitiveness, 49, 166

I Am 20, 203–204
IBM, 32, 55, 70, 224
IBSA, 215
IFCI Venture Capital Funds Ltd, 134
IIM, 4, 46, 78–79
IIT, 46
India Against Corruption (IAC), 97, 201
Indian Administrative Service (IAS), 106–107, 178
Indian bureaucracy, 106, 112–113
Indian Civil Services (ICS), 82
Indian Foreign Service (IFS), 106
Indian Merchant Chambers (IMC), 129
Indian Penal Code (IPC), 161
Indian Plumbing Skills Council, 125
Indo-Danish relations, 102
Indo-Japanese friendship, 51–52
Indus Entrepreneurs (TiE), 163
Industrial Entrepreneurs' Memorandum (IEMs), 144
Industrial Training Institutes (ITI), 122
Infosys University, 68

Infosys, 68, 124, 163
INSEAD, 38
Insolvency & Bankruptcy Code Bill, 90
Insolvency and Bankruptcy Code 2016, 142
Insolvency, 47, 90, 141–142, 165
Intellectual Property (IP), 168–171
Intellectual Property Rights (IPR), 56, 90, 239
International Comparison Program, 11
International Monetary Fund (IMF), 18, 94, 94, 215, 226
Invest India micro Pension Services (IIMPS), 218
Investment
  funds, 34
  domestic investment, 109
  foreign investment, 8, 16
  by NRIs on non-repatriation, 109
  related regulatory service, 145
  strategic investment, 83
  undeniable investment destination, 3
IPO, 196
IPS, 175
Irani, J.J., 133
ITES, x
Ivy League MBA, 116

Jaitley, Arun, 143, 153, 188
Jan Dhan Yojana, 10, 192
Janata Party, socialist phase of (1977–79)
Japan, 2, 6, 9, 12, 52, 61, 100–101, 126–127, 161, 228
Jasmine Revolution, 66
J-curve, 8, 191
JK Group, 44
JOBS Act (Jumpstart Our Business Startups Act, 2012), 126
Joshi, Bharat, 117
Jugaad, trap of, 62–66
Justdial, 206
JV partner, 83

Kalam, A.P.J. Abdul, 229
Kanoria, 78
Kargil war, 231
Kejriwal, Arvind, 4, 66, 97–99, 201
Kelloggs, 49–50, 85
Khan, A.Q., 229
Khan, Salman, 41
Khan, Shah Rukh, 56
Khosla, Vinod, 163
Kingfisher airlines, 47
Kini analyses, 58
Kini, Venkatesh, 55, 160, 172

Labour
  disputes, 142
  intensive farming, 122
  laws, 56, 119, 177
  reform, 22, 128
  unions, 14, 118
Larsen and Toubro (L&T), 102
Leapfrogging, 217–220
Least developed country (LDC), 78, 215
Libel laws, 172–173, 177, 179
Liberalization (1991–circa 2001), 226–228
Liberated territory, 210
Licence Raj (1947–91), 36, 111, 222–226
Limited Liability Partnerships (LLPs), 109
Lok Sabha, 87, 231, 232
Lokayukta, 201
Lokpal (Ombudsman), 97

Maira, Arun, 124
Make in India, 9–10, 17, 35, 123, 126–127, 143, 145–146, 163, 169, 239
  Digital India, 10
  Jan Dhan Yojana, 10
  key features of, 239–240
  Skill India, 10
  Stand-up India, 10
  Start-up India, 10
  Swachh Bharat Abhiyan, 10
Malaysia, 44, 84
Maldives, 43, 81, 214
Malhotra, Sanjay, 156
Mandal Commission, 36–37, 132
Mani, V.S.S., 206
Maoist ideology, 209
Maoist monopoly, 210
Maoist movement, 210
Market strategy, 212
Market Welfarism, 66
Mast, Adriaan, 6, 81, 83
MasterCard, 117
Mauritius, 101, 153
Max Telecom, 22
McDonalds, 48, 55, 160
MEA, 100, 104
Media Trials, 171–173, 177, 201
  Coke, 172–173
  Maggi, 171
Mehta, Zubin, 203
m-governance, 207
MicroPension Foundation, 174
Microsoft, 32, 117, 163
Minimum Alternative Tax (MAT), 144
Ministry of Corporate Affairs, 75, 199
Ministry of Entrepreneurship and Skill Development, 125
Ministry of Human Resource Development, 79, 124
Mitsubishi, 128
Modi, B.K., 227
Modi, Narendra, 5, 8–10, 15, 87, 98–99, 100, 102–103, 114, 125, 128, 140, 189, 191, 213, 225, 231–232
  campaigning for the BJP and against AAP, 98
  commerce and economic development, 103
  demonetization, 189–192
  development plank, 128
  first year government, 102
  foreign policy, 100
  pariah for some of the Western world, 103
  pushed hard for legislation, 87
Most Favoured Nation (MFN) Treaties, 101
Mukherjee, Pranab, 153
Müller, Max, 82
Mumbai attacks (2011), 59

Nair, T.K.A., 52, 113
Nanda, Ashish, 4, 64, 78, 184, 200
NASA, 39
Nath, Aman, 219, 238
National Association of Software and Service Companies (NASSCOM), 129
National Council of Applied Economic Research, 88
National Democratic Alliance (NDA), 52, 228, 232
National Disaster Management Authority, 101
National Payment Corporation of India (NPCI), 191
National Pension Scheme (NPS), 218
National Rural Employment

Guarantee Act 2005 (NREGA), 209, 230
National Skill Development Agency (NSDA), 124
National Skill Development Council (NSDC), 124
National Stock Exchange (NSE), 164
National Trade Union Congress (NTUC), 14–15
Neemrana, 233, 234, 235, 238
Nehru, 206, 222–224, 229
Netherlands, 6, 8, 101, 150
Nilekani, Nandan, 124
Nirbhaya case, 176
Nokia, 117, 159–160
Non-adversarial and investor friendly tax system, 144
Non-Aligned Movement, 223
Non-discriminatory Market Access (NDMA), 101
Non-governmental organizations (NGOs), 15
Non-politicization of the labour union, 160
Norgay, Tenzing, 47
Northeast, 43, 210

Obama, Barack, 96, 99
Obstructionism, 96
Ola, 166–167
Original Equipment Manufacturers (OEM), 63
Orwellian constitutional provision, 224
Overseas Indian Affairs, 33
Oyo Rooms, 163

Pai, Mohandas, 163
Panda, Jay, 99
PAP, 14
Parallel economy, 187–189

Parsi population, 136
Patanjali, 220
Patel, Nadir, 34
Paytm, 166, 191
Pending litigation, 142
PepsiCo, 49, 55–56, 117, 160, 163, 172, 225
Personal security, 59
Persons of Indian Origin (PIOs), 32–36, 204
PHD Chambers of Commerce and Industry (PHDCCI), 129
Pinckney, William S., 156, 161
Pitroda, Sam, 124
Planning Commission, 27–28, 124, 222
PMO, 104, 128
POC, 216
Police Reforms Commission, 158
Policy paralysis, 11, 107
Pollution Control Board, 37, 160
Prasad, Chandrabhan, 129
Presidency Towns Insolvency Act 1909, 142
Prevention of Corruption Act, 1988, 107
Private Sector Corruption, 195–202
Prize Chits and Money Circulation Schemes (Banning) Act, 161
Progressive Age, 96
Progressive reform of laws, 96
PSU banks, re-capitalization, 144
Public distribution system, biometrics to plug leakage, 185
Public Interest Litigations (PILs), 173
Public-Private Partnership (PPP), 11, 124
Pudong, 80, 81

Quality of Death, 141

Quasi-juducial roles, 112
Quraishi, S.Y., 188, 202, 207

Rai, Vinod, 182, 184, 187, 202
Raja, A., 23
Rajasthan State Industrial Development Corporation (RSIDC), 37, 42
Rajasthan State Pollution Control Board (RSPCB), 37
Raju, Ramalinga, 69, 71, 75
   announcement of this diversification, 70
   confession, 70
   Ernst and Young Entrepreneur award, 70
   Letter from Raju, 71–75
   'poison-pill' strategy, 70
Rajya Sabha, 87, 232
Ramachandran, Reena, 178
Ramadorai, S., 124
Ramdev, Baba, 220
Ranvir Sena (landowners muscle), 210
Rao, P.V. Narsimha, 226–227
Raymonds, 78
Real Estate Bill, 90
Red Tape, 5, 53, 85, 92, 146, 189
Red wheat' import from USA, 4
Reebok, 84, 197–200
Reform
   big bang reform, 86
   in bureaucracy, 113
   by stealth, 114
   labour, 22, 128
   legal, 207
   legislative, 16, 155
   police, 158
   police-judicial, 158
   policy, 11
   rate of, 35
   reform, 18–19, 52, 86, 227–228, 231
Reform, 19–20, 94
Reliance, 35, 65, 212, 223
Religion, 135–140
Reserve Bank of India (RBI), 139
Respect for religious sentiments, 138
Right to Education Act (2009), 230
Right to Employment, 230
Right to Food (National Food Security Act), 230
Right to Information (RTI) Act, 97, 201
Right to Information (RTI) activist, 97
Right-wing vigilantes, 208
River Ganga, cleaning, 6
Robin Hood model, 51
Rogers, Steven, 163

SAARC, 213–216
Satyam, 69–76, 120
   acquired by Tech Mahindra, 76
   collapse of, 75
   crisis management, 76
   managerial bailout, 75
   no financial bailout for, 75
   See also Raju, Ramalinga
Saxena, N.C., 158
Schiphol Amsterdam Airport, 81
Sector Skill Councils, 125
Securities and Exchange Board (SEBI), 75, 107, 111, 165, 180, 196
Securities and Exchange Commission (SEC), 112
Semi-feudal society, 60
Sentiment-driven holiday business, 42
Sesame Street, 50–51, 111, 168
Sexual Harassment of Women

Workplace (Prevention, Prohibition and Redressal) Act, 2013, 177
Sexual Harassment, 176, 180
SEZ, 7, 16, 19
Shah, Naman, 34
Shah, Pradip, 50
Sharif, Nawaz, 213
Sharma, Anand, 9
Sherpas, 47–48
Ship of Theseus, 107–108
Shiva, Niraj, 134
Shringi, Dhruv, 36, 62, 158, 185
Shriram, Kavitark Ram, 163
Shyama Prasad Mukherji Rurban (Rural-urban) Mission (SPMRM), 139
Sidhu, Harinder, 34
Silicon Valley, 116, 162–163
Singapore Model, 14–17
   'Clean and Green' Singapore, 15
   focus on labour-intensive industries, 14
   industrialization, 14
   legislative reform, 16
   workforce education, 15
Singh, Amar, 193
Singh, Analjit, 22, 110, 126, 196
Singh, Choudhary Charan, 225
Singh, Manmohan, 18, 226–227, 229, 231
Singh, V.P., 37
Singhania, Hari Shankar, 227
Singhania, Shrivats, 43
Single-window clearance, 33, 64, 183
Skill India, 10, 123
Skin whitening creams, 205
Smart Card, 185
SME, x, 190
Snapdeal, 163
Social and political stability, 207
Social media, 173
Society of Indian Automobile Manufacturers (SIAM), 129
Socio-cultural and economic challenges, 1
Socio-economic hierarchy, 123
Soft Bank, 163
Somany, R.K., 125
Stand Up India, 128
Standard & Poor's (S&P), 50
Stand-Up India campaigns, 163
Startup India, 9, 123, 128, 163, 166
Steel Frame, 99
Steel use, 3
Steinruecke, Bernard, 79, 159
Sting operations, 98, 201
Stock transfer, 92
Subramanian, Arvind, 86
Sukhram, 23
Sulabh, 15
Suzlon, 109–110, 148–150
Svane, Freddy, 103
Swachh Bharat programme, 15–16
Swades, 39
Switzerland, 226
Symbology, 97

Talent pool, 68, 115, 166
Tanti, Tulsi, 77, 109
Tariff jumping, 54
Tata Nano, 63
Tata, 35, 68, 124, 133, 170
Tax Avoidance Treaties, 101
Tax evasion, 65, 190
Tax reform, 88
Tax terrorism, 152–156
   Amway case, 155–156
   retrospective taxation case, 152
   Vodafone case, 152–153
TaxiForSure, 166
Technological and institutional

reform, 21
Telecom Regulatory Authority of
    India (TRAI), 111
Thapar, Lalit Mohan, 227
The Raj, (1858–1947), 221–222
Three-pronged reform programme, 15
Tijara Fort Project, 233–238
Transferable skills, 45
Transnational corporations, 118
Transparency International, 182
Trump, ix, 189
Tully, Mark, 16, 25, 60, 128, 155,
    157, 189, 230
Twin deficits, 27–29

Uber, 63, 166–167, 218
UN, 100, 182, 215
Unfriendly Nations, 101–106
UNICEF, 51
Unified Payment Interface (UPI), 191
Unique Identification Authority of
    India, 124
UPA 1 and 2 (2004–2014), 229–232
UrbanSpoon, 167
US presidential poll, 231
USA, ix, 1, 2, 4, 18, 66, 101, 162,
    203, 214, 225

Vajpayee, Atal Bihari, 52, 228
Verma, Richard, 34
Vibrant Gujarat Summit, 100,
    103–104
VIP Culture, 58, 60, 98
Virtual monopoly, 57
Virtual warehouses, 92
VISION 2019, 145–147
    customer-centric, 145

Digital India, 146
Make in India, 146
objective of ease of doing business,
    145
Vodafone, 117, 122, 152–153
Volkswagen, 80

Wadhwani, Ramesh, 163
Wahi, Diviya, 116
WalMart, 49
War of Independence in 1857, 221
Warren Buffet Notes, 123
Welch, Jack, 215
Westminster-style elections, 231
Williams Jr, Hank, 86
World Bank, 2, 9, 11, 23, 28, 35,
    100, 141, 143, 146–147
    Ease of Doing Business Rankings,
        23, 141
    'Protecting Minority Investors'
        indicator, 146
    rankings, 100
World Trade Organization (WTO),
    19, 94, 215

Xiaopeng, Deng, 19

Yadav, Akhilesh, electoral promises of
    laptops, 66
Yatra.com, 36, 39–47, 62, 85, 158
Yew, Lee Kuan, 14, 23

Zemin, Jiang, 20
Zendesk, 167
Zero defects and zero negative effect,
    10
Zomato, 115, 167, 206

Praise for the book

'One of the best books on the subject. A balanced account of India, that steers away from clichés and stereotypes, to decipher a rising economic superpower.'

Vinod Rai, *Chairman, Banks Board Bureau and Former Comptroller and Auditor General (CAG) of India*

'India is a land of contrasts—and more than that, it is a chaotic, bewildering and intimidating market for the uninitiated business person. *Navigating India* is written for these keen, but fearful, investors. Bharat tells it like it is... India is not for the faint-hearted. But for those willing to take time to get to know India, this book is an excellent place to start.'

David Lim, *Former Deputy Chairman, Ascendas India Trust*

'A must read for all budding entrepreneurs, written in a very easy going and matter-of-fact way.'

Sumit Mazumder, *Chairman & Managing Director TIL Limited, Former President CII (Confederation of Indian Industry)*

'Replete with real-life examples and case studies, and written in easy-flowing conversational style, Bharat's book is a practical guide for anyone, not just foreigners, wanting to do business in India. Even for the experienced Indian entrepreneur, this is a handy reference book to dip into from time to time for inspiration to address the inevitable bureaucratic and market challenges India offers.'

Pradip Shah, *Chairman, IndAsia Fund Advisors Pvt. Ltd, and founder, CRISIL*

'There are business books and there are business books. Bharat Joshi has done a remarkable one that is ground-up with stories and tales of success and hassles that describe the incredibly complex market that is India where it's tough to do business and yet very profitable. With compelling flair and a loose open-ended style Bharat captures both your interest and time. Enjoy the read!'

Dr A. Didar Singh *Secretary General, FICCI (Federation of Indian Chambers of Commerce and Industry)*

'I congratulate the timely publication of *Navigating India*, which provides firsthand insight into Indian market when the world is eyeing on its robust growth and vast business potential. As Japan has a long history of growing economic ties with India and has been one of the biggest foreign investors in the country, I myself witnessed great opportunities as well as challenges in doing business in India. This book provides a great introduction and experiential guidance to complicated Indian market.'

Kenji Hiramatsu, *Ambassador of Japan to India*

'*Navigating India* deftly articulates the most compelling opportunities and challenges of India with refreshing candour. A must read for professionals and entrepreneurs alike.'

Justice Sistani, *Judge, Delhi High Court*

'*Navigating India* is a very interesting and real life experience novel. I would suggest it as a must read for anyone who wants to do business here.

Many anecdotes and stories of how business has actually unfolded. One must also remember that India is changing and the huge change in business environment over the last two years must be appreciated and understood. It is not the same as doing business in many of the other developing economies because the market is far larger, far more complex and far more developed than most.

Kudos to Bharat Joshi, the author.'

Alok Shriram, *Vice Chairman & Deputy MD, DCM Shriram Industries Ltd and Former President, PHD Chamber of Commerce and Industry*

'Highly recommended for entrepreneurs, diplomats and policy makers to get a head-start in India.

If you think you cannot miss India in your global business strategy, this is the book for you.

If you are still skeptical, this book will clear your mind.

Bharat Joshi is a member of the young business leaders forum, who will create tomorrow for India.

India will grow to the one of the biggest economy of the world.

If you are looking for someone who can tell you the truth amid confusion, this is the book for you.

Bharat Joshi is a business leader representing most brilliant young generations who share the value for tomorrow.

When a country like India starts dancing, how would you dance together?

This is the book for you if you want to grow your business in India and beyond.'

Hideaki Domichi, *Former Ambassador of Japan to India*

'You will not find detailed charts of how to navigate the Indian market in Bharat Joshi's book, but you will receive a wealth of information based on real life experiences. Bharat Joshi, who is himself an accomplished businessman, has brought together a treasure of testimonies from entrepreneurs who were or are active on the Indian market.

Indian as well as non-Indian readers will find this book to be of great interest to them.

The main question for anybody who wants to do business in India is how to approach such a difficult market. *Navigating India* gives you a vivid account of the complexities of doing business in a country the size of a continent, unparalleled in its diversity.'

Jan Luykx, *Ambassador of Belgium to India*

'Observers and practitioners of business in India would do themselves a favour when they read this book.

Navigating India is a brilliant account of the challenges and opportunities of the world's most compelling emerging economy.'

S.Y. Quraishi, *Former Chief Election Commissioner of India*

'This book is not the run-of-mill stuff self-help book on India. Entrepreneurs, and anyone who wishes to engage with India: do yourself a favour and pick up this one.'

H.E. Cho Hyun, *Vice Minister of Foreign Affairs, and former Ambassador of Republic of Korea to India*

'Even though the word "navigating" is associated with the covering of marine distance, Bharat Joshi's use of this for a land mass the size of Europe, suggests the difficulty of the quicksand that India has been for novices. But for the seasoned optimist-entrepreneur, India also lets itself be navigated—as it did for the East India Company!

This is a very different read on India. The text races ahead as it hopes that the country also will! Such optimism keeps the reader afloat—navigating even on rocky and steep terrain. Joshi is much younger and he can see the 800 million Indian youth soaring and flying sooner than some of the pessimist economists.'

Aman Nath, *Author & Founder-Chairman, Neemrana Hotels*